Left:
*Liv Kjørsvik Schei
in her national dress*
© G. Moberg

Right:
Gunnie Moberg
© Staffan Joffell

LIV KJØRSVIK SCHEI is a writer who is especially interested in the history and culture of the lands once settled by Norway, and has written several books on the subject. Her first two were *The Orkney Story* and *The Shetland Story*. Working with the late Hermann Pálsson, professor of Icelandic at Edinburgh University, she translated *The Book of Settlements* and *The Ramsta Sagas* into modern Norwegian. She lives in Kristiansand, Norway, is married to a metallurgists and has two children.

GUNNIE MOBERG comes from Sweden but lives in Orkney. She has collaborated with Liv Schei on a number of books on Orkney and Shetland, the most recent of which, *The Islands of Orkney*, was published in 2000. She has illustrated two books by George Mackay Brown, *Stone* and *Portrait of Orkney,* and also worked with him on *Pictures and Poems*. She exhibits her photographs regularly at home and abroad. She is married to Tam MacPhail who runs a bookshop in Stromness, and has four children.

The distinguished Faroese artist TRÓNDUR PATURSSON has illustrated several books by Tim Severin and sailed across the Atlantic with him on the Brendan Voyage.

THE FAROE

ISLANDS

LIV KJØRSVIK SCHEI AND GUNNIE MOBERG

WITH DRAWINGS BY TRÓNDUR PATURSSON

Birlinn

Published in 2003 by
Birlinn Limited
West Newington House
10 Newington Road
Edinburgh
EH9 1QS

www.birlinn.co.uk

ISBN 1 84158 242 5

British Library Cataloguing-in-Publication Data
A catalogue record for this book is available
from the British Library

Page make-up: Mark Blackadder

Printed and bound by Book Print SL, Barcelona, Spain

CONTENTS

ACKNOWLEDGEMENTS

We would like to thank the Mentunargrunnur Føroya Løgtings (Cultural Committee of the Faroese Lawting) and Det faglitterære fond (Norwegian Non-fiction Fund) for their contributions towards the publication of this book.

Our walks and climbs in the Faroe Islands did at times put our courage and physical stamina to a serious test, but they gave us unique experiences of scenic beauty. They also brought us into contact with a warm and interesting people, who helped make our stays in the islands thoroughly enjoyable.

We would like to express our gratitude to all those who in various ways contributed with advice and criticism. We thank Sofus Olsen of Tórshavn specially for his interest in and support for our work on this book, and for introducing us to people who, like him, gave generously of their time and knowledge to help us.

GUNNIE MOBERG
LIV KJØRSVIK SCHEI

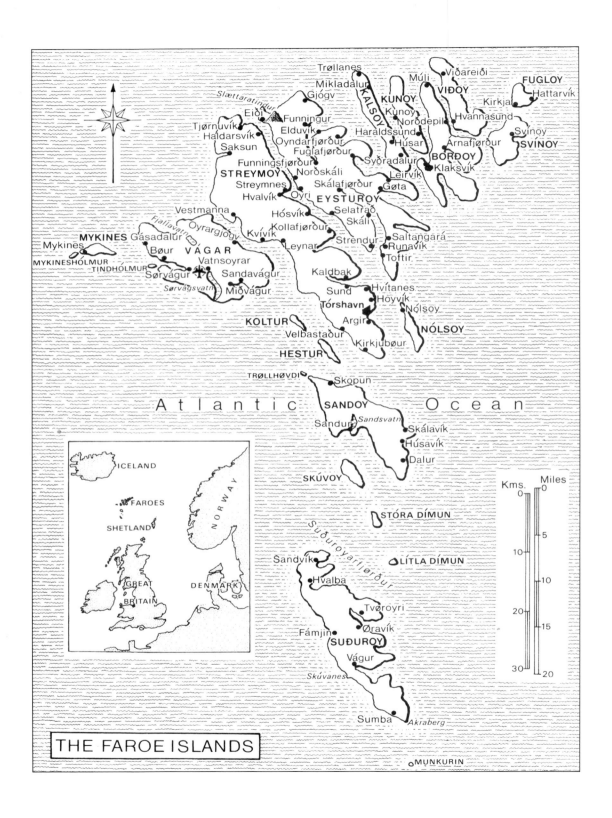

THE FAROE ISLANDS

INTRODUCTION

The føroying's way is like the bird's
        one spring day the seas will call:
Come, child, we will rock you gently –
        come, flee from your islands' basalt!
Come down from the sheltering mountains
        and up to the shining north.
We will take you, will lift you, will promise you
a voyage with life and death,
while you rock in the sea.

Nis Petersen

The Faroe Islands rise in austere beauty steeply from the sea. From afar they appear as a dark, inhospitable mountain mass that gives authority to the legend of Atlantis, the Utopian island overwhelmed by an earthquake in the western sea, leaving only its highest peaks visible above the water. The clean, sharply-defined lines of the mountains seem the work of a master sculptor with a taste for the abstract. Large valleys look as empty and untouched as if they had only recently been fashioned by the glaciers of the Ice Age.

The intensity of colours in the scenery therefore takes us by surprise. The lush grass of the cultivated land and mountain pastures seems greener than anywhere else and contrasts dramatically with the savage shades of black, grey and brown of the peaks and crags. Daisies and marsh marigolds abound. The purity of the air makes it difficult to judge distances, and what look like rocks strewn in the landscape sometimes turn out to be sheep grazing on steep slopes or narrow plateaux, seeming to defy the laws of gravity. Indeed they sometimes venture too far out or the wind pushes them off the cliff, but generally the birds nesting along the grassy edges see to it that the sheep are kept in their place. Sea-birds by the thousand make the cliff-faces teem with life.

The light is always changing, so that the most awesome rugged cliffs may be transformed into a gentle fairy-tale land of ethereal beauty. The light seems to come from all directions, and so does the mist; suddenly the top of a mountain rises from billows of thin wool, only to disappear again as the

Streymoy's most northerly coastline, with Stakkur

mist forms and re-forms into fantastic shapes. During the short and intense northern summer the nights are never really dark, and in the muted light of dawn and dusk the islands become a magical place.

And yet the Faroe Islands should not be thought of as idyllic. There are some hundred settlements of varying size, many of them clinging precariously to the shores of the basaltic islands, as if one storm would be enough to blow the homes into the sea. This has happened often enough in the past, as in the winter-time the islands are subjected to a combined attack by sea and sky; during a December storm a few years ago several houses vanished. Mountains surround many settlements on three sides with the fourth facing the sea, above a shore so inhospitable that even in a calm sea it may be difficult to land. It is often said that the Faroese did not settle in their islands by choice, but because they were too seasick to carry on with the voyage to Iceland!

The sea is friend and foe, loved and hated. It has beckoned and enticed, giving generously at times and taking savagely at other times, through accidents and attacks by pirates. A boat was a necessity; in the words of a Faroese proverb, *'Bundin er bátleysur maður'* – 'a man without a boat is a prisoner'. As a young child a føroying would learn to handle one, and as a youth he would be ready to take his place in a crew. His work at sea was full of challenge; forever wrestling with the waves and the wind around the Faroe Islands, he acquired patience but also an ability to give his best at a critical moment. Sometimes the odds were against him or he took one risk too many: the sea was a fearsome widow-maker, and the lot of Faroese women was often hard.

Today the old, beautifully-worked wooden boats are no longer a necessity, and the rowing is mostly done in competitions. Modern trawlers with the latest navigational aids have reduced though not removed the danger and the toil of life at sea. Going north – to the rich fishing grounds south of Iceland or around the Greenland coasts – is still not without risks, as these are treacherous waters. But no longer are the charges of the life insurance companies in Copenhagen five times greater for the Faroe Islands than for Denmark, as they once were.

The fish in the sea are today the be-all and end-all of the islands, and their dependence on such an uncertain resource gives cause for worry. Still the idea of oil development does not meet with much favour. In the popular song 'Føroyar' – 'The Faroe Islands' – Steintór Rasmussen voices a view held by many:

Flúgva fagrir fuglar byggja reiður her	Lovely birds come here to nest
og fiskur býr í sjónum so langt sum eygað ber	and fish live in the ocean as far as the eye can see
at vitja fjallatindar mangur gleðir seg	many wish to climb the mountains
og spríkja goymdar keldur um vit bora ígjøgnum teg	but hidden springs well up if we bore through you
og verða vit ríkari tá Føroyar	and will we be richer then, Faroes?
og hvør verður ríkari tá Føroyar?	and who will be richer then, Faroes?

The Faroe Islands are not just sea, sky and basalt, they are the home of a strong little nation with a culture and a social pattern that are unique. The

Faroese belong to the Scandinavian group of peoples. Their social weave is strong and has been amazingly tolerant – the Faroe Islands have the impressive record of being the only country in northern Europe where no fire was ever lit for the burning of witches.

In the course of a century and a half, life in the islands has changed drastically. From being for centuries mainly a farming society with a small, stable population, the Faroese have become one of the world's most technically advanced fishing nations, and the population has grown tenfold. Their standard of living is high, and in many ways they have become the victims of their own success, as with restless energy they plan another road, tunnel or school. At the same time they have learned once again to take their heritage seriously.

Life in the islands is not geared to mass tourism, so every visitor is treated as a welcome and honoured guest. Signs are not always considered necessary – after all every Faroese knows where things are! Sheer geographical distance has made the islands into a self-contained world.

> To these cliffs
> To these rocks in the great ocean
> The world is anchored,
> Here is the place
> Where everything begins
> And where everything returns in the end.
>   *Gunnar Hoydal*

Isolation has made the islanders lords of all they survey, in an island country that has the complexity of a modern community yet is small enough for everyone to know most people.

Suðuroy. Sign at Beinisvørð, the 469-metres-high mountain

1

NATURE

Once all the Faroe Islands were floating islands. They drifted unclaimed around in the fog until they found their permanent place. But not until *iron* was brought to them did they make fast and put down roots in the bottom of the sea.

William Heinesen

This tradition of floating islands, reclaimed from unknown seas, is common to many maritime cultures. It is not difficult to see how such an illusion arises when in changing lights the blurred outline of the land blends with the surrounding sea and sky.

The Faroe Islands landed as outposts in the North Atlantic between latitude 61° 20' N and 62° 24' N and longitude 6° 15' W and 7° 41' W. From north to south the islands measure 113 kilometres and from west to east 75 kilometres. The nearest land is Shetland to the south-east, some 300 kilometres or 187 miles away. Due north there is only the small island of Jan Mayen between Faroe and the North Pole.

There are eighteen islands of some size; of these sixteen are inhabited. The population has doubled since 1930, and is now close to 50,000. Centralization is still going on, with more and more people moving to Tórshavn, the capital and largest town. It now has a population of 15,000 – three times what it was in 1945.

The total land area is about 1,400 square kilometres (540 square miles), with a heavily indented coastline some 1,100 kilometres long. Today most communities are connected by roads and tunnels; indeed, Gásadalur on the island of Vágar is now the only settlement without a road of any kind.

Topography

The islands have the shape of an irregularly spiked battle-axe.

G. H. Harris

Apart from Suðuroy and Stóra Dímun and Lítla Dímun in the south the Faroe Islands form a compact group. A striking feature of them all is that they extend, long and narrow, almost parallel from north-west to south-east. On the north and west coasts high, steep cliffs face the fierce onslaught of the Atlantic. An impressive cliff is Enniberg in Viðoy, rising 725 metres perpendicularly from the sea, and considered the highest headland in the world. From the high mountain areas of the west the islands slope slightly towards the east, and not surprisingly most settlements are found there. Slættaratindur in Eysturoy is at 882 metres the highest mountain, but even if none of the Faroese mountains is of great height, there are many of them, so that the average altitude of the islands is 300 metres above sea level. And the absence of trees and bushes makes the mountains seem higher than they are.

Fertile land has always been precious in Faroe. Most of the hamlets, known as *bygdir,* which are so characteristic of all the islands, were traditionally built to take up as little of the cultivated land as possible, and they are all curiously alike. Seen from afar they resemble blobs of paint on an artist's palette, with houses in all the colours of the rainbow, some of them with turfed roofs. Tarred or painted white, the church always has pride of place. The green patch surrounding the cluster of houses is the *bøur* – the cultivated infield. Today the *bøur is* usually given over to grass and a few potatoes, but barley used to be grown on it as well. All around the *bøur* runs a stone dyke; the land beyond this is known as the *hagi* or outfield. A fenced-in, cultivated plot can sometimes be found in the outfield, and is then known as a *trøð.*

Many *bygdir* are built in a short valley, known as a *botnur,* which is open to the sea so that boats can land, although in many places with difficulty. Such a *botnur,* like Tjørnuvík in Streymoy, is half circular, almost like an amphitheatre, and rises in slopes, known as *brekkur,* up to the characteristic *hamrar* – terraces – of the mountains. The ridge between two *botnar is* often very narrow; a naturally-formed pass through it is known as a *skarð.* The deep cleft formed in the coastline where the less resistant rock has worn away is known as a *gjógv* and is a very striking feature of the landscape. The many rivers hang like shining white ribbons down the mountain slopes and fall into lakes or directly to the sea. Rivers or brooks may be short but are often rich in fish. The first settlers knew what they wanted, and most *bygdir* are old.

In the sounds between the islands the tidal current runs swift and strong. When it presses its way in from the Atlantic at high tide it is known as *vestfall,* and in the same way the low tide is called *eystfall.* The current flowing at full speed through the sound can be an impressive sight. But it is also dangerous, and should be treated with due respect. Through the centuries it has been a determining factor in all communication between the islands, and the Faroese became masters not only in making the best of it, but also in making good use of it.

Left:
Gjógv. The bygd *gets its name from the deep cleft formed in the coastline*

Right:
Streymoy. The 140-metres-high waterfall, Fossá, tumbles down over several hamrar *before it falls into Sundini*

Geology

> The cliffs of the Faroes are among the scenic glories of Scandinavia.
>
> *Brian John*

At one time the cliffs of the Faroes were part of an unbroken mountain chain, the Wyville Thompson Ridge, which stretches from Scotland across the sea to Greenland and keeps the cold water of the polar regions away from the Atlantic. It is from the Wyville Thompson Ridge that the fjords and sounds of the Faroe Islands got their pronounced north-west – south-east axis. During subsequent upheavals the bed of the Atlantic Ocean was split and widened and the ridge subsided. The Faroe Islands were then carried to the east of the ridge, which Iceland still straddles, and are today well away from the scene of volcanic activity.

The Faroe Islands were formed in Tertiary times, millions of years ago, from submarine outpourings of basaltic lava, and belong geologically to the

Syðradalur, Streymoy. The alternating dark hamrar and softer shelves of tuff give the mountainsides a stepped appearance

North Atlantic basalt province. Lava and ashes from volcanic eruptions have formed basalt plateaux, shown through drillings in Suðuroy to continue down to at least 2,200 metres below sea level.

The layers of basalt are 10 to 30 metres wide and dip gently to the south-east. They form steep mountains, very often looking like natural pyramids. In between the basalt flows are sandwiched softer layers of so-called tuff, a kind of stone made up of volcanic ashes and other sediments. This alternation between the hard, dark *hamrar* and the softer shelves of reddish tuff gives to the mountainsides a certain stepped appearance, and takes some of the monotony away from the otherwise stark slopes. Cleverly built to run parallel with the *hamrar,* a road will hardly show in the landscape.

Thus it seems that there have been periods of intense volcanic activity followed by long, quiet intervals when a rich vegetation was possible. The layers of coal found in Suðuroy point in this direction: the coal-bearing shale layers are up to fifteeen metres thick; they have been found to contain a rich pollen and spore flora, and could only have been formed during a long pause in the volcanic activity.

The coal in Suðuroy has been worked for 300 years for local household consumption. Mining is still carried on, but the demand for coal is declining. The basalt was once used for building the dykes separating the infields from the outfields and to some extent also for building houses. There has been some production of basalt slabs for the building industry, for home use as well as for export, but transport costs limit the scope for commercial exploitation. The hard red tuff at Argisfossar in Streymoy was at one time used to produce a rust-preventing paint. Generally speaking, the Faroese basalts are poor in the minerals that are worth exploiting economically.

Climate

The isolated position of the Faroe Islands, far away from any large land mass, leaves them at the mercy of the elements in the North Atlantic. But because the warm waters of the Gulf Stream in this area meet a cold polar current deflected from Iceland, a typically mild and damp oceanic climate prevails. In fact, there are few other places in the world with such an equable climate; the difference between the warmest and the coldest month of the year is only seven degrees. To find milder winters we must go as far south as the French Riviera. The highest temperature so far measured is 22°C, and the lowest is −14 °C. Such extremes very rarely occur, but in winter and early spring the temperature can change suddenly from one day to the next.

The islands are right on the route of the wandering low-pressure belts of northern Europe, and the steep cliffs of naked rock are natural rainmakers. The annual rainfall is therefore considerable, but there are large local variations: Vestmanna in Streymoy has 3,108 millimetres of rain a year, whereas the island of Mykines surprisingly has only 769 millimetres. Strange though it may sound, periods of drought are not uncommon in the summer months. But on average there are 280 days of rain a year, mostly in the autumn and winter. However, the rain comes as showers, and the daily rainfall is usually very small. Between the showers the sun may shine brightly.

The most striking characteristic of Faroese weather is in fact its changeability. It is possible to leave one end of an island in brilliant sunshine and reach the other end in dense fog. The islands are a battleground for the winds, where north and south winds especially struggle for supremacy. The wind tends to change direction often and abruptly owing to the passage of cyclones.

Storms are violent and sudden, though mostly fairly brief. They come in fierce gusts, howling down the valleys with such force that stones are flung upwards and the turf can get torn up like a loose carpet and carried out to sea. The 1988 storms ruined the beautiful wooded plantation in Tórshavn and ripped the roofs off houses. Past experience has taught the Faroese that houses must be solidly built, even chained to the site, to withstand the force of the wind. Stories abound of earlier disasters. On a night in early January 1886 the church of Sørvágur was wrecked by a storm; ten years before, the same had happened to the church at Mykines. To be out at sea in such weather can be fatal: in 1913 the final chapter was written in the saga of Skarð in Kunoy, when all the men of the village were drowned during a storm.

The Faroe Islands are also known for their fog, but the number of foggy days varies greatly from one island to another. Thus on average Mykines has 100 days of fog, which is twice as many as occur in the Tórshavn area. The mist known as *skadda* can lie around the mountain tops at any time of the year. *Mjørki,* the dense type of fog that covers everything, occurs mostly in summer-time. For anyone caught in the mountains by such a fog it is dangerous to stray from the cairned routes; but usually the fog lifts as suddenly as it came, and the best thing is to sit it out: fog and rain may suddenly change into the most glorious summer weather!

There is no midnight sun in Faroe, but the nights are light throughout the summer, so that the lighthouses are not lit between mid-May and mid-July.

The Faroese climate may be capricious, but it offers many compensations. As the air is almost free of dust, it is unusually clear, and this makes the colours contrast sharply. To watch the shadows of the clouds dance across the greens and browns and greys of the landscape and bring out new and bold colour effects is enchanting. In the early morning, at sea or in the mountains, there is a strange and beautiful solitude: a shower of rain is caught by the wind; a waterfall is scattered on the air in a luminous rainbow; the fog suddenly lifts to reveal a village in bright sunshine. The landscape changes its shapes and yet never changes; no wonder that this is a land of many painters.

Nobody can predict the weather in Faroe and tell what the morrow will be like. It is best to come prepared with rainwear and a warm sweater at all times, so as not to fight the weather but to allow for it and enjoy it. Plans should be provisional. The Faroes have been called 'the land of maybe' because the changeable climate has shaped the life of the people. It used to be difficult to make an appointment on another island because if the wind changed, you might have to wait six weeks to fulfil it, and it was always better to say *kanska* – maybe. A climate like this teaches patience, as the Faroese proverb confirms: 'He will get wind who waits.'

Flora

One of the most striking features of the Faroe Islands is the lack of wild trees and bushes. According to an old tradition the islands were once full of trees, and fragments of good-sized birch and juniper are said to have been found in peat bogs. But today there is not one tree that has not been planted. The climate with its fierce gales and salt-laden air does not allow trees to grow, and the ubiquitous Faroese sheep are a further hindrance.

However, small woods have been successfully planted in sheltered areas. The first plantation, which was named Viðalundin but is popularly known as Plantasjan, was established in Tórshavn in 1902. It is a lovely park with winding paths among larch and white spruce. Other such plantations later came in Kunoy and Selatrað. Among the more recent woods is one at Mikladalur.

Quite exotic trees can thrive in Faroe when away from the wind and the salt spray, as we can see in many private gardens. But on the whole garden plants must be hardy to survive the vicissitudes of the Faroese climate. 'Many plants struggle along doubtfully through the alternate soakings and freezings, the pitiless downpours, and violent gales; sprout often in February, and are frozen in March; sprout again and are cut down in May; get the better of their troubles, show great promise of a flowery future, and then die quietly in June' (Elizabeth Taylor).

Most of the soil is acidic and lacking in minerals. The cool summer makes it difficult for many plants to set seeds. This rather favours perennial plants and those spreading vegetatively; few Faroese plants are annuals. But considering all the natural disadvantages of climate and soil, the vegetation can seem quite lush in places, and 400 different flowering plants can be found in Faroe. These grow mostly in the lower areas, and what they do not produce in fruit they make up for in flowers and leaves. On the higher slopes we find only about half the number of species. A typical flower in the mountains is the Alpine buttercup, or *Ranunculus glacialis,* with its hardy white flowers. Like all mountain plants it is anchored to the soil by deep-diving roots. In the mountain areas above 600 metres mosses and lichens predominate; many are arctic varieties which can be found in most arctic regions.

Only one plant has been considered endemic to the Faroe Islands: the Faroese Lady's Mantle – Føroya Skøra or *Alchemilla faeroënsis* – with its yellow flowers which are in bloom in June and July, and geometrically shaped leaves. It can grow up to 40 centimetres high and produces seed without pollination. It grows on cliffs and ledges and is common throughout the islands. The Reyð Várhagasólja or *Taraxacum rubifolium R.R.*, on the other hand, has not seen in any other place in the world apart from Tórshavn, where it was discovered in 1909 by Rasmus Rasmussen.

Animals

Of wild animals there are only rats, mice and hares, and these have all been brought to the islands fairly recently. Originally there were no wild animals at all, not even toads or reptiles. This shortage of species is probably due to isolation and the lack of natural habitats. However, the newcomers to the islands have adapted surprisingly quickly to different conditions and have developed local strains.

In 1854 three northern hares – *Lepus timidus* – were brought from Telemark in Norway and let loose in Streymoy. With no natural enemies such as foxes to harass them, they thrived and multiplied rapidly. Today they can be found in the mountain areas of most islands, in such large numbers that they are hunted every year between 3 November and 1 January. An amazing change took place as early as 1882; only a quarter of the hares turned white in winter, the rest becoming bluish-grey, as they now all do. The hares changed in other ways too; they became smaller, with a shorter skull and smaller teeth. Today the Faroese hare is considered a new variety – *Lepus timidus seclusus*.

The mouse has been in Faroe for centuries, and like the hare it has changed, and has developed four new varieties which are not found anywhere else, but in some respects resemble the St Kilda mouse. They are larger, have thicker tails, and are of a more reddish colour than the mouse they descend from. Besides, they are really no longer house mice, but live outside, many of them in the bird cliffs. Thus there is a mouse special to Nólsoy, another, much larger, in Mykines. So far Vágar and several of the northern islands have remained free of mice.

According to tradition the brown rat first came to Faroe in 1768 on board a wrecked Norwegian ship which drifted ashore in Suðuroy. Within a few years it had ousted the black rat, which disappeared. There are now rats on most islands and they are a great pest, both in the *bygdir* and in the bird cliffs.

The tjaldur *or oyster-catcher is the protected national bird of Faroe*

Birds

Oyster-catchers swoop overhead, the lucky bird of the Faroes, where it is called *tjaldur,* just as it is in North Ronaldsay. They are Saint Bride's pages, who hid the Christ-child from Herod, under seaweed, and in flight they show a white cross on a black ground. Their brilliant orange beaks are easily spotted.

Christine Muir

The *tjaldur* or oyster-catcher – *Haematopus ostralegus* – is the protected national bird of Faroe. Its unmistakable plaintive and piercing cry can be heard everywhere, from the time it arrives in the middle of March as the certain messenger of spring in the islands, until it leaves again in the autumn. A few stray ones even stay for the winter. To kill a *tjaldur* is unlucky and dishonourable. Through the ages the Faroese have come to feel a close affinity with this fearless and colourful bird, which chases away any trespasser and will fiercely defend its young and any weakling in the flock against attack. The idea that the *tjaldur* represents the Faroese people themselves, or anybody trying to resist oppression, can be found in old ballads and especially in *Fuglakvæði*, the satiric verses of Nólsoyar-Páll from the beginning of the nineteenth century.

Another popular bird is the small northern wren that is endemic to the islands – *Troglodytes troglodytes borealis*. *Músabróðir* – the mouse's brother – the Faroese call him, and 'indeed, except as to the tail, he is much like a mouse in size and colour; the same bright eyes and darting motions; the same fashion, too, of whisking in and out between the slats of the *hjallur,* or outside store, and stealing the dried meat. He is seen on the moors and mountains and bird crags as well as near the houses, and more than any other Faroese bird is associated in my mind with the free outdoor life of the light summer nights' (Elizabeth Taylor).

The wren and the *tjaldur* are not without enemies. Although the sea eagle became extinct before 1700, ravens and hooded crows have through the ages taken their toll of the bird population; the ravens have also been charged with killing newborn lambs. So these predators have had a price put on their heads and have been hunted mercilessly. A whitebreasted raven, an ornithological rarity not met with anywhere else, used to be quite common in the islands, but it became extinct in about 1900. The threat posed by the ravens was considered so serious that for a long time a beak duty was in force; it is mentioned as early as 1555, and was not abolished until 1881. The beak duty required all grown men to deliver one beak of a raven to the magistrate each year, or pay a fine. The beaks were collected and burned in a bonfire at Ólavsvøka on 29 July.

Another bird known to have been under the beak duty at one time is the great skua – *Stercorarius skua skua* – and this led to its almost complete extirpation from the islands in the 1890s. But there were other reasons for this as well, as the story of the last pair of great skuas in Vágar illustrates. They were a male and a female, shot by a proud Englishman who had hunted them long and hard and was looking forward to having them stuffed and displayed at home. He was tired and sent his Faroese guide ahead with the two birds, telling him to take good care of them. And so the man did. When the hunter arrived an hour and a half later his dinner was awaiting him: nicely roasted skuas with cranberry sauce and new potatoes. Most of us will feel a certain glee at his chagrin. When the great skua became a protected species in 1897, it was in the nick of time, as there were only four pairs left in the islands. The stock of this bird has since increased; their largest colony is in Svínoy and numbers 500 pairs.

The number of gannets has also grown, but this large white ocean flyer keeps to its one colony at Mykineshólmur and the surrounding stacks. The gannet has been known to go there for centuries, and in 1669 it was referred to as a bird which 'has this nature in it that it does not set foot in any place in all the islands, except only on a small holm lying close to the island of

Mykines ...' (Tarnovius). The gannet is known in Faroe as the *súla*. In 1860 an albatross was sighted among the gannets. For thirty-four years it would come every February to Mykineshólmur and live among the *súla*, then leave with them in September. The bird became an ornithological wonder, and was popularly known as the *kongasúla* or king of the gannets. In the end the albatross was accidentally shot by a Mykines man who had merely wanted to see the bird on the wing. It was sent to the Nólsoy ornithologist Peter F. Petersen, who found it to be a well-developed female bird in beautiful plumage. Strangely, the story has been repeated. In recent years an albatross has returned each year to the same ledge at Hermaness in the Shetland island of Unst, to sit on its solitary nest right in the middle of a large gannet colony.

As in Orkney and Shetland the fulmar has flourished and is now one of the most common birds in Faroe. It was first observed nesting in Suðuroy in 1839 and rapidly spread, so that by the end of the nineteenth century it could be found in all the islands. The growth in its numbers coincided with the development of fishing, and this may in part explain its expansion. So far the fulmar has not been able to oust the puffin, or *lundi*, which is still the most numerous bird despite its having been hunted for centuries. A record one-man catch of 1,200 puffins was taken in Viðareiði.

In the 1930s an epidemic of a previously unknown infection broke out in the islands. It was a virulent fever, described as alveolar pneumonia, and several people died from it. At first it was confined to the southern islands but gradually it spread to the whole of Faroe. A general practitioner at Eiði began a systematic study of all the cases and concluded that the infection was psittacosis or 'parrot fever' and that the source was probably the young of the fulmar, which in Faroe were caught in August and September. His diagnosis was proved correct in 1938 when the psittacosis virus was found both in fulmar chicks and in the patients who died that year. Since then the fulmar has largely been left in peace.

Generally speaking, wild life in Faroe is completely dominated by the bird population. There are overwhelming numbers of a surprisingly large variety of species, most of them sea-birds: puffins, guillemots, razor-bills and gulls. In fact there are few other places with such a concentration of sea-birds. Altogether there have been definite sightings of 227 different birds, as compared with 543 in Britain, but most of these are migratory birds or stray guests. The number of resident birds, however, is large compared to those wintering in other Scandinavian countries.

2

EARLY TIMES

The great narrative *Navigatio Sancti Brendani* describes the voyages supposedly made in AD 560–7 by the Irish abbot Brénaind – St Brendan – across the western oceans to find the 'Promised Land of the Saints'. The book tells how he sailed for many years and lived through many adventures before he reached his objective. The story is a strange weave of many strands, of both Celtic and classical origin, and it was long considered a legend, a moral fable. St Brendan was after all a pious man who founded many monasteries in his native country. Added to that, the story was probably not written down until some time in the ninth century, and the original manuscript is lost. But there were scholars who thought that much of the story rang true, and in 1976–7 it was put to the test. In the *Brendan,* a light skin boat which was a replica of the old Irish currach, a small crew sailed across the Atlantic to Newfoundland, although not without difficulty.

In his story St Brendan tells of the Island of Sheep, which some take to be the Faroe Islands. There they went ashore and slaughtered a sheep to celebrate Easter. A messenger 'with white hair and young eyes – for he had lived a long life in peace' brought them greetings from God and the bread of the land, 'big, white and unleavened loaves'. He reported that the sheep were so large in the islands because no ewe was milked, the winter was mild and no animal ever died of sickness.

In 825, some two and a half centuries later, the Irish priest Dicuil in his book *De Mensura Orbis Terrae* gives us another glimpse of the islands:

> There are many other islands in Britain's northern sea. They can be reached from the northern islands of Britain by sailing for two days and two nights on a straight course under full sail and with a fair wind. A devout priest told me that he navigated this route in two summer days and one night, in a small two-benched boat, and landed on one of the islands. These islands are for the most part small, and there are mostly narrow sounds between them, and in these islands hermits, coming from our country, Ireland, by boat, have lived for almost a hundred years. But as they have always been uninhabited from the beginning of the world, so have Norse pirates caused them to be devoid of anchorites, but

One of the Brendan
crew, *Faroese artist,*
Tróndur Patursson

they are full of innumerable sheep and many different kinds of
sea birds. I have never seen these islands mentioned in the books
of other authors.

When Dicuil wrote his book about the dimensions of the earth, he tried to
introduce new geographical knowledge. The story he told of anchorites in the
islands does not come as a surprise to us, because not only has St Brendan's
tale prepared us, but also in Iceland, Shetland and Orkney the presence of
Irish monks in that period has been much discussed. We would expect these
hardy travellers, whose stated purpose it was to find 'a hermitage in the
untravelled ocean', to have appreciated the loneliness and wild beauty of the
Faroe Islands, and not to have passed them by. For these islands to have been
continuously occupied by monks for a century or more, the sea route from
Ireland and the way to navigate it must have been fairly well known. That this
was true is borne out by the tale of sea adventure ascribed to St Brendan –
clearly based on authentic seamen's accounts.

For some time archaeologists have believed that certain fields in the island
of Mykines were in fact cultivated before the Norse settlers came. This theory
was given added weight by the research of Faroese botanist Jóhannes
Jóhansen. In his 1985 dissertation at the University of Copenhagen he claimed
that as early as AD 600-50 the long sloping fields in question had been used
for growing corn, first oats and later barley. Analyses of pollen from Mykines,

Tjørnuvík in Eysturoy, and Hov in Suðuroy show the same result: there have indeed been two land occupation phases in the Faroes, one some time in the years between 600 and 700, when oats were cultivated, and the other in the Viking period, when the crop was barley. Fields similar to those in Mykines can be seen in Suðuroy. they are generally found in the *hagi* or in almost inaccessible slopes facing south and west. The fields are long and narrow, separated by low banks of earth, which are actually old stone dykes, rather like those found in western Ireland.

In an old churchyard in Skúvoy a number of puzzling gravestones have been found. They are decorated with crosses in a way that points to Celtic influence, possibly even Celtic origin, so that the possibility that they were made by Irish *papar*, or priests, must be entertained. In Suðuroy a tale has been told of holy men living on the island before the coming of the Norsemen. They were alleged to work wonders such as healing all wounds and diseases both in animals and people; they also foretold the weather and whether the fishing would be plentiful. They kept to themselves and lived on milk, eggs and seaweed, for they would not kill any living thing. Although there are various factors indicating a pre-Norse presence in Faroe, many scholars point out that as long as no archaeological finds are made, the evidence remains circumstantial and nothing has been proved.

During the eighth and ninth centuries the *vestrvíking* expeditions from the west coast of Norway were carried out with ever-increasing momentum. As their range and scale grew so did the westward expansion, with a large-scale Norse emigration first to Orkney and Shetland, then to the Faroe Islands and finally to Iceland. The long voyage to the Faroe Islands meant sailing for days across the open sea, as a later ballad-writer describes it in the 'Sigmundar kvæði' – 'The Ballad of Sigmundur Brestisson'*:*

Nætur tvær og dagar tríggja	Two nights and three days
fyrr enn han fekk Føroyar at síggja.	before he sighted the Faroe Islands.

To find the Faroe Islands in the rain and the fog without the help of a compass was no mean feat!

A swiftly rising population at home was perhaps the major cause of this emigration, which the Norwegian historian A. W. Brøgger calls 'the drive to the west':

> The choice of northerly regions by the majority was due to fundamental and primitive causes. It was the craving for surroundings where something of the old was to be found in their new activities. They asked for sea and fjord, mountain and hill, the fowling cliffs and sealing grounds. They needed the pastures, meadows and heather to which they had been accus-

tomed in the land of their birth, and the light summer nights which brooded softly over farm and field in Norway. No sentimental spirit of homesickness lay at the back of all this, but the simple fact that the whole of their mentality, fostered by the toil of countless generations before them, was adjusted to a life in which all these things were to be found.

The settlers would at once have seen and appreciated the green pastures and the rich resources of birds and fish found in the Faroe Islands.

Whereas the sagas describe the settlement of Iceland in detail, they do not pay much attention to the Norse *landnám,* or landtaking, of the Faroe Islands. Of course the most probable explanation for this lack of interest is that the settlement in Faroe was not well known to the saga writers. According to *Færeyinga Saga – The Saga of the Faroese –* the first settler in the Faroe Islands was a man named Grímur Kamban – '*Hann bygdi fyrstr Færeyjar*'. It may have been the landtaking of Grímur and his followers that caused the anchorites to leave. This landtaking must have taken place quite soon after 800 as we are told in the Icelandic *Landnámabók – The Book of Settlements –* that Grímur Kamban's grandson Tórolvur Tórsteinsson went north to look for Iceland around 870. The nickname Kamban is probably Gaelic and one interpretation is that the word refers to some physical handicap, another that it may point to his prowess as a sportsman. Probably he came as a young man to the Faroe Islands by way of Viking Ireland, and local tradition has it that he settled in Funningur in Eysturoy. Grímur Kamban seems to have played much the same part in the settlement of the Faroe Islands as Ingólfr Arnarson in that of Iceland.

Iceland was discovered by the Norsemen when, around 850, the Viking Nadd-Odd was driven off course by a storm while on his way from Norway to Faroe. He was born in Agder in the south of Norway, but had been outlawed and had settled in the Faroe Islands. We are told that forty years later Aud the Deepminded, daughter of the Norse chieftain Ketil Flatnev, left Scotland for Iceland after her husband Olaf the White and her son Torstein the Red died. She stayed for some time in Faroe and married her granddaughter Olúva Tórsteinsdóttir to a chieftain at Gøta in Eysturoy, thus establishing the famous and powerful family of the Gøtuskeggjar. It is the only Faroese family to be mentioned in the Icelandic sagas.

We know from saga sources that in Iceland Aud claimed a huge area, which she later shared with family and friends – an area large enough for eighty farms. This is probably what happened in Faroe too, as much of the place-name evidence suggests that at the time of the first settlement the land holdings were few and large, in some cases including whole islands. The *landnám* was probably organized by a few powerful families, who would then favour their own and keep others out of the islands. These families came

Overleaf:
Tróndur Patursson – Sighting land.

mainly from the Norwegian west coast, but they would have been joined by friends and relations from the Norse settlements in Ireland and the Western Isles as the Norsemen were always conscious of family ties and obligations. In fact, there are archaeological as well as linguistic indications of a fairly close and long-standing connection with the western settlements. Also some practices of the old farming culture, such as the use of tormentil roots as tanning material, were clearly adopted from Gaelic areas.

The settlement history of Faroe seems to indicate that there were three separate areas in the islands at first – the North Isles with Borðoy as the centre on one side, Suðuroy with Dímun and Skúvoy on the other, and between them the large central area of Streymoy and Eysturoy. Each of these areas would have been the domain of a chieftain and his family. This division probably lasted for some time, as can to some extent be inferred from *Færeyinga Saga*, which deals with a later period. Thus the saga tells us of the chieftain Bjarni in Svínoy and his tax rights, of the Gøtuskeggjar in Eysturoy and of Havgrímur in Hov on Suðuroy. But the chieftains probably let tenants run some of their farming area. With the passage of time the land holdings would also have been divided among heirs according to Norse law, and thus split up into smaller units.

The islands were organized in accordance with the Norse way of life. Among the most characteristic features of Norse settlements in the west were their systems of law and order. There were local tingsteads – among them í Køtlum in Borðoy and Stóragil near Øravík in Suðuroy – but the main meeting-place would have been at Tinganes in Tórshavn; site of the Løgting, or Lawting, where matters concerning all the islands would have been discussed and settled. This was also the main place of worship; it is even possible that the original name was Tórsnes. As the name tells us, Tór was an important god in the islands. He was the god of the weather and therefore master of the crops. From the eleventh century the Faroese Løgting was opened on 29 July, the day King Olav Haraldsson the Saint died in 1030, and it has been the only Norse ting opened on that day. The conversion to Christianity of the Norse areas coincided more or less with the death of St Olav, who seems quickly to have assumed some of the functions of the god Tór. King Olav became the saint for corn and other produce in the north, and in the Orkney islands the 'Fair of St Olla' was held to give thanks when the corn was cut, a custom that persisted into the nineteenth century.

Systematic archaeological excavations in Faroe began as late as the 1940s, and were largely the work of Sverri Dahl, the founder and for long the only practitioner of this science in the islands. The first major burial find from the Viking age was made in 1956 close to the village of Tjørnuvík in Eysturoy. At least twelve persons had been buried close to the shore in a dune of shifting sands, which had been covered by later landslides. They were all placed with their heads towards the north, and at least one of them had been buried in woven textiles. They had been given everyday articles as grave-goods. The most interesting of these is a ring-headed pin of bronze, with pieces of cloth still hanging from it, which is recognized as Scottish-Gaelic and dated to the tenth century. This pin thus suggests that communication between the Norse settlements in the west lasted for some time.

The earlier building finds show great variations in size and structure and reflect a stratified society. In Kvívík in Streymoy we find the best-known example of the excavated houses. It is a rather traditional Viking longhouse 20 metres in length, with an open fireplace in the middle. Alongside the longhouse is also a cowshed – so far the only one identified in the islands. It probably had room for twelve cows. The animals were placed in two rows opposite each other. The southern parts of the buildings had been washed away by the sea. Evidently the land must have subsided several metres since the Viking age. A number of finds made on the site give an interesting picture of life as it was lived on a major farm of the period. Among these finds are characteristic shoes, similar to those found in Borgund in Norway, and children's toys of carved horses and boats with oars. A habitation very similar to the Kvívík farmhouse has been excavated at Fuglafjørður in Eysturoy.

A number of excavations have been made at Gøta in Eysturoy, and it is interesting to see that they do not in fact disprove the story told in *Færeyinga Saga*. When the chieftain nicknamed Gøtuskegg died, his two sons cast lots for the main farm at Gøta because they both wanted it. Tróndur won, and his elder brother went away. So did Tróndur for a while, after letting out the land at Gøta for as large a rent as he could get for it. After making his fortune he came back to put his place at Gøta in order. Today Gøta is divided into three bygdir: Norðragøta, Gøtugjógv and Syðragøta. Traditionally Tróndur's farm was at Norðragøta, and here a settlement has been discovered on the beach. At high tide it is covered by water. The remains of a medieval churchyard have been found on the beach at Syðragøta, and according to tradition this was the site of the church during the Middle Ages. Along the edge of the old infields at Syðragøta are scattered five small farm sites. They have not as yet been fully excavated, but both shape and size distinguish the small buildings from the larger longhouses.

These simple houses clearly represent a different social level from that of the longhouses, and may well have belonged to Tróndur's tenants.

3

FÆREYINGA SAGA

The only written source to throw any light on life in the Faroe Islands during the Viking Age is *Færeyinga Saga* – the Saga of the Faroe Islanders. It is a story told on many levels: it describes how the kings of Norway try to win the islands by political efforts rather than war; it is a dramatically told tale of family feud and bitter strife through three generations; and it depicts a time of religious and ideological upheaval, when conflicting values meet and clash as the old faith is being replaced by Christianity.

Færeyinga Saga does not exist as a separate manuscript. The story was pieced together as early as 1832 from different sources, of which the most important is the *Flateyjarbók*, a manuscript from *c.* 1380 containing sagas about the kings of Norway. Although there are obvious gaps in the present story, it has the stamp throughout of one writer, and various factors indicate that there was at one time an original *Færeyinga Saga* which today is lost. As much of the saga involves affairs of state, the historian Snorri Sturluson drew on it heavily when, some time between 1220 and 1235, he was writing his sagas of Norse kings, and he even refers to it in places – '*svá sem segir í Færeyingasǫgu*' – 'as it is said in *Færeyinga Saga*'. The original saga must therefore have been written before that period, probably just after 1200.

Færeyinga Saga describes the period from *c.* 980 to *c.* 1040 in the history of the Faroe Islands, and takes place partly in the islands and partly in Norway. Probably it is to some extent based on authentic Faroese tales, but the Icelandic writer may never even have visited the islands. His geographical knowledge of them seems to have been rather sketchy, otherwise he would not have made the mistake of describing an attack on Stóra Dímun and insisting that it takes place in Skúvoy, as the two islands are simply too different topographically to be confused. Certain characteristics of style have made scholars cautiously conclude that the writer may have come from the district around Eyjafjörður in northern Iceland.

When the saga begins the Faroe Islands have already been settled for a long time and some families are firmly entrenched in positions of power. Later incomers seem to be tenants and owe loyalty to their chieftains. It is a period of political unrest; Norse rulers are trying to gain a foothold in the islands for taxation purposes, and they are succeeding in making some of the chieftains become their vassals, but there are others who oppose this incipient

24

dependence on the crown of Norway. It is a classic example of how a divide and conquer policy can undermine the independence of a people. When Christianity becomes part of the picture the scales are tipped in favour of the Norse kings, as the question of power now becomes an ideological issue. This is the background of the two main protagonists – Tróndur í Gøtu and Sigmundur Brestisson, who both belong to the family known as the Gøtuskeggjar. The theme of the saga is a fight to the death between these close kinsmen – Tróndur is fighting against Christianity and for independence from Norway, while Sigmundur becomes a Christian and the close friend and ally of Norse rulers.

Ironically Tróndur has brought this state of affairs on himself. At the beginning of the saga his two cousins Brestir and Beinir, who own farms on Skúvoy and Stóra Dímun, are attacked by the chieftain Havgrímur í Hovi from Suðuroy, and all three die in the battle. We are told that these men between them hold the Faroe Islands in feu from Norway: Havgrímur from King Harald Greycloak and the brothers Brestir and Beinir from the king's successor, Hákon, the powerful Earl of Lade. Tróndur is present during the battle but does not take an active part in it. Sigmundur and Tórir, the small sons of Brestir and Beinir, are also witnesses, and when Tórir cries, Sigmundur tells him not to weep but to remember … They are sent to Norway to be sold as slaves by Tróndur, who now rules the islands alone. He brings Havgrímur's son Øssur to his farm in Eysturoy, to be brought up there, and later lets him take over the property which by right belongs to the other boys.

Sigmundur and Tórir are freed, grow up in Norway and become the close friends of Earl Hákon, who knew their fathers. After an eventful time in the earl's service, Sigmundur returns as a seasoned man with a well-equipped ship to retrieve his property and avenge his father. He reaches an uneasy truce with Tróndur at an assembly meeting at Tinganes in Tórshavn. Sigmundur is the earl's man in Faroe and brings him taxes from the islands. There is, however, a political change in Norway – King Olav Tryggvason seizes power and begins to convert the country to Christianity. The saga tells us that when he has been on the throne of Norway for two years, he sends for Sigmundur, who spends the winter with the king, and is rated highly by him. Sigmundur becomes a Christian and promises to convert the Faroe islanders. When he returns to the islands, he summons the farmers to a Ting meeting and puts the matter before them. Tróndur advises the farmers against accepting the new faith, and Sigmundur has to promise in front of witnesses that he will never again try to convert them.

Sigmundur grudgingly keeps his promise for a year, but the next spring he secretly sails to Eysturoy, surrounds Tróndur's farm during the night and forces him with an axe to his head to be baptized. With Tróndur as an unwilling companion Sigmundur goes around the islands and makes people

Overleaf:
Tróndur Patursson –
Gøtuskeggjar going
up on Skúvoy.

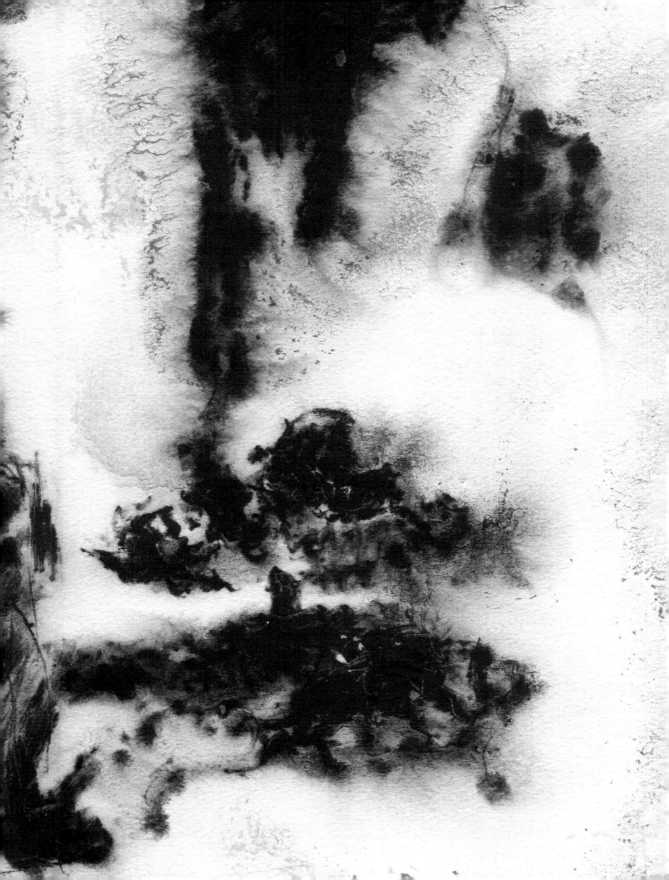

accept the new faith. Some years later Tróndur and his men carry out a surprise attack on Sigmundur's farm on Skúvoy. Sigmundur tries to save his life by swimming across to Suðuroy, and makes it to Sandvík, only to be murdered by Tróndur's tenant, who covets his gold arm-ring. Tróndur arranges a marriage between Leivur Øssursson, the grandson of the Suðuroy chieftain Havgrímur í Hovi, and Tóra, Sigmundur's daughter, thus effectively reconciling two contending families. The rest of the saga describes Tróndur's continued fight, by fair means and foul, against Norwegian overlordship in the islands. But when he dies in 1035 the fight is over, and Leivur Øssursson accepts allegiance to Norway.

However, in the imagination of the Faroese people the strife among the Gøtuskeggjar lived on, and a number of ballads and dancing songs tell again the stories of Sigmundur and Tróndur and all the others. Sigmundur stands tall in all the stories and songs about him – he is the shining hero both as a young Viking and later as a Christian crusader. In a long speech King Olav Tryggvason, who excelled at all sports himself, compares their fates: both of them lost their fathers for no reason; they themselves were sold as slaves; both of them later had great honour conferred on them by important men; and eventually they came into their own again in the land of their birth. The saga writer takes the comparison further and tells us himself that Sigmundur and King Olav tested their skills at swimming and shooting and other sports and, although the king always won, Sigmundur came closer to him than any other man.

Tróndur is a central figure in the saga from beginning to end. We are told rather harshly at the beginning that he is sly and untrustworthy; indeed, by drawing attention to his red hair and freckles, the saga writer may want us to associate him with a fox. Through his practical common sense he makes a good deal of money for himself at a market in Denmark; the means thus earned are often referred to later as the basis of his power at home. But we also note that he is respected for his knowledge of the law, and at the Ting he is deferred to by the others. He is also shown to be a master of old rites which can call forth the dead.

We must bear in mind that this saga tells of events that took place long before they were written down. The saga was composed by a Christian Icelander who was assured enough in his faith and his art to play with his characters and his listeners; there is much sleight-of-hand in the unfolding of his narrative. Thus Sigmundur is going to take Tróndur against his will to King Olav in Norway, but the ship is driven back by storm and current. A second attempt fares no better. The saga narrator does not in fact tell us that this is magic worked by Tróndur, but he very skilfully leads us towards such a conclusion.

As the narrator is a Christian it follows that he is biased in favour of the Norse kings and their chosen man, Sigmundur. Moral values are therefore coloured by other considerations: Faroe must be won for the new faith by whatever means, even if this means that the islands will lose their political as well as their economic independence. Sigmundur's own motives may very well be a mixed bag too: through the command given him by King Olav he has been handed not only power over the islands, but also a unique tool for revenge. And he has no compunction about breaking his word, given at the Ting to all the people there, that he will not try again to make them change their faith. In fact, after he has forced Tróndur to become baptized, he cleverly uses him as a hostage to make sure that the farmers will follow his example, depending on Tróndur being a man of his word.

Perhaps the narrator's view of his subject and his characters is more ambivalent than we are at first led to suppose? Many incidents in the saga lend themselves to different interpretations. Thus the gold ring that Earl Hákon gives Sigmundur before he returns to Faroe is meant to bring him luck. When Sigmundur later becomes King Olav's man and is sitting one day at his table, the king asks Sigmundur for his ring, saying that he will give him a better one in its place. But Sigmundur will not part with it as 'I promised the earl when he generously gave me the ring never to part with it, and that promise I shall keep, for the one who gave it to me, the earl, seemed to me a good man who was kind to me in many ways.' There are deeper reasons behind the king's request; it is his way of asking Sigmundur to renounce his friendship and loyalty to Earl Hákon, and Sigmundur refuses to do so. The King, we are told, turns red as blood, and prophesies that the ring will cause Sigmundur's death; the relationship between the two cools after this. Friendship in the face of obstacles – loyalty to the two contending parties – is an idealized theme in the sagas, and it says much for his character that Sigmundur remains loyal to a man whose name, according to Snorri Sturluson, had become a bad word, who was the king's defeated enemy and a heathen to boot. When the ring is the cause of Sigmundur's death it seems like bitter irony – is he being punished for not embracing Christianity whole-heartedly? But the saga writer leaves us guessing as to the answer; his story has so many twists and turns, so many layers of meaning, that we never learn just where his loyalty lies.

Tróndur comes across as the more interesting of the two; he is one of the inscrutable characters of saga literature. The saga writer's indictment against him at the beginning of the story remains unsubstantiated, for the only crime we actually witness is his betrayal of his family. Although he did not kill his cousins Brestir and Beinir himself, he did not in any way try to prevent the assault on them; and he sells his own kinsmen as slaves – when the young boys are sent off they have already had their hair cropped short and are dressed as slaves. In a community where family loyalty was an integral part of the social pattern and a question of personal honour his behaviour is difficult to understand, but then the origin of this family feud is never really explained.

When set beside Sigmundur, the Christian courtier endowed with so many heroic qualities, Tróndur comes across as a pragmatic politician who, when necessary, is able to concede defeat and is willing to compromise. In many ways he seems strangely modern in his outlook. When Tóra, wife of Leivur Øssursson, protests that the Creed Tróndur has been teaching her son sounds quite new to her, he says: 'As you know it is like this, that Christ had twelve disciples or more, and each of them had his own Creed. Now I have my Creed, and you have what you have learnt, and there are many Creeds, and even if they are not the same they are just as right.' It seems as though the saga writer wants to portray Tróndur as a rugged individualist who may have suffered the utter humiliation of being forced to accept a faith he is opposed to, but still goes on keeping his own counsel. If this is what the saga writer intended us to think, then the Iceland of his times must have been a tolerant society.

Although the saga is logically constructed, there are many fairy-tale incidents that are obviously tacked on to the story, so that its purpose seems to be to entertain rather than instruct. Still, it seems probable that the historical core is in the main correct; the fact that the historian Snorri Sturluson used *Færeyinga Saga* may also vouch for its historicity. The saga throws some light on legal practices in the islands, but we learn surprisingly little about the routines of daily life. It also gives some idea of how Christianity was introduced. We are told that Sigmundur built the first church in the islands on his own Skúvoy, and that both he and his cousin Tórir were buried there. A large stone, the 'Sigmundarsteinur', where a Latin cross has been carved, still stands in the old churchyard in Skúvoy.

Færeyinga Saga has meant much to the Faroese as a national epic. Tróndur í Gøtu has remained respected. Sigmundur may be the man of action, the romantic hero, but he is perhaps more the king's man than a man of God, and it was Tróndur who fought to keep the islands independent. In the ballad of the Gøtuskeggjar we are told:

Tróndur alskaði Føroyaland	Tróndur loved the land of Faroe
í sína ævi alla	for all his living days

4

LATER HISTORY

Færeyinga Saga ends with the islanders converted to Christianity and under Norse rule. As the saga implies, this conversion did not come about because people no longer believed in the old gods, but because the new faith was forced on them. The Church expected each individual, whether chieftain or slave, to conform to its values. This effectively broke up the old social order based on family allegiance and power. Chapels and churches were built, yet it took centuries before all the old customs and beliefs disappeared: they survived as part of a subculture.

Throughout the eleventh and twelfth centuries economic conditions were relatively good in the Faroe Islands, as they were in the Nordic countries as a whole. And yet we see the islands becoming increasingly isolated and dependent on the king of Norway during this period. The old shipping connections, mostly run by the Faroese themselves, came to an end, and in 1273 King Magnus the Lawmaker undertook to send two trading ships a year, probably in an attempt to set up a royal trading monopoly. He was not able to keep this promise, and gradually the trade on the islands was taken over by the Hanseatic merchants, whose boats were better suited to the transport of goods. In 1294 and again in 1302 Hanseatic trade in the Norse areas was prohibited, but to no effect. Finally, in stiff competition with the Dutch and the British, the Hansa in 1361 gained the same trading rights as Norwegian merchants in the Norse areas of the North Sea and the North Atlantic.

Towards the end of the thirteenth century some 4,000 people lived in the islands, and for centuries to come the population remained roughly this size. It is around this time that the Faroese nation emerged. Historical sources are few, but it appears from the Seyðabrævið or Sheep Letter of 1298, which regulates the keeping of sheep, that the large land holdings of the first settler families have been split up into smaller farms, and that on the whole the settlement has become more scattered. The Church gained in importance, both because a bishopric was established and because the Church became the largest landowner in the islands. The islands were probably a flourishing community when the building of the Magnus Cathedral at Kirkjubøur was begun sometime around 1300. Even so, people are said to have revolted against bishop Erlendur because of the financial burdens imposed on them in connection with the building of the cathedral.

There was considerable economic decline in the islands later in the fourteenth century, as indeed there was in Norway. Many reasons have been put forward for this change, such as a serious deterioration in the climate, which is believed to have become colder and wetter. This cannot be proved, however, nor is there any scientific proof that the Black Death ever reached the Faroe Islands, although in some places farm ruins lend support to the popular stories of death and depopulation. To explain the striking gap in the oral tradition of this period the theory has been put forward that the Black Death may have killed off such a large part of the population that new immigration from Norway became necessary. It was probably because the trade connection with Norway became so difficult to maintain that Hanseatic merchants in 1361 were given the same trading rights in the islands as Norwegian merchants. Still, there is really no satisfactory explanation of why within a few decades a seemingly prosperous community declined so far that it would take centuries to recover.

For dynastic reasons there was a fusion of the crowns of Norway and Denmark in 1380, but this was of little consequence for the islands at first, as at least nominally they were governed as a part of Norway until 1709. Gradually much of the land became the property of the Catholic Church, the Crown or prominent Norwegian families, so that by about 1500 less than half the land was owned by the Faroese themselves.

The sixteenth century was a time of profound and painful change. Raids by French, British, Irish and Algerian pirates became frequent and much feared. The Algerian pirates, who were popularly known as Turks, were perhaps feared more than the others. Neither man nor beast was safe from abduction, as there was little people could do to protect themselves except hide in the mountains. Old hide-outs in almost inaccessible places can still be seen in most *bygdir,* as well as look-outs where a watch would be kept.

For a while the Dutch gained trading rights in the islands alongside the Hanseatic merchants, and the rivalry between merchants became fierce. On two occasions King Henry VIII of England was offered the Faroe Islands and Iceland by the Danish kings in exchange for a loan, as the Danes were always desperately in need of funds. King Henry turned them down, however, and in 1529 King Frederik I gave the Faroe Islands in fief to the Hamburg merchants Thomas Koppen and Joachim Wullenweber for 100 marks per year. They also obtained a trade monopoly and the right to collect taxes.

The Norwegian State Council was dissolved in 1536, and both Norway and the Faroe Islands became Danish provinces, although constitutionally the islands remained 'really and truly the land of Norway's crown'. The Catholic Church, which represented the last bulwark against royal power, was abolished when the Reformation was introduced between 1535 and 1540. This change was imposed from above, and in many ways it meant a death-blow to the old culture. Whereas in both Germany and Sweden the Reformation led

to a flourishing of the national language and culture, it meant a decline in
Norway and the Faroe Islands, because Danish replaced Latin as the church
language. Priests had been educated at Kirkjubøur, but when the school there
was closed down ministers had to be educated in Copenhagen, so that in due
course there were more Danish ministers than Faroese.

King Christian III at once confiscated two-thirds of church land and later
let it to Thomas Koppen. When in 1557 the bishopric was abolished and the
islands made part of the bishopric of Bergen under a *próstur*, or dean, the
remaining church land was also seized by the king. The king's land – the
kongsjørð – was rented out to tenants who became known as *kongsbøndur*
(king's farmers), who often owned some *óðalsjørð* of their own as well. As the
ownership of land was necessary to settle in the *bygdir*, the *óðalsjørð*, or
private land, was divided among family members again and again. As the
king's farms, on the other hand, could not be split up, and the tenancy was
inherited by the eldest son, a class of powerful families arose. In this way the
kongsbøndur came to represent the most stable and influential factor in the
Faroese community in the centuries to come. The ministers as a rule had
numerous offspring, who tended to marry into the families of the *kongsbøndur*, and often a minister's son was given the tenancy of a king's farm
when it became vacant. People with no land rights became the servants of
this new class of farmers and government officials.

On the whole the history of the islands in the period between 1500 and
1700 presents a dark picture. Political and economic power became concen-
trated in the hands of the king in Copenhagen. For a short time the trade
monopoly was in Faroese hands, after it had been given in 1579 to Magnus
Heinason (1548–89), an adventurer who was born and bred in the islands but
learned how to fight a war while serving with the Dutch. In order to clear
Faroese waters of pirates King Frederik II gave Heinason wide powers, such
as the right to equip a naval ship and build the fort of Skansin. His feats have
not diminished in the telling and he has remained a hero in his homeland,
even though he appears in his cavalier way to have cheated them shamelessly.

In 1619 the Faroese trade was moved from Bergen to Copenhagen, where
it remained, and thus a connection that had lasted for some 800 years was
severed. At the same time the Church was transferred from the bishopric of
Bergen to that of Sjælland in Denmark, but the islands went on being ruled
according to Norwegian law. Although all legal trade in this period was
confined to the Trade Monopoly, records show that a lot of smuggling did in
fact take place. Then in 1661–2 the islands were given in feu to Christoffer
Gabel, who obtained absolute power both economically and politically.
When he died he was succeeded by his son Frederik. They both used the title
of governor, and both have been condemned for cruelly usurping their rights.
Imports became dearer while the price of woollen goods and dried fish fell.
The work of further fortifying the Skansin in Tórshavn was imposed on the

landless townspeople without pay. In 1673 their minister Lucas Debes, who wrote the famous description of the Faroe Islands and the Faroese called *Færoæ et Færoæ Reserata,* helped his parishioners compose a formal complaint to the king in Copenhagen. The same year almost all the buildings of the Trade Monopoly at Tinganes in Tórshavn as well as the house of the Løgting were burned down, and the store of gunpowder kept at Tinganes blew up. There seems no doubt that the fire was intentional. Then in 1677 the town was looted by French pirates. Lucas Debes also got into trouble for his intervention in the struggle, but the king did take a stand for his subjects against Gabel. All in all the Gabel period is held to be the nadir in Faroese history, when life in the islands was difficult and unhappy for many reasons – not least because this was a time of armed conflict and unrest in North Atlantic waters.

In his novel *The Good Hope* the Faroese writer William Heinesen uses these conflicts in a masterly way. His main character is a minister, who is described as no better than he should be – he is perhaps rather too fond of the bottle; he comes to the oppressed island country and becomes shocked and disgusted by what he sees. To some extent William Heinesen uses the historical character of Lucas Debes for the portrayal of the Tórshavn minister, but he emphasizes that 'the book is not concerned with historical and biographical facts; it is the general situation that is important to me. I have tried to draw a character who represents what I admire most of all, struggling humanity. It always triumphs in the end over evil and brutality.'

After the death of Frederik Gabel a royal commission was sent to the islands to examine conditions there, and the outcome was that King Frederik IV decided to take over the trade monopoly himself. Thus from 1709 until 1856 the Faroe trade was carried on to serve the needs of the people and not private interests, and the change from a feudal to a bureaucratic regime was almost immediately noticeable. To most people it seemed a change for the better: corruption came to an end, Faroese products could be sold and a reasonable supply of goods be bought in return, all at set prices. People were not hounded if they could not pay. On the other hand very little was done to promote any kind of trade or industry between the islands themselves, and the Faroese had to sail in all kinds of weather to Tórshavn if they wanted to deal with the Trade Monopoly. This naturally affected Suðuroy especially badly, and in 1720 people reportedly starved to death on that island. In the 1830s branch stores were established in Tvøroyri, Klaksvík and Vestmanna.

The Royal Trade Monopoly served to conserve the old order of things. All power in the islands was once more centralized under the Crown, and government officials such as the clergy were given unprecedented authority. Thus in 1777 the *kongsbøndur* and the government officials succeeded in introducing the law known as the 'slave-law', which stipulated that anybody wanting to marry must own enough land to be able to support a family. The purpose of this law was to keep the population down to a level which the land could support, and it therefore seems illogical that at the same time nobody could leave the islands without paying a large sum of money for the privilege. Probably the proletariat was needed as a cheap labour force at times when trade flourished and extra hands were needed; they also had a duty to serve as boat crews on the fishing boats and whenever transport was required. The law was not repealed until 1846. The first faint opposition to this concentration of power in the hands of the ruling class was expressed by Jens Christian Svabo in his *Records of a Journey in Faroe 1781-82*, but nobody paid much attention to him. Another blow came in the 1790s when the Latin School in Tórshavn was closed down, thus making it difficult for the islanders to obtain an academic education.

For a short period towards the end of the eighteenth century the private company of Niels Ryberg drew the Faroe Islands into international trade, when groceries were smuggled into Britain. Ryberg also tried to make the islanders take up commercial fishing. Another colourful individual in Faroese history is Nólsoyar-Páll, or Poul Poulsen of Nólsoy, who became the first Faroese after Magnus Heinason to own a ship, the *Royndin Fríða* – the *Good Endeavour*. Inspired by the ideas of the French Revolution he turned courageously against the rule of the corrupt and inefficient government officials that strangled any development in the islands. He tried to convince his countrymen as well as the Danes of the benefits of free trade, and plans were actually made to introduce free trade as from 1 January 1796, when the outbreak of the Napoleonic Wars halted them. During the war Nólsoyar-Páll tried to bring corn from England, but he disappeared at sea in 1809, on his way to the Faroe Islands. The supplies he was bringing were sorely needed, as what little there was in the way of food and supplies had been taken. In 1808 the English brig *Clio* under the command of Captain Baugh entered Tórshavn and captured Skansin. Later the same year an English privateer owned by the Baron von Hompesch shot at the town and the sailors robbed the buildings of the Monopoly and the Church as well as all public coffers. In Tórshavn von Hompesch has been remembered as Brillumaðurin – the man with glasses.

When by the Treaty of Kiel in 1814 the union between Norway and Denmark was dissolved, the Faroe Islands remained with Denmark. There is no record of the Faroese reaction to this breach. Politically the ties to Norway had become broken, but the feeling of cultural kinship was to become an important factor in the national awakening towards the end of the century. Norwegian laws remained in force, and Danish laws had to be specially adapted.

The old social order was, however, disintegrating. In spite of the attempts to curb the population, it was growing larger than the *bygdir* could absorb, and some new *bygdir,* such as Skopun in Sandoy, were built. Even though potato growing had made farming more productive, the islands grew increasingly dependent on imported food, especially corn. At the same time the climate seems to have become warmer, and the fishing improved to the extent that commercial exploitation could be considered. Reforms were urged by the governor Christian Pløyen and by Nólsoyar-Páll's younger brother, who for twenty years managed the Monopoly store in Tórshavn. In 1839 Christian Pløyen made his famous trip in the company of three føroyingar from Eiði, Nólsoy and Hoyvík, to Shetland, Orkney and Scotland to study both fishing and farming methods.

The Monopoly began buying all kinds of fish for export, and by the 1840s fish and fish products accounted for almost 40 per cent of all export. When a census was taken in 1850, fishermen had already become the largest group. With the development of fishing each *bygd* grew in size, as it could now support more people. In the 1850s we therefore find people moving back to the *bygdir*, so that the population of Tórshavn actually declined. The *bygd* was not always the same, however, as the old communal way of living had to some extent been replaced by a more individually-orientated culture. As the fishing began to take the men away for long periods at a time, the tasks and responsibilities of women also changed. And whereas the ministers in the old days often came to stay for life, now they tended to see their stay in the islands as a first step on the career ladder, and disappeared to Denmark after a few years. This made the ministers strangers to the society they worked in.

Governor Pløyen described the Royal Trade Monopoly as 'the great hinge upon which all the affairs of the islands turn', but in the end it had become a straitjacket, and the demand for reform came from the Faroese themselves. It is perhaps true to say that structural changes had already come about and precipitated the reform, rather than the other way round. On 1 January 1856 the Faroe Islands were opened to the world. During the following summer the Trade Monopoly buildings in Tórshavn, Klaksvík, Vestmanna and Tvøroyri were sold to private companies, which largely carried on as before. As a consequence of the economic and cultural changes taking place in the second half of the nineteenth century a national movement was born which viewed the prospects for the future optimistically. This national awakening was inspired by a wish to preserve the best in the old peasant culture, but as time went on it took on a political character.

5

POLITICAL AWAKENING

The Faroese Løgting is one of the world's oldest parliaments. It began as an Allting where all free men could meet to discuss island matters. The smaller administrative unit was a *sýsla*, with a local Ting that would meet every spring. There were six of these units: The Northern Islands, Eysturoy, Streymoy, Vágar, Sandoy and Suðuroy. Today Streymoy has become divided into two units; otherwise the system remains unchanged. More important matters were passed on from the local Tings to the Løgting which convened every year on 29 July in Tórshavn. The leader of the Løgting was called the Løgmaður. The Løgting also functioned as a court of law, which, after the islands came under Norse rule in 1035, came within the jurisdiction of the Gulating, the legal authority for western Norway and 'west over sea'.

The law of the Gulating was followed for generations before it was written down. As has been pointed out by Poul Petersen, a former member of the Løgting and an expert on old Faroese law, not even in Norway have Norse law and ideas of justice been preserved so perfectly as in the Faroe Islands. The law of the Gulating is still the basis of many of the rules and regulations in force today, such as the rights relating to property, fishing, driftwood and fowling. Even the rule that everybody has a right to a share of the *grind* (whale-meat) stems from the old law. A dispute in the 1960s about the right to take sand on a beach in Tórshavn ended up in court, which ruled according to the law of the Gulating: the right to the land extends 'as far out as a horse can wade at high tide'.

The expert on old Faroese law, Poul Petersen

37

The work of King Magnus the Lawmaker was aimed at making one common law for the whole Norse area, but he also decreed special regulations for certain areas. Seyðabrævið – the Sheep Letter – of 28 June 1298 is the only known special regulation for the Faroe Islands, which were at that time ruled directly, with Shetland, by King Magnus' younger son, Duke Hákon. Seyðabrævið decreed among other things how many sheep could be kept in the islands, and many of its regulations have been followed to this day. Sometime in the sixteenth century the Kirkjubøur *kongsbóndi* Peter Jákupsson, who was Løgmaður from 1588 to 1601, took the Faroese law book, containing both King Magnus' Norse Law and Seyðabrævið, to Bergen to be bound. What happened to it after that is a mystery, but in 1680 it turned up at auction in Stockholm, and sometime later became the property of the Royal Library. The Faroese believe this manuscript, which they call Kongsbókin, to be the original copy of Seyðabrævið and that it should therefore by rights belong to them. Although reluctant at first, the Royal Library agreed to return the manuscript to the Faroe Islands, so it has now come home, hopefully for good. The only other extant copy of the Seyðabrævið belongs to the University of Lund in Sweden; it is one of the most beautiful of Nordic manuscripts.

In 1380 the Faroe Islands, along with Orkney, Shetland, Iceland and Greenland, came with Norway into a dynastic union with Denmark, and gradually all power became centralized in Copenhagen. By the Treaty of Kiel in 1814, at the end of the Napoleonic Wars, Denmark was forced to cede Norway to Sweden. The Swedish negotiators were in a hurry to get the matter settled and so did not protest when the Danes at the last minute wanted to keep for themselves the former Norwegian islands. Nobody asked the people concerned. Probably it would have made no difference if they had protested, because the 'great powers' would not have accepted an even stronger Sweden.

Two years later the Faroe Islands were made a Danish *amt* or county. The Løgting was abolished, and an *amtmaður* or governor became the highest authority in the islands. The position of the Løgting and the Løgmaður had in fact over two centuries become gradually weaker. In the von Gabel monopoly period both civil administration and trade were in the same hands, and the Løgting was left virtually powerless. Christian V's Norwegian law of 1687 turned the judicial power over to royal officials. The Løgmaður still participated, but from 1709, when the government took over the trade monopoly, he was a paid government official. This position was not always given to a Faroese: one was an Icelander who never showed up in Faroe at all, and two others were Norwegians who just saw their stay in the islands as a stepping-stone in their career.

The Danish parliamentary constitution of 1849 was made to apply in the Faroe Islands too, so that, paradoxically, just as the islands were taking their first steps towards becoming a modern state, they were finally made part of

Denmark. In 1852 the Løgting was nominally reinstated, but did in fact serve mostly in an advisory capacity with the limited political powers of a county council. It consisted of twenty members: the dean and the governor as a matter of course and eighteen members who were elected to represent their various districts. The Danish governor was a co-opted member and the speaker; he presided at all meetings and it was he who called the tune. He represented the king and later the government in the islands and possessed the power almost of a viceroy. The Faroe Islands were represented in the Danish Parliament: the Løgting would elect a member to the upper house, and the votes of the people would send another member to the lower house. But political interest was very low and sometimes only some five to six per cent of the electorate would vote.

The turning point came in 1856 with the end of the trade monopoly. Faroese society became vulnerable to the winds of change, and foreign influences began to be felt in all areas of life. The old agricultural communities were weakened when the men turned to fishing, and the pattern of life appeared to be under threat. Iceland's struggle for freedom from Denmark became an inspiration to many, and a Faroese (J. P. Gregoriussen) visiting Iceland in 1868 describes his feelings on hearing a sermon in the church at Bessastaðir thus:

> It was not just his good sermon that touched my heart; the Icelandic language also moved me; for I was hearing with some variations my own tongue spoken in church, and that I had never heard before …Then I asked myself: Why are the Icelanders so great and we so small … What the Icelanders have kept through adversity is language and love of country, and those are the very things that I believe the Faroese lack.

But a national movement was coming in Faroe too, and at first it would centre mainly around the language question. Only Danish could be used in churches and schools. But the Danes were indignant when their former countrymen in the southern province of Schleswig had to learn German. The young Danish linguist Svend Grundtvig pointed out in his famous pamphlet *Dansken paa Faroerne* – The Danish language in Faroe – that the kettle was in fact calling the pot black, as the Danes were acting in the Faroe Islands in exactly the same way as the Germans did in Schleswig. Ever since then this title has denoted the abuse of power to the Faroese, and we can still see it referred to when people feel that the Danes go beyond their mandate.

On 22 December 1888 the newspaper *Dimmalætting* carried this advertisement: 'Everybody is invited to come to the house of the Løgting on Boxing Day at 3 p.m. where we will discuss how to protect the Faroese language and the Faroese culture'. Nine young men had signed the advertisement, which drew such a crowd that there was not enough room for everybody. Rasmus Effersøe, the editor of *Dimmalætting,* read a poem written for the occasion by the 22-year-old and still unknown Jóannes Patursson, which opened with the now famous line 'Nú *er tann stundin komin …*' – now the moment has come – for the Faroese people to look after their heritage. In his rousing speech Effersøe said: 'Now it is up to ourselves whether we shall be destroyed or whether we shall be like our freedom-loving and enterprising ancestors and develop our country through industry and hard work.'

A national organization called Føringafelag was founded as a result of the meeting. Its double task was to increase the status of the Faroese language and to improve the lot of the Faroese people in all respects so that they might become self-sufficient. Although the national movement began with these aims, as time went on it inevitably became involved in politics, and the question of home rule became crucial.

Over the years many Danish officials and businessmen who had originally come only for a short time chose to settle in the islands. Their children also stayed, and became a hybrid group of Danish–Faroese, who sometimes were more pro-Danish in their sympathies than the Danes themselves. They were also worried lest home rule should result in tax assessments. In 1906 the Danish authorities were willing to listen to Jóannes Patursson's proposal for giving wider powers to the Faroese Løgting with a view to future home rule, but this was at once foiled by the unionists. They founded their own political party, which they called the Sambandsflokkur – the Union Party. This was the first of its kind in the Faroe Islands, and was dedicated to as much association with Denmark as possible. As a counter-move Jóannes Paturson and the other supporters of the national movement founded the Sjálvstýrisflokkur – the Self-Rule Party – which advocated home rule. Political life – and strife – had come to the Faroe Islands with a vengeance.

In 1927 a third party entered the scene: Føroya Javnaðarflokkur, a social-democratic party which steers a middle course in national questions. Until 1940 it held a majority in the Løgting, together with the Sambandsflokkur, thus blocking any devolution of power from Denmark. In 1939 Jóannes Patursson broke with his old party and founded the Fólkaflokkur, where he was joined by many of his old followers as well as by a faction of businessmen.

On 9 April 1940 the Germans invaded Denmark; three days later the British sent troops to Faroe to prevent a German occupation. Overnight the political situation changed dramatically. The sloop *Eysturoy* from Sørvágur was on its way under the Danish flag to Aberdeen with a cargo of fish on ice when she was hailed by a British warship and told: 'Take down that flag. Haven't you got anything else?' The skipper Hans Mikkelsen said that they had their Faroese flag. 'Then hoist it!' The British disregarded the protests of the Danish governor, and on 25 April the BBC announced that from then on all Faroese ships should fly the Faroese flag. In Tórshavn people filed past the British headquarters to show their gratitude for this decision, and since then 25 April has been an official flag-flying day. The Faroese flag is the Merkið; it was designed by Jens Oliver Lisberg and his student friends in 1919. Even in 1931 a proposal was before the Løgting to accept the Merkið as a national symbol, but it was not passed.

The Second World War was a milestone. The price both in human lives and ships was heavy – the Faroese kept on fishing and sailing with their catches to Britain under conditions so dangerous that everybody else gave up. They carried legislative and fiscal responsibility during the war years and had reserves of six million pounds in British banks. To all intents and purposes they had had home rule for five years, as the British had not meddled in domestic affairs. Surely a return to the status quo was not possible?

A referendum was held on 14 September 1946. There were two choices: full independence – *loysing* – or a degree of self-government within rather narrow limits that were defined by the Danes. The Fólkaflokkur wanted four different alternatives, but the majority, the Sambandsflokkur and the Javnaðarflokkur, made clear to them that this was a take it or leave it proposal, an ultimatum. These shock tactics were employed in the hope of making the Faroese toe the line; but they did not work, as in the referendum 5,650 voted for independence and 5,500 for the union. The Danish prime minister declared at once that a parting of the ways had been reached, as that was what the Danes had promised. The Faroese Løgting with a narrow margin decided to accept the result of the referendum as binding.

Then the Danes seem to have panicked. Somehow it became widely believed in political circles that a Republican coup d'état had taken place in Faroe and that Danish national prestige was at stake. The prime minister was forced to retract his statement, and let the king for the first time in history dissolve the Løgting and call for a new election. The majority of the Løgting objected to this, claiming the proceedings were illegal, but to no avail. A new election resulted in a political majority in the Løgting for an alternative of increased independence within a union. Negotiations led to the passing of the Faroese Home Rule Act, which took effect from 1 April 1948.

In *Færeyinga Saga* the choice is between freedom on the one hand and the security of belonging to a larger community on the other. The choice was the same in 1946, and among many of those who had worked for independence and believed they had won through at last the reaction was strong. They felt that a new party was necessary, because although the Javnaðarflokkur might be a socialist party, it was far from radical in its nationalistic stance, and the two parties with independence as a party programme were in other ways conservative. The new party that was formed in 1948 is the Tjóðveldisflokkur, and its objective is full independence: in short it wants the result of the 1946 referendum to be accepted.

The Home Rule Act represents a compromise, in so far as Faroe became 'a self-governing community within the Danish realm'. To some extent this status means a return to the relative independence of early Norse rule. The Danish *amtmaður* was replaced by the *ríkisumboðsmaður,* who may sit in on the Løgting meetings and can speak but not vote. The Løgting has between twenty-seven and thirty-two members. Today the Løgmaður is the leader of the Landsstýrið – the cabinet – and has the status of prime minister. The Løgting has the right to reject any Danish laws not considered suitable for the islands and can also legislate on matters of local importance. This creates a minefield through which it is not always easy to steer a safe course. Thus a newly appointed Danish minister in Fuglafjørður caused an uproar one Confirmation Sunday, which is a great family event, when he chose to use his sermon to rant against a Danish law about homosexual partnerships. This was a law that did not apply in Faroe, but as the minister was new he did not know that.

The Faroese are responsible for most matters of government, such as taxation, customs, electoral rules, all schools, sanitation and the post office. The issuing of Faroese stamps has turned out to be a source of considerable income for the islands. The Danes still have control of the police force, who receive their orders from the Ministry of Justice in Copenhagen, as well as

The issue of Faroese stamps is a source of considerable revenue for the islands

military defence policy and currency. The Danish language must be taught in schools. Although Denmark in principle takes care of all foreign relations, foreign trade is in fact left to the Faroese, who can also negotiate with other countries. They entered into bilateral agreements when the fishing limit was extended in 1977. The Faroese have chosen to stay outside the EC, as they are afraid that the Community's fishing policy would threaten the industry that provides most of their income. No direct taxes are paid to Denmark, and the subsidies received from that country represent some 14 per cent of the Faroese gross national product. In return the Danes have had the Faroese market in consumer goods practically to themselves.

As part of Denmark the Faroese are in Nato, which has a small radar station just north of Tórshavn. It is manned by a Danish military crew, as there is no military service in Faroe. The Løgting has decreed that in peacetime there will be no soldiers or arms in the islands, so the station is undeniably a source of conflict. And yet the islanders have to face the fact that they are in the middle of an area which is crucial to the control of the North Atlantic.

In 1954 yet another party was formed, representing a middle of the road view, so that there are now six different political parties represented in the Løgting. The political scene is confused, and confusing to an outsider, as all the political parties seem to have coalesced with each other. Measured by the political yardstick of any other country, some of the collaborating parties have had irreconcilably different views, and the coalitions have been surprising to say the least. But in spite of an often extremely heated political atmosphere, the Faroese are pragmatists, and no party is ever deterred from practical collaboration by ideological considerations.

The Faroese still send two representatives to the Danish parliament, although there is now only one chamber. On occasions the Faroese votes have tipped the scales in an unpopular direction, thereby giving the Danes a dose of their own medicine! The outspoken Erlendur Patursson, representing the Tjódveldiflokkur, insisted on using the Faroese language when speaking in parliament.

The islands have also had independent status in the Nordic Council since 1970, with two of the eighty-seven members.

It is necessary to bear in mind that in Faroese politics there is always a double dimension: there are the usual economic and social dividing lines between right and left, but the stance taken towards the union with Denmark is always the primary issue. For close on two hundred years the Faroe Islands have been bound to the one Scandinavian country with which they have the least in common. They have had to learn a foreign language that is of little use to them, as spoken Danish is difficult for other Scandinavians to understand and opens no European doors. Still, the Danish presence represents a political and financial safety net that it might be difficult to manage without.

6

PEOPLE

Cairns
were built
across the mountains
between the many *bygdir*
at the bottom the largest stones
exquisite stones meant to support
the smaller stones that made up the cairn,
and the hollows filled with the broken pieces.
Oðin Oðn

The cairns were a lifeline to people crossing the mountain from one *bygd* to another. They were path markers and built so close to each other that the walker need not leave one cairn before the next one had been sighted, even in bad weather. Today the cairns are falling into disrepair, as the mountain paths are no longer used or needed. Excellent motor roads circle the mountains or pass right through them.

Like handfuls of colourful toy bricks the *bygdir* cluster close to a river mouth or a harbour, sparing as much as possible of the valued *bøur* or cultivated land. Sometimes the church is in the centre of the *bygd,* but quite often it is built close to the sea, so as to be seen from afar. There are about a hundred such *bygdir,* and to the stranger they often seem curiously alike. A *bygd* makes a strong visual impression and must be a painter's dream; where an artist like Sámal Joensen-Mikines sees striking shapes and lines, another like Frimod Joensen is more concerned with the bright colours of the houses contrasting with the green *bøur.*

Traditionally people have lived in a *bygd,* as life outside the community was not really tenable. Before fishing became an industry, every *bygd* had to be more or less self-sufficient, and there was a limit to how many people it could support. Thus for some time a man who wanted to marry had first to prove that he owned land or had other income sufficient to support a family. Failing that, the couple had to work as servants for at least four years, and then be able to produce good references. Thus the number of inhabitants remained stable, at around 4,000 to 5,000 people, for a long time, but then doubled during the nineteenth century.

The long low farmhouses in use until the early twentieth century did not differ much from the Norse longhouses. They seemed to be as much at one with the surrounding landscape as if they had grown out of it. The grass roof would almost merge with the hill. This was true even of the houses in Tórshavn, and at a short distance away from the harbour they seemed to disappear as if by magic:

> Nine-tenths of the little capital is composed of weather-worn cabins, built on and among ledges of basaltic rock. The roofs are covered with turf, the grasses growing long and thick, so that the town harmonizes with the surrounding fields, and at a short distance one can define its limits only by the curling blue smoke from the peat fires.
>
> *Elizabeth Taylor*

The log-built house was often shipped from Norway; there are also stories of buildings having drifted across, such as the bishop's house in Kirkjubøur and an old church in Vágur in Suðuroy. The log house would, however, have outside stone walls and this building method prevailed for a long time.

Inside the old house was divided into two main parts: the *roykstova* and the *glasstova*, which was a later addition. The *roykstova* had not changed much in its function or the way it looked since medieval times. The word means a smokeroom and refers to the open fireplace, which was used for cooking as well as heating the room. There were no windows or ceiling; the light came from the *ljóari* in the roof, and the smoke would leave through the same opening. Later the *roykstova* would boast a stove instead of the open fire, and a glass window in the roof. There would be box beds and narrow benches along the walls.

> If you have never sat on the peat-box beside the stove, enjoying the heat while the winter storms are howling outside and the rain is drumming against the pane, the spinning-wheel is turning and the carding combs are whishing, then you will not know what Faroese cosiness is. Soon it will begin to grow dark, and the lamp with the large flat metal shade will be lit; then everything is as it should be …
>
> *Børge Kielberg*

The *glasstova* was the best room and used for special occasions only. It had a wooden floor, a ceiling and a small window. There was usually a big bed in addition to a table and an iron stove, which would double with the stove in the *roykstova* and be heated from there. Any treasured knick-knacks would be placed in the *glasstova,* of which a very good example can be seen in Norðragøta in Eysturoy.

The *roykstova* was the focal point of all life on the farm. This was where the family slept and ate and did most of the indoor work. The men did the carding and spinning while the women knitted. Although the old Norse weighted loom was used in Faroe until the end of the eighteenth century, it was cumbersome, and the weaving was therefore often done in special weaving sheds. The knitting was of high quality; stockings and patterned sweaters in natural colours were sold through the Trade Monopoly, and as early as 1567 Norwegian sources mention imported Faroese stockings. For a long time the knitting brought in the only cash there was.

The social and cultural aspect of the *roykstova* evenings is apparent in all stories of life in Faroe. It was through the *kvøldsetur,* as such evenings were called, that the language and the old literature were preserved. There were good listeners and magnificent story-tellers:

> I have heard many of the *roykstova* stories several times. On winter evenings much was related for amusement's sake, but what we children and young people liked best was when someone began to talk about old things from our village. The listeners were keen, and the tellers no less keen; they lived in the story, and they seemed scarcely to notice what was happening in the house.
>
> *Mikkjal á Ryggi*

Through the centuries playing chess was also a popular pastime in the *roykstova* evenings, especially during Lent, when many other activities, such as dancing, were frowned upon. In Faroe and Iceland there seems to have been an uninterrupted interest in this game ever since Norse times.

From early in the twentieth century onwards the old houses were gradually replaced by two-storeyed houses with a high basement, which was often used as a byre for a cow or two and might house a few hens as well. These houses, which seem to defy the wind and the land around them, are built of concrete and corrugated iron and painted in bright, even gaudy colours. Individually few of them are pleasing to the eye, but in many *bygdir* the houses huddle as close together as in any medieval community, and the total effect is quite charming. Beside the house or built on to it is often the shed known as *hjallur,* a small house with trellised walls where the wind blows right through. This was used for drying fish and meat. Down by the shore lie the *neyst* or boathouses, with gables facing the sea. In the places where the surf is strong, such as in Trøllanes and Mikladalur, the *neyst* are on the cliff edge and the boats had to be winched up to them.

Today modern well-equipped houses appear everywhere. Often they are ready-made houses imported from Norway or Denmark, so that in new areas there is a certain uniformity with the other Scandinavian countries. These houses are made of wood and are usually quite large. They are often built in new plots outside the boundaries of the old *bygd,* as respect for the *bøur* is no longer so great. Interest in the old building tradition has made some architects experiment with combining the old style and modern materials, in private homes as well as in public buildings like Hotel Borg and the Nordic House in Tórshavn. Owing to the recent affluence in Faroe, modern homes lack nothing in the way of material comfort, while still retaining their functional simplicity of style.

Home and family mean much to the Faroese, even though social patterns are changing. The old *bygd* and the cairn are both symbols of a way of life which forced people to live and work close together. Adaptation to the community was necessary, and the innovative and creative were too often met with scepticism, so that work habits took a long time to change.

Apart from the cairned paths across the mountains there was for a long time only a short road from Tórshavn up the side of Kirkjubøreyn. To the islanders the natural road from *bygd* to *bygd* or to another island was the sea. It used to be that in every *bygd* the *amtmaður,* or governor, appointed an official known as a *skysskaffer,* whose task it was to provide travellers with transportation. No man he summoned to serve as guide or oarsman could refuse, as this was considered a civic duty parallel to military service. In an emergency or time of danger the village boat crews would again be alerted, and then

> there are no bolder, more fearless men in the whole world over. In Viðareiði, for example, in times of dangerous storms when the *need-sending message* goes through the hamlet, many men risk their lives to bring the doctor from Klaksvík ten miles away. Not for a case of ordinary illness would they go in need-sending weather, but for a woman in childbirth danger, for a serious surgical case, for a child struggling with membraneous croup, for such a need eighteen men go (for the doctor must be sent back with a fresh crew) and forty miles of treacherous sea are rowed; and for this service no payment is ever taken.
>
> *Elizabeth Taylor*

Today the Faroese have taken to the automobile in a big way, and the density of cars is among the highest in Europe. A network of good motor roads and an efficient bus and ferry service link the various *bygdir* with each other. The number of tunnels or *berghol,* as they are called in Faroese, has been steadily growing in recent years. Communications have been improved as part of a plan to stem depopulation of the *bygdir.*

For obvious reasons cycling is difficult in many places, and the islanders do not seem to care for walking. To walk across the mountains was perhaps at one time so much of a necessity that people became blind to the beauty of their surroundings. The Faroese live in a natural wonderland, yet today they

Football has become one of the most popular sports and is played in many bygdir

make little use of it. They are good sportsmen and would rather beat the Shetlanders at football, driving a car back and forth to the stadium! Football has become the most popular sport beside swimming, and altogether there are twenty-two football clubs, with 5,300 registered players.

Together with San Remo the Faroe Islands was accepted as a member of the International Football Association in 1988. The qualifying match in 1990 for the 1992 European Championship was the first international game for the Faroe team since receiving recognition by UEFA, the governing body of European football. They played against the Austrians, who were the veterans of the World Cup tournament of the year. The match had to be played in Sweden because there are no grass football fields in the islands – they would quickly turn to mud – and UEFA will not allow games to be played on artificial surfaces. An incredible thing happened – the Austrian team lost 0–1! Austrian newspapers insisted their team had become the laughing-stock of Europe for losing to 'the dwarfs of the Faroe Islands'. In Tórshavn the team were received as giants and given a heroes' welcome, and the performances of Torkil Nielsen, who scored the winning goal, and the goalkeeper Jens Martin Knudsen will be remembered for a long time in the islands.

It has often been said that to get to know the real Faroe one must stay for some time in a *bygd*. There is usually a *handil* (grocery shop) but finding it can be a problem for the newcomer, as it does not advertise its existence: after

Meat drying, from the pilot whale

all, everybody knows where it is! Mostly the shop will deal in non-perishable goods, as people are still surprisingly self-sufficient and have well-stocked larders of dried fish and the delicacy known as *skerpikjøt,* which is dried and hung unsalted mutton, said to contain more energy than any other food. There is fresh fish as well, and this is often made into the dish known as *knettir,* consisting of large lumps of creamed fish mixed with strips of mutton suet. Some people have potatoes from their own patch. Meat and blubber from the pilot whale are a treasured part of the diet, and it has turned out to be a healthy one: it has been medically confirmed that whale fat lowers the blood cholesterol level.

On the whole the Faroese are a healthy people. Infant mortality has always been low and the average life span very high. Indeed in 1846 a Danish scientist proved that the average length of life of the Faroese was the highest in the world. In the old days there were in most *bygdir* people knowledgeable about illness who would be sent for in less serious cases. During the first half of the twentieth century tuberculosis was the scourge of the islands, as it was in most of northern Europe. It has recently been found that the number of rheumatic disorders found in Faroe is nearly twice as large as in countries like England and Holland. The Faroe Islands have also made their mark in medical history, as any study of the causes of multiple sclerosis must necessarily refer to them. The disease was unknown in Faroe before 1940, but an epidemic was diagnosed in the years after the British troops were stationed in the islands, and it could therefore be established that the disease was caused by an infectious agent.

It used to be said that a føroying's riches were his dram and his many children. A drink was cheap and readily available, and there are many stories of what happened when the one drink turned into many. A funeral procession once crossed the mountains to the church, decorously singing a hymn, only to discover that the coffin had been left behind in the mountains! Likewise a wedding was due to take place at a set time in the office of the *sýslumaður* when word came that the marriage ceremony had to be postponed for a few hours, as the bridegroom was drunk. Some time later the groom was back on his feet, but by then the *sýslumaður* was drunk, and it was the wedding couple's turn to wait! For some time now the Faroe Islands have lived under probably the strictest drinking laws in northern Europe. A light, locally-produced beer can be bought in most grocery shops and restaurants, but those who want wine or spirits must order by the case from Denmark.

Almost every *bygd* has its own church. The older tarred churches which today are a treasured part of the historical heritage, were typical vernacular buildings, and often they could be distinguished from the farm houses only because they were longer, and because they usually had a small white belfry at the west end of the roof. The interiors of these churches have the same simplicity of form, and the unpainted wood adds to the feeling of space and light. Scholars have pointed out that in shape the Faroese village church is rather similar to the rectangular stone churches that were common in Norway after 1250. The cathedral and the parish church at Kirkjubøur also have this shape. The excavations of a succession of foundations at the church site in Sandur in Sandoy have shown how church architecture has developed and have also indicated links between the thirteenth- and the nineteenth-century churches.

The Faroe Islands are divided into thirteen parishes with nineteen ministers and a bishop, based in Tórshavn. There used to be just six ministers, led by the *próstur,* or dean. As each minister was responsible for several churches, services would be read in his absence by a layman, and this practice is still followed. A German ornithologist who went to such a service in Sørvágur in 1828 was not impressed, writing that the layman sang like a red-striped guillemot (*Colymbus septentrionalis*)! Still it may be this sharing of responsibility which accounts for the high level of involvement in church matters that is commonly found. The Faroese are naturally devout but, like most Scandinavians, they tend to regard Christianity as more a question of moral principle than of mystical religious experience.

> The service seemed to be pervaded by an ethical atmosphere, one felt that the moralities were out for an airing, and that virtue was

receiving its weekly justification. The congregation could not be said to worship in the same way as the Celts worship or the Latins worship.

G. H. Harris

A minister of Viðareiði wrote in 1824 of how he had listened to a discussion among the guests at a wedding about superstitions and lack of faith 'in which I felt myself to be more in the company of Christian philosophers than among unphilosophical Christians.'

Today almost all ministers are native Faroese, but at one time they were mostly Danish. They were well-educated men, and many of them fell under the spell of the islands; the written records some of them left behind are invaluable for our understanding of social history. Usually they came straight from university, and the transition from town life in Copenhagen to a storm-tossed island in the Atlantle proved traumatic for some ministers and their wives. And yet they came in many ways to a privileged existence, as the glebe usually had some of the best soil in the district, and the holdings were large. Not everybody exploited the system but, as the Faroese are quick to point out, some of the ministers came with nothing but the clothes they stood up in, and left as well-to-do men. Sometimes the more discerning among the ministers felt the incongruity of their position:

> Here I as a rule felt so small and unworthy. For one thing I would preach in a language that was never spoken in the homes and in any case was stranger to the young listeners than German or English is to us; secondly I knew of course that several of my old listeners daily – or at least often – occupied themselves with their Bible, their only book, sitting there during the long winter evenings studying the Old as well as the New Testament, though mostly the Old, and interpreting it in *their* way.
>
> *Jørgen Falk Rønne*

It was disconcerting for a young minister who had perhaps worked long and hard over his sermon to have it courteously but completely taken apart by an old, white-bearded fisherman who had been 'speculating about these things'.

At the turn of the century most people belonged to the Lutheran church. There was only one Catholic in the islands, an old woman living at Hvútanes outside Tórshavn. She had a small chapel of her own, and once a year a priest would come up from Copenhagen to say mass. Today a small Catholic congregation has its own church in Tórshavn. In the first few decades of the twentieth century a number of different denominations established themselves in the islands, and many people left the Lutheran community to join a dissenting group. Among the first to come were the Plymouth

Brethren, an evangelical sect that got its name from an association formed in 1830 in Plymouth in England. It was established in reaction to the formality of church practices, and has no set organization or ordained ministers. The sect reached Faroe from Scotland via Shetland. Today the Brethren make up the largest dissenter group with thirty-four meeting houses throughout the islands. It is believed that they make up some 10 per cent of the population, but the nature of the organization makes it difficult to calculate their exact number.

Families traditionally go to church together, taking their children with them. Until recently there was, in accordance with Scandinavian custom, a men's side and a women's side in the village churches, and the women had to defer to the men: '. . . in the sod-roofed church where never was a fire made, she will sit with her mother on the women's side, waiting meekly after service until the last man and the last boy have left their seats' (Elizabeth Taylor). In the household the men would eat first and the women afterwards. The beauty of the women has often been commented on by visitors to the islands. And yet their life has often been rugged, as they have had to keep the home fires burning on their own when husbands and sons went off to sea, and experienced sorrow and hardship when one or more of them did not return. Today the young women are leaving the *bygdir*. Some of them decide '*at fara niður*' – to go down to Denmark – or '*at fara út*' – to go abroad – but most of them go no further than Tórshavn, where the job prospects are better than in the *bygdir*. There is a lack of women of marriageable age in many *bygdir*, and in

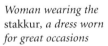

Woman wearing the stakkur, *a dress worn for great occasions*

order to make *konufólkið* want to stay, jobs have to be found for them, which may require the men to change some of their ways.

Faroese men still wear their national costume on many occasions, and they wear it with dignity and style. The costume consists of homespun kneelength trousers, embroidered waistcoat, silver-buttoned coat and buckled shoes, and it makes most men look handsome. The young men wear red caps with a narrow black stripe, whereas widowers and older citizens choose dark blue hats. The older men, accustomed to walking in the mountains, move with particular ease and grace. The women ceased to use their national dress for everyday wear long before the men. Today it has won a new popularity, and at Ólavsvøka and other festive occasions there are women in costume everywhere. Some women will also wear the *stakkur,* a dress that has been worn for great occasions, especially weddings, for centuries. It was first described by Lucas Debes in his Faroe description of 1673, but in the old days only rich farmers' wives could afford it. It is usually made in blue or deep red silk, rather in the style of French court dress.

The old communal way of living, in which social responsibility was ingrained, has supported and strengthened the islanders in the transition to modern life. And the changes have been great. A people who have created one of the most technically advanced fishing fleets in the world have had of necessity to give up some of the old traditions and beliefs. One of the most fascinating aspects of contemporary life in Faroe is the mixture of the cautious and the daring, of the traditional and the ultra-modern.

The old communal farming system, with small fields built up in terraces, is today used mostly for grass. Funningur, Eysturoy

7

FOLKLORE

If trolls and other such creatures exist, then this is where they are, let loose to sweep howling and screaming in their wild dance through mountain and bygd.

Børge Kielberg

The folklore of Faroe comes down to us not only through the make-believe of fairy tales but as much through the more realistic stories known as *sagnir,* or folk tales, which are presented by the story-teller as though they were true. The *sagnir* faithfully record where events take place, and thus they often contain valuable historical material. The old pagan beliefs died slowly, and a subculture connected with them lived on into the twentieth century, side by side with an orthodox Christian faith. People would shy away from talking about these beliefs openly, and direct questions would only get evasive replies.

Most of the creatures of Faroese popular belief belong to the common folklore heritage of the Scandinavian countries in general, and Norway and Iceland in particular. Thus the troll of Norway, the trow of Orkney and Shetland and the *trøll* of Faroe are closely related, but have taken on characteristics of the landscape they live in. Most of the themes are familiar too, and it is interesting to see how they have been adapted to life in Faroe.

In a story taken down in Sandoy we are told that a man living in Sandur was one day riding east to Skálavík to a wedding. As he passed under Tróndardalslíð he heard a voice crying, 'Listen, you, man that rides by! Take word to the house where the wedding shall be that Bembil is dead, and the child is burned.' When the man came to the house where the wedding was being held, he opened the door and called out, 'Bembil is dead, and the child is burned.' Then someone ran out from under the table, crying, 'That was my son!' This story of the *huldufólk,* or the other people, seems a genuinely local story, and it therefore comes as a surprise to find that this is one of the folk tales found in different versions all over Europe. In a version found just north of Oslo the message is given to a boy who is bringing the food for a wedding by horse and sled; in the tale taken down in the Shetland island of Fetlar there is no mention of a wedding at all. As it happens, the tale was first told by the Greek writer Plutarch in AD 100!

The tales are realistic in their description of daily life. Most of this life is bound up with the farm and the boat, but even rock climbing is worked into the stories. The lack of trees is very cleverly dealt with; instead of getting lost in a forest the Faroese characters have the fog to contend with. In one story Øskudólgur, who is the Faroese version of the Ashlad so popular in Norwegian folk tales, has to explain to his two brothers how he knows about the mysterious rider who tries three times to reach the top of the glass mountain to win the princess. He knows it for the good reason that he himself was the rider, though ostensibly he was at home, poking the ashes as usual. Øskudólgur claims he has seen what happened respectively from the *hjallur,* or drying shed, from the *gróthús,* or stone shed, and from the *hoyggjhús,* or hay shed, thus giving us a picture of a Faroese farm. As the rider progresses up the glass mountain, so the height and size of the look-outs increase, in the way of fairy tales. Thus the use of realistic pictures of everyday life serves to make the fantastic parts of the story more credible.

Giants and trolls, known in Faroe as *risar* and *trøll,* are part of the old lore, but by the time the material was written down they belonged to the fairy tale world, and there was no longer any sharp distinction between them. Even though such creatures seem to grow naturally out of the Faroese scenery, they were clearly no longer really believed in. The cheeky hogboon of Orkney has in Faroe become the beneficent *vættur,* who will only stay where the people are kind and God-fearing. The *sjódreygil,* or water-dreel, which in Norway was greatly feared, has also undergone a metamorphosis, and has become a helpful but rather pathetic creature. On dark nights a kind of phosphorescence could be seen in the sea; this came from the *sjódreygil's* mouth when he uttered his plaintive cries.

But there were still sinister creatures to be reckoned with. The female demon Marra would sneak up on people while they were peacefully sleeping, and if she succeeded in counting their teeth, they would not live out the year. And the *nykur* was perhaps the most frightening of these creatures: looking like a beautiful pony with a long silvery mane he would make people want to ride him, and, when he succeeded, would plunge with his prey back in the tarn or lake where he belonged. Sometimes he would lure people by appearing with a light on his tail, and for this reason a meteorite or a shooting star is known as a *nykbrandur.* The only way of saving oneself from the *nykur* was to call out its name, as that would make it lose all its strength. That is what happened to some Sørvágur children in Vágar when they went to Leitisvatn to play. They could not resist mounting the lovely horse they found, but it was too high for the smallest boy, so when the horse made for the lake, he ran after it, calling his brother Niklas. As he was too small to pronounce words clearly, it sounded like the *nykur's* name, and thus the children were saved. Variations of the same story are told in Norway as well.

About a hundred years ago the belief in the *nykur* seems to have been as strong as ever. An Englishman fishing for trout in Leynavatn in Streymoy tells this story of how he learned about the *nykur:*

> An old fisherman at Leynavatn, by the banks of which we were encamped, was a firm believer in this animal, and warned me, almost on his knees, to remove the camp from the side of the lake, and seemed really quite upset when I was in the water up to my waist wading. He begged me over and over again to come out before the *nykur* could catch me.
>
> *Joseph Jeaffreson*

The belief in the *huldufólk* has survived the longest and has played a very great part in the life of the people. A number of *sagnir* tell us about the *huldufólk,* who are never part of fairy tales, perhaps because to the story-tellers they were no less real than neighbours and friends. Their name is believed to derive from the verb *hylja,* which means to hide. The *huldufólk* are visible only when they want to be; they are the grey people or the 'other people'. Their hidden world is close, and their life goes on more or less as it does in the human world; in fact it mirrors life in Faroe. They keep cattle and go fishing. One popular story has a man from Gásadalur taking his place in an *áttamannafar* (an eight-man boat) thinking he is joining a Bøur crew. He catches a lot of fish and is allowed to keep it all. When he does not thank them, they comment on his bad manners, but he has in fact taken care not to do so, for that would give the *huldufólk* power over him. Thus he is in a quandary. Even if the *huldufólk* can often be kind and will always try to return favours, care should be taken not to cross them, as they do not forget a slight and can bear grudges for ever.

According to an old saying a knifeless man is a lifeless man, and no Faroese would ever go without his knife. It might come in handy in many situations, and steel was the only protection against the powers of darkness. As it was better not to use such a word as knife when the *huldufólk* might hear it, the word *hvast* – a sharp one – would be used instead. This belief in the magical qualities of steel persisted into the twentieth century. Thus a young man, who in a terrible gale was on his way home along a rocky trail where the *huldufólk* were known to dwell, was found dead in the morning, with his face, hands, feet and knees badly lacerated. A group of men were talking about it the next evening, and one of them said he did not think that all was as it should be, meaning that the *huldufólk* had had a hand in it. Then another said, 'He had no knife with him.' No more was said – it was not necessary.

> These men had seen the carcasses of sheep whirled up and cast down again and again on sharp ice and jagged rocks until they were a mass of broken bones and crushed flesh. Yet they gave no

thought to the cast-wind as the cause of that tragic death. No, the lad, passing over those slopes where the *huldufólk* dwelt, had no protecting steel with him; he had met the *huldufólk,* had striven with them – and they had conquered.

Elizabeth Taylor

The *huldufólk* could be met anywhere in the mountains or at sea, and many strange stories have been told about those who disappeared because the 'other people' had taken them. In his description of the Faroe Islands from 1673 the minister Lucas Debes ends his work with a long chapter called 'On ghosts and Satan's temptations in Faroe', where he gives numerous examples of mysterious happenings. The Rev. Debes, who was not only the *próstur* but also the rector of the Latin School in Tórshavn, is able to name places and people, and it is evident that he himself wholly believes in the *huldufólk.* Thus he tells the story of how the Rev. Ganting's daughter Kirstine disappears while playing with other children in the fields close to the vicarage in Miðvágur in Vágar. The father looks everywhere for her, and after more than a week she is found unhurt and peacefully sleeping at the very edge of a high promontory. The child said a big man had brought her there, and she thought it was her father himself. And one Saturday when the Rev. Taalle was minister in Eysturoy, everything was ready for a wedding when the bridegroom went missing and could not be found anywhere. After some time he turns up, and tells a wondrous tale of a beautiful woman trying to tempt him and make him leave his fiancée for her sake. He had seen the men who were looking for him, but was unable to answer them. Of course, as he could not be tempted, the seductress let him go in the end.

Some people had the gift of seeing the *huldufólk* when they did not mean to be seen. Such a person was known as *framsíggin,* one who has second sight. People with this gift could also see into the future and sometimes predict death and disaster. Nobody wanted to be *framsíggin* if they could help it, and other people would therefore take care not to touch the seers or walk behind them for fear of becoming one themselves. At a christening the water must on no account run down into the baby's eyes, as that might cause second sight. An unchristened baby was in danger, as the *huldufólk* might take it. In its place they would put one of their own, and such a changeling would always seem half-witted among human beings. The baby's name must never be revealed before the christening, so one should not ask what it is. The idea that harm will follow if an enemy uses one's name is very old in Nordic culture.

The belief that a child born secretly and then murdered would haunt the place where it was killed has existed in all the Nordic countries. In Faroe such a child would return as the dreaded *niðagrísur*. It was a creature with a large head and a small body, and it would roll like a ball; any man who got it between his feet would not see the year out. The legendary Guttormur í Múla once laid the troubled spirit of such a child, who was pestering the minister of Viðareiði for Christian burial, and we are told that the minister gave him a cow for doing this. Another way of putting such beings to rest was by baptizing them or giving them a name. A story from Skáli in Eysturoy illustrates this. In the infields of Skáli there is a stone called Loddasasteinur, and a *niðagrísur* used to haunt this place, rolling about before the feet of people passing in the dark. But one day a man grew angry and exclaimed, 'Oh, that Loddasi!' Then the ghost buried itself in the ground and was never seen again, because it had been given a name.

It was said of many ministers that they knew the Black Art, but there were others, both men and women, who were supposed to have supernatural powers and know about witchcraft, or *gandur* as it was called. There were those whose predictions, often made in anger, tended to come true. Many people had great fear of such a *gandakona* or *gandamaður,* who would sometimes use their fear to extort money. Thus fishermen would pay a sort of tax to such people before going to sea, so as not to have accidents. And if they refused to pay, their family would pay for them.

The seals used to be more numerous around the Faroe coasts than they are today, and it is not surprising that they were an important part of popular imagination. They tended to be confused with mermaids. A strange belief found in Faroe as well as the other Scandinavian countries links the seals with the soldiers of Pharaoh. These were lost in the Red Sea, but did not drown. Instead they turned into seals and swam northwards, to the Faroe Islands. The classic story about seals and people is *Kópakonan* – The Seal-wife – which is set in Mikladalur in Kalsoy. The seals would once a year take off their skins and dance the night through by the shore. A young man watching them at one time took the skin of a seal-maiden and hid it, so that she could not get back into the sea. She became his wife, and they had children, but all the time her skin was there, locked in a chest. One day while out fishing he discovers that he has left the key to the chest behind. In despair he calls out that now he will lose his wife! He rows home in a frenzy, but she has gone – back to the sea and her seal husband. The fire has been put out and all the knives locked up, so that the children shall not come to any harm. *Kópakonan* never comes back, but sometimes when the children come down to the shore, there will be a seal there, watching them.

This story is known in all North Sea countries. Perhaps the Orkney version is the most lyrical. But the Faroe version does not stop there; perhaps it has been added to in order to explain why so many have died in the surf around Kalsoy. In the old days many seal-hunts were held in Mikladalur because the seals would gather there in the large caves to breed. The story tells in gruesome detail how all the Mikladalsmen go seal-hunting and then sit down for their dinner, when *Kópakonan* descends on them like an avenging fury and cries, 'Here lies my old man with the upturned nose, the hand is Hárek's

The seals are an important part of the popular imagination, often confused with mermaids

and the foot is Fríðrik's – vengeance will be wreaked on the Mikladalsmen until enough of them have been lost to link arms around Kalsoy!' And indeed, many men have since gone to their death in the mountains and at sea, but not enough, as yet! To prove the truth of this story the story-teller will point out that the descendants of the seal-wife have webbed fingers. Perhaps the story of *Kópakonan* explains why many people in Faroe would not eat seal meat. The story has been turned into a ballet, which a group of Faroese dancers took with them on a tour of the Baltic states. The scene in which the seals shed their skins and dance on the shore in joy at their freedom is hauntingly evocative.

Many large boulders that might be split in a peculiar way were believed to be the homes of the *huldufólk*. Often these boulders have been much in the way, lying right in the infields, but nothing could be done about them. Sometimes Viking graves and other antiquities have been saved for posterity because people believed them to be haunted by the *huldufólk* or even more frightening creatures. It must have been easy to begin looking over one's shoulder while walking in the mountains or rowing a boat in a stormy sea. A man of imagination might start asking himself whether perhaps such creatures as the *huldufólk* really did exist. A stay of more than six years in a lonely parish was therefore considered unwise for a young minister:

> A pastor confessed to me that on one wild and lonely trail over mountain and moor that he had to traverse alone, he always felt a presence that accompanied him, heard a soft footfall just one step behind him and a little to one side, that again and again he has reasoned with himself, saying 'it is only an echo – a nervous fancy; I will *not* turn and look!' Yet at last he has wheeled about suddenly, desperately, to find – nothing; and to go on unhappily, feeling again that invisible presence, hearing again that hushed footfall.
>
> *Elizabeth Taylor*

Perhaps living close to an awe-inspiring natural world always makes it difficult to draw a clearly defined line between fantasy and reality. What to some seems like fantasy and superstition may to others appear as objective reality. In the *bygdir* the world has existed on two levels, a visible and an invisible but equally real one.

8

THE LANGUAGE

> Their language had words for everything the eye saw and the ear
> heard. Words which opened your eyes to the distinctive beauty, to
> what was graceful and gentle under the harsh and stern exterior.
> Words with the heavy undertone of a roaring sea and pounding
> surf, of untamed savagery and crushing, tormenting strength.
> Words which conjured up fantastic images and enticing wonder-
> lands beyond the horizon, where sea and sky fused in the evening
> glow.
>
> *Asbjørn Hildremyr*

In this romantic and poetic way a Norwegian writer describes his feelings
about the language of the Faroe Islands, where as a seven-year-old boy he had
fled with his family when Norway was invaded in the spring of 1940. While
he soon learned to speak Faroese he found it difficult to read, as the language
looked so different in print.

The language of the Faroe Islands is closely related to the dialects of
western Norway, more specifically to those of the districts north and south of
Bergen. This is not strange, considering that most of the original settlers
came from those areas more than a thousand years ago, and that until the end
of the seventeenth century there was still regular contact. 'The intonation, the
flexible diphthongs, the burred r, the sharp consonant clusters – I had heard
them before, from speakers of Sogn and Voss, Hardanger and Rogaland, even
among immigrants in far-away America' (Einar Haugen). Modern Faroese is
still closely related to Norwegian and Icelandic. It is close to Middle
Norwegian, the language used in Norway around 1400. Some scholars have
linked this fact with the Black Death, theorizing that the islands may have
been left almost empty at the time, so that a new immigration from Norway
took place, but this remains pure speculation.

Words of Celtic origin exist in the language even today, and point to an
early contact with Celtic speakers – a legacy of the Viking Age. Among these
few but interesting loan-words are *tarvur* for a bull and *blak* for sour milk.
With Christianity came foreign influences, mostly from English, thus *sál* was
adopted for soul, *hvítusunna* for Whitsun and the now archaic *blessan* for
blessing.

Early sources are extremely sparse. The few rune stones that have been found are comparatively recent. The Lund version of the Seyðabrævið dates from *c.* 1310 and is believed to have been written by a Faroese. It is therefore considered the oldest known Faroese text. Although in the main the language is Norse, it shows special Faroese features, which in later documents become even more distinct, so that it may be said that by *c.* 1400 Faroese shows signs of developing into an independent language. The main source from this period is the six Húsavík letters from 1407 concerning the property left by the lady Guðrun Sjúrdarðottir of Húsavík in Sandoy. These letters are not only linguistically important but also give a fascinating picture of how people lived on a major Faroese farm in the Middle Ages.

The Reformation in *c.* 1540 did irreparable damage to the Faroese language and cultural life in general. Danish was introduced as the language of the church and administration, and Faroese ceased to exist as a written language. No attempt was made to produce a Faroese Bible, and the earliest extant records of the Løgting, from 1615, are in Danish. Court records had to be drawn up in Danish even when everybody concerned, including the officials, were Faroese speakers. Thus Danish left its mark on the abstract, and in particular the religious, vocabulary. The Danish language was for centuries learned through the Bible, so that when people in the *bygdir* tried to make themselves understood in Danish, it would sound as if they were reciting from the Old Testament.

During the following centuries the language was exposed to a thorough-going Danish influence. This did not at once affect the spoken language. Thus the Icelander Jón Olafsson, popularly known as Jón Indíafari, commented after his visit to the islands in 1616 that the Faroese would read Icelandic books without difficulty, 'for there was no great difference between their tongue and ours, and it was the same in many ways with their customs … but Danish manners have come in, both in church and outside it, and also ordinary Danish speech.' During the next two centuries the contact with English sailors was strong enough for more loan-words to be adopted, such as *fittur* for neat, *sáttligur* for softly or calmly, and *ánari* for owner.

A young student wrote the first known description of the Faroese language, but this was lost in the Copenhagen fire of 1728. In the years 1781–2 Jens Christian Svabo (1746–1824) went to the Faroe Islands to collect material for a description of the spoken language. He had undertaken to record for posterity what was believed to be the remains of a dying language. With his purist conception of language Svabo considered Faroese a kind of corrupted Norse, and did not believe it had a future. As he saw it there were only two possible roads to travel, either to restore the lost purity of the language by going back to its Norse roots or to accept Danish. He considered the latter the only practicable solution, but industriously set about the work of describing the language as he found it. There was no tradition he could build on, so Svabo had to start from scratch by making his own orthography. This he based consistently and accurately on the pronunciation of his own dialect from Vágar.

As it turned out, Svabo's work did not become a memorial to a dead language but instead the foundation stone for its restoration. In the 1820s came the first two books printed in Faroese, a collection of ballads by H. C. Lyngbye and a translation of the Gospel according to St Matthew by J. H. Schrøter, a Suðuroy minister, whose pioneer work was received with consternation by some – this did not sound like the word of God! Danish had over the centuries become firmly entrenched as the holy language, and many bastions had to fall before the islanders could communicate with God in their own language. Both Lyngbye and Schrøter, who later also translated *Færeyinga Saga* into Faroese, largely followed Svabo's orthography.

With the Romantic Movement of the first half of the nineteenth century, language came to be viewed as a national heritage that reflected a people's individuality, and the work of collecting ballads and legends began all over the islands. In 1840 the Faroese student N. Nolsøe wrote:

> It must certainly be regarded as a miracle that all the ballads found in this country should be preserved so well for so many centuries, even though they were not written down. But this is true of our Faroese language as well; it has remained to this day just as pure and unmixed as in the days of Sigmundur Brestisson, even though the Danish language has been forced on us …

But as the compilers all wrote idiosyncratically, it was becoming more and more obvious that a standardised norm for the written language was necessary.

On 19 December 1844 a Copenhagen newspaper carried an article called 'The Faroese Language', signed only 'A Føroying'. It was written by the young divinity student Venceslaus Ulricus Hammershaimb (1819–1909), the son of the last Løgmaður at Steig. The article was prompted by the provisional ordinance for a compulsory elementary school in the Faroe Islands with all teaching conducted in Danish only, as the Faroese language was defined as a dialect, and a Danish one at that. A few months later Svend Grundtvig (1824–83), the son of the famous founder of the folk high school movement, published the protest that would become the gospel of the national movement: 'The Danish language in the Faroe Islands. A Parallel to the German Language in Schleswig'. He insisted that education should serve to set a nation free and not be used as a weapon to deal a fatal blow to its nationality and language; in short it could not be tolerated that the Danes should do to the Faroese what they did not want the Germans to do to themselves in Schleswig.

Hammershaimb had become convinced that he must act at once if his mother tongue was to be saved. Assisted by the famous Icelander Jón Sigurdsson he worked out in 1846 a written language which, with only minor changes, is the form used today. It builds on the etymological principle, that is, in its written form Faroese is based on the original Norse language. By rooting the orthography in the past, the language was given a historical perspective. Thus the fricative ð, like the English *th* in they or this, is used in the written form almost as in Norse, despite the fact that it is not pronounced in any Faroese dialect.

The etymological spelling is more easily understood by Icelanders and to some extent by other Nordic speakers, and also works as an instrument of unification: because the visual picture of the words does not reflect the phonetic changes that have taken place over the centuries, all the many dialects that have appeared can co-exist within the same written form. On the other hand it cannot be denied that the difference between pronunciation and spelling makes it difficult for Faroese children to learn to spell correctly, but then that is a problem in England too! The linguist Dr Jakob Jakobsen, who is known for his study of the Shetland Norn, thought that it was not too late for the islands to give themselves an easy, phonetic spelling, and he therefore introduced his own version. This led to a vehement orthographical dispute, which ended in a compromise – a spelling known as *broyting* – but as it turned out Dr Jakobsen was practically the only person to use it.

The Faroese national movement thus began among students and intellectuals in Copenhagen, and the first literary attempts were soon made in the new written language. At the 1888 Christmas meeting in Tórshavn a programme was laid down for restoring and developing the language, and a national revival began. It quickly became apparent that the national struggle for the language could not long be kept separate from a struggle for political rights, but the fact that the Faroese did not always agree among themselves about what course to follow made the situation far from simple.

In spite of Hammershaimb's work, compulsory elementary education in Danish was introduced in 1846, but it met with such opposition that the ordinance was withdrawn in 1854. For a whole century afterwards there was a bitter dispute about the medium of instruction. In 1870 a teachers' college was established in Tórshavn. A law passed in 1912 stated expressly that Danish was the mandatory language of instruction for older pupils. This represented a step backwards and poisoned political relations between Denmark and the Faroe Islands for years to come. Of course, it gave young students a welcome thrill whenever their teachers broke the law by addressing them in their own language! The writer William Heinesen, who had left school before any instruction was given in written Faroese, describes his school days thus:

> The school with its garden and enclosed yard was a world of its own. Although it was called *Færøernes Mellem-og Realskole* – The

Faroe Islands Junior High School – it had really not much to do with the Faroe Islands. It was a Danish school, where the pupils learned about Danish scenery and Danish culture, and the language of instruction was Danish, even when there were Faroese teachers and Faroese pupils. We learned everything about the history of Denmark from the Stone Age to the present, but nothing about the historical fate of the Faroe Islands, which after all is only in part connected with that of the Danish realm. And it was the same with the other subjects.

Faroese was finally acknowledged as the language of instruction in schools in 1938; the struggle had been long and hard. The question of the language used in church was equally important in the national debate, and in some ways even more difficult. When Hammershaimb as an enthusiastic young minister preached his New Year sermon in the native tongue to a shocked Kvívík congregation, there was an uproar. There were dire predictions that Faroese as a church language would mean 'the destruction of Christianity in the Faroe Islands'. But in 1902 the high church minister A. C. Evensen gave respectability to the language by using it for his sermon in the church at Skopun, and from then on there was really no turning back. The man responsible for the Faroese church language was Jákup Dahl, the *próstur* who was the last minister to live at the lovely old manse of Sandagerði in Tórshavn. His translation of the New Testament came in 1937 and the complete Bible appeared in 1961, at the same time as the Faroese hymn book.

Jákup Dahl belonged to the circle of nationalists who had Jóannes Patursson as a natural and forceful leader. Their political aims were always to transfer more power to the Løgting and gain full acceptance of the Faroese language. But the church in general came to accept the idea of Faroese as a church language because the Plymouth Brethren adopted it. As early as 1907 Jóannes Patursson ascribed their instant success to their use of the native tongue for preaching. They sang in Faroese too, and by 1920 they had their first hymn book printed. The Plymouth Brethren preacher Victor Danielsen (1894–1961) had translated the whole Bible by 1949.

The Home Rule Act of 1948 established Faroese as the principal language of the islands. However, it also stipulated that Danish should have equal status in public affairs, and this has been a cause of resentment as well as friction with the Danish authorities. Thus the language of the courts has remained mainly Danish, and the laws of the Løgting are printed with parallel texts. Still, most of the bastions have been won, and the work of consolidation has begun. When *Fróðskaparsetur Føroya* was established in the 1960s it became possible to teach the native language and literature at university level. Led by Professor Jóhan Hendrik W. Poulsen the language committee *Føroyska málnevndin* has been active since 1985 as a watchdog for the language. Its main objective is to keep Danish and Faroese apart as two separate languages, and today this is made difficult, among other things, by the insidious influence of the glossy Danish magazines that flood the Faroese market. Another task is to try to stem the flow of international technical terms by inventing new Faroese words. Some of these have become instantly popular, such as *tyrla* for helicopter and *telda* for computer. However, new words can only be suggested, as these days nobody tells a føroying how to speak!

The headstone of Jóannes Patursson, in St Olav's churchyard, Kirkjubøur, with St Magnus Cathedral in the background

9

PLACE-NAMES

Faroese place-names, when correctly interpreted, often tell us something not only about an epoch and an area, but also about people. Sometimes the names contain clues to the history of an area, even to the extent that archaeologists can study them for the corroboration of their theories. The majority of place-names are Norse, but there is also a small, interesting group of names shown to be of Gaelic origin. The presence of Irish hermit monks does not seem unlikely but cannot be proved; either way it gives no clear answer to the question of why Gaelic names would come to be used in Faroe. One possibility has been suggested by Fridtjof Nansen:

> The Celtic place-names may have been brought by Norwegians, who before they came to the Faroe Islands had lived with Celtic-speaking people in the Scottish islands or in Ireland; but it still seems unlikely that they should have used a foreign language to give names to their new home. It is a more natural explanation that they have got the names from the earlier Celts, no matter whether these were just the Irish hermits or larger groups.

In the north-west of Mykines we find a *botnur* by the name of Korkadalur. The Faroese word *korki* refers to a lichen used to produce a reddish dye. As this lichen grows everywhere, it seems improbable that it would ever have been brought from Korkadalur. An old Gaelic word *corka* means oats, so that Korkadalur might mean the valley where oats grow. By comparison *korkakost* was at one time used in Foula in Shetland for oat bread. The Faroese botanist Jóhannes Jóhansen points out that such an interpretation of the name Korkadalur would agree with his pollen analysis, which reveals the growing of oats in Mykines as early as the seventh century.

Place-names like Paparøkur near Vestmanna and Papurshálsur in Saksun seem to refer to the Irish hermits, as the Norsemen called them *papar*, and several such place-names are known in Shetland and Orkney, as well as in Iceland. But we also know that the Norsemen would sometimes jokingly refer to the puffins as *papi*, and both Paparøkur and Papurshálsur are names for exposed places that do not seem habitable even for hermits, *røkur* meaning ledges and *hálsur* an outcrop in a hill ridge, so probably the names refer to puffin ledges! The name Vestmanna has been shortened from Vestmannahøvn, which means 'the harbour of the westmen'. The name may therefore refer to the Irish, but not necessarily, as westmen is also used for people coming from the other British Isles. There are, however, other names referring directly to the Irish, such as Iraliðgjógv near Uldalið in Mykines, and Irakøstar just west of Gøtueiði in Eysturoy. Sometimes vague tradition connects such names with priests; such a name is Baglahólmur in Suðuroy as the Norse *bagall* means a bishop's staff, and is believed to derive from the Irish *bachall*. Such staffs were found in Iceland, 'and,' says the *Islendingabók*, 'from this it could be concluded that they were Irishmen.'

Until the studies of the Faroese linguist Dr Christian Matras were published, historians did not know that the system of taking cattle to a summer farm, known as a *sæter* in Norway and a *shieling* in Gaelic Scotland, had at one time existed in the Faroe Islands as well. Dr Matras found out that place-names where the element *ærgi* (from Gaelic *airge*) occurs are used of shielings or summer pastures. Probably the name was brought to Faroe by Norsemen coming from the south, and then it stopped there, as it is not known in Iceland or Norway. In Scottish Gaelic it means a pasture with huts for farm workers to stay in during the summer. The element appears as *argi* in the northern islands and as *ergi* in Suðuroy, and there are many such place-names in Faroe, although the spelling varies. Argir in Tórshavn is one of them. The philological discovery of Dr Matras was followed by archaeological excavation of a most interesting site in Ergidalur at Hov in Suðuroy. It turns out that all names containing *ærgi* are situated rather high up and far away from the oldest farm in the district, and of course that is the reason why they were built: to husband and harvest the land as economically as possible.

From their names it is possible to establish that some of the *bygdir* were once large settlement farms; among these are the *bygdir* with names ending in *bøur*, such as Sumba from Sunnbøur, Hvalba from Hvalbøur, and Froðba from Froðbøur, all in Suðuroy. A few original farms have names compounded with personal names. Then there is Hov in Suðuroy, a place of worship in pre-Christian times, which was the home of Havgrímur, who *Færeyinga Saga* tells us was wont to keep up the old ritual practices. And just north of Kirkjubøur we find the name Velbastaður, which may derive from Vébólstaðr, where *vé* refers to a holy place in pre-Christian times, and *bólstaðr* means a farm. All these names refer to major farms at the time of settlement. Other farm names may end in *garður*, *skáli*, *hús* and *toftir*.

The place-name pattern in Faroe is different from that found in Shetland and Iceland. Velbastaður may be the only -*bólstaðr* name in Faroe, but its derivation is not undisputed: it may be the only -*staðir* name instead! In Shetland -*bólstaðr* names are very common, ending today in -busta or -bister. Other common Shetland name elements such as -land and -setr are lacking in Faroe, and so is the -*staðir* element compounded with personal names that is so common in Iceland. There are *-staðir* farms in Shetland too, and at one time they were all important settlements. There is no obvious explanation of this, but it does perhaps point to the date of settlement – the Faroe Islands were settled after Shetland, but some time before Iceland, and there seem to have been fashions in name giving. If *-staðir* names were the vogue in the early tenth century when so much of Iceland was settled, it may simply mean that in the Faroe Islands the land was already taken at that time so that there was no room for any more large farms, whereas in Shetland it was perhaps still possible to found a large farm.

The origin and meaning of the name Føroyar have also been much discussed. The name is pronounced as 'føryar' and believed to mean 'sheep islands'. To some extent this seems to be corroborated by Dicuil, who informs us that the islands were 'full of innumerable sheep'. The form Føroyar is recent; the Norse form was Færeyjar, and the name appears in Seyðabrævið from 1298 in the expression 'í Færøyium'. The monk Theodricus in his history of Norway (*c.* 1180) wrote of the islands 'quas nos Pharias vocamus' – 'which we call Pharias'. On the Hereford map, the Mappa Mundi (*c.* 1280), the name Farei is used. As early as the seventeenth century Norwegian writers pointed out that the Norse word commonly used for sheep was 'sauðr'. The historian A. W. Brøgger maintains that as in the names of Orkney and Shetland the first part of Føroyar is probably a Celtic word, and suggests that the Norse settlers knew this name as part of the common geography of the northern seas. Dr Matras, on the other hand, points out that only the plural form distinguishes the old name from Færøy which occurs as an island name in several places in Norway, and from the names of Faray and Fara in Orkney. And as P. A. Munch points out, the word *fær* does occur as an example in an old Icelandic grammatical treatise, although it was probably not a commonly used word. For the foreigner, Faroese place-names can be confusing as they vary according to grammatical use, thus in Føroya Løgting the genitive form of the name is used, and 'í Føroyum' is in the dative. Most of the other island names also end in -oy, for island.

Fugloy
: The bird island. The name may be explained by the many birds in the cliffs. On the other hand the island may have resembled a bird when used as a landmark, so that it was perhaps referred to as 'the bird'. There are islands named in such a way in Norway. A third possibility is that the island name refers to the first settler, as Fugl was a Norse man's name.

Svínoy
: The pig island. This may originally have referred to one of the mountains in the island, as such a naming practice was not unusual.

Viðoy
: The wood island. Probably this refers to the drift-wood that has always collected in the large bay on the north side of the island.

Borðoy	This is probably derived from *borða*, meaning an edge or a steep promontory, of which there are five in Borðoy. The steep southern part of Nólsoy is known as Borðan.
Kunoy	The wife island. Kunoy and Kalsoy are believed to be named for the two stacks at the north end of the islands, Konan and Kallurin, the wife and the husband. As with Risin and Kellingin just off the north coast of Eysturoy, Kallurin was tall and slim while Konan was shorter and more rounded, just like the two islands.
Kalsoy	The husband island.
Eysturoy	The easterly island. Probably the island was named from Streymoy, which therefore must have been settled first.
Streymoy	The island in the current. The tides rip past on both the western and eastern sides of Streymoy. In these narrow sounds the current has been known to run at 20 knots per hour and stop any boat going against it.
Nólsoy	is named nors-oy in a document *c.* 1400. The name probably derives from the Norse noun *nór* (Gen. *nórs*) meaning a narrow stretch of land in a river, sound or lake. It is an old place-name element, as it is found in combination with *heimr*, e.g. Norheimsund in Hardanger. It refers to the northern isthmus, which is perhaps the most striking topographical feature of the island.
Hestur	The horse. A name describing the ridge of the island, which resembles the back of a horse. A similar name can be found near Sumba in Suðuroy: Hesturin hái means 'the high horse'.
Koltur	may be derived from *koltr*, a rounded mountain peak. There is a Kultersfell in Cunningsburgh in Shetland.
Vágar	is the plural form of *vágur*, meaning bay. The name Walls in Shetland is derived from the same word.
Mykines	has been believed to derive from *myki*, meaning dung or muck. This may perhaps refer to bird droppings. The element *nes*, meaning promontory, is unusual in an island name. An old story has it that Mykines was once a floating island. A fisherman, who had brought cow dung to throw at the whales in order to scare them away from the fishing ground, saw an island rise out of the fog. He threw the dung at a *nes*, at once making the island keep still – and this is how it got its name, or so they say. The Faroese scholar Ulf Zachariasen suggests that the origin of the name is the Celtic *muc(c)inis*, meaning pig island, and recently this interpretation has become accepted as likely.
Sandoy	is named for its sandy beaches or dunes.

Skúvoy	is probably named for the *skúgvur* – the skua – as large numbers of this bird used to breed in the island.
Dímun	is of Celtic origin. It is a combination of *di* (two) and *muin* (ridge or top), the use of two similar features being characteristic of Irish place-names. The name seems to have been fairly common: there is an island called Dimna on the Norwegian west coast, the name de Dimons is used of two stacks east of Yell in Shetland, and the name Dímunarvágr is mentioned in the Icelandic *Book of Settlement*, the *Landnámabók*.
Suðuroy	The south island.

Much local information and history can be drawn out of the place-names. Thus Árnatindur in Tindhólmur and Árnafjall, which is found both in Mykines and in Gásadalur, show the breeding places of the sea eagle – *Haliaetus albicilla* – which was once numerous but disappeared sometime before 1700. At Selberg on the south-western coast of Vágar the seals would whelp at a time when they were more common in the islands. Kópasker is a skerry where the seals would gather. In a place like Hvannagjógv the plant *hvann,* or angelica (*Angelica archangelica*) which at one time was much used, grows wild. Kleystrajorð means 'the land of the monastery', and tells us that this place in Norðoyri in Borðoy, was in pre-Reformation times a part of the landed estate of the Munkeliv monastery in Bergen. Punthavn and Krambatangi near Øravík in Suðuroy probably go back to the time of the Hanseatic merchants, and refer to places where they carried on their business.

Some place-names are connected with particular incidents. Thus Fútaklettur near Oyrargjógv in Vágar got its name in the following way: one day the bailiff, or the *fúti,* wanted to go from Tórshavn to Sandavágur in Vágar. He came to Leynar in Streymoy and asked the farmer Dávur í Leynum to take him across, but as the weather was bad Dávur would not go. The *fúti* refused to listen and told Dávur he had to go, but when they were about halfway across Vestmannasund, he took fright and wanted to turn back. 'Since you have taken to the sea, you must stay at sea,' said Dávur. When the *fúti* came ashore in Vágar with his baggage, he insisted that Dávur should help him get to Sandavágur, but Dávur calmly pushed off, saying that from now on the *fúti* would have to look after himself. And from then on the place has been known as Fútaklettur.

The 621-metre-high mountain Sátan dominates the coastline between Leynar and Skælingur. *Sáta* is the Faroese word for a hay-stack, and *sátan* is the definite form of the word. When used of a mountain it refers to its rounded form. But there are also several small rounded skerries in the fjords known as Sátan. At one time a new minister was coming to Viðareiði. He was

Danish and knew nothing of Faroese place-names or of the Faroese language. The boat crew was bringing him in bad weather, and the minister was rather the worse for wear. The poor minister got the shock of his life when suddenly one of the boat crew said, 'Well, it will soon be over, for now we can see Sátan.'

For some time it has been common to use the prepositions *í* (in), *á* (at) or *av* (from), combined with a place-name in the dative for surnames. This is perhaps to counteract the anonymity of the -sen names that have come from the Danish. Even in a small community there might be several people called Mikkjal Mortensen, but probably there would not be more than one Mikkjal Mortensen á Steig. Also the place-names give a sense of belonging to a place. Thus we find Steingrím av Vollanum and Símun av Skarði, as well as Dánjal í Buð and Annika á Lava. Sometimes a more detailed geographical description is given: Jóhannes norðan fyri Vegg – Jóhannes from north of the wall, and Hanus uttan fyri Á – Hanus from the other side of the river.

10
CULTURE

Norðurlandahúsið í Føroyum – the Nordic House in Faroe – is the centre for cultural co-operation between the Nordic countries, with their bond of individuality and community. The house is the result of a joint effort to create a centre that would bring the culture of the Faroe Islands and the other Nordic countries together for the benefit of all. A strikingly beautiful building with all kinds of technical equipment, Norðurlandahúsið in Tórshavn offers the Faroese people a variety of events, from an exhibition of Orkney art to an all-islands meeting of the folk-dance societies, with some 700 people doing the *føroyskur dansur* all through the night.

Sculpture outside the Útvarp (the radio station) by Tróndur Patursson

Cultural contact with others is not new in the islands. In Norse times there was a lively cultural intercourse with Norway, and perhaps even more so with Iceland. It even came about at times that Norwegian tradition reached Faroe through Iceland. The languages were so close that until the Reformation people in the Faroe Islands would sometimes learn Icelandic poetry by heart as if it were their own. This is what happened to the long religious poem *Ljómur* which has by some scholars been ascribed to Jón Arason, Iceland's last Catholic bishop, who was beheaded in 1550. For 300 years this poem lived in the Faroe Islands as oral tradition, faithfully handed down from generation to generation. But a terrible fate was said to befall anyone who learned the whole poem, so it was always known in bits and pieces. Jens Christian Svabo (1746–1824) wrote down nine verses of it. Before the Rev. Jensen of Sandoy was killed while going down the path on Stóra Dímun, he had for some time been trying to collect all the verses of *Ljómur*.

Traditional Faroese literature was based on such individual recollection and oral transmission, which thrived in most of the *roykstovur*. In the *roykstova* culture a good story-teller was appreciated, but there was room for everybody, and it was a school for language-learning too, as the writer Heðin Brú tells us:

> I came from a farm with many people, where we sat talking in the evenings so that I got a language schooling that really mattered. The primary school meant nothing to me. I did go to school – but the teacher did not know much Faroese, not that we were allowed to use it anyway. When I myself started writing, I was not short of words. You must remember that Faroese was never dead or dying, and everything that concerned the work, the nature, the sea, the land, the air and the people – and also their minds and feelings – all that could be described in a rich and varied language.

Education

The first school in the islands was the priest school at Kirkjubøur, whose most famous student was Sverri the Priest, who became King of Norway. It was closed down at the time of the Reformation, which in many ways had a disastrous effect on the old culture and language. For some time there was a Latin school in Tórshavn, but this closed at the end of the eighteenth century. The people of the *bygdir* were taught the basics of reading, writing and arithmetic, mostly so that they would be able to read the Bible, and in 1673 the minister Lucas Debes reported that people were indeed well schooled in Christianity. Another minister wrote in 1800 that 'the parents teach the children themselves, and a great number of them not only know how to read but can also write and do mental arithmetic, even fractions they can do rather well' (J. Landt).

In the second half of the nineteenth century all communities were expected to provide regular schools with trained teachers, and in 1870 a two-year teacher training course opened in Tórshavn. At first the new system was resisted, but towards the turn of the century many new schools were built all over the islands. Some schools were too small to have one teacher to themselves, but had to share with one of the neighbouring *bygdir*. Thus the teachers were involved in a lot of walking, but they seemed to put up with it. For example, at the turn of the century the *bygdir* of Árnafjørður and the now derelict Skálatoftir in Borðoy shared a teacher, who himself lived in Klaksvík. His walk to Skálatoftir must have taken a couple of hours each way; even so, he once walked all the way back to the *bygd* with a box of matches he had forgotten to return and knew was needed! The way to his other school was shorter in miles, but the mountain separating Klaksvík from Árnafjørður is some 600 metres high and the ascent is steep. However, when the teacher reached the pass, he could see whether there was any point in going down on the other side – if all the boats were out in the fjord to catch a shoal of herrings, the children would be on board also, as all hands were needed.

It is still a general principle in the Faroe Islands that where there is one child there is a school, and there are thirty-two schools with only one teacher. Some schools still share teachers: Gásadalur, Stóra Dímun and Mykines have the same two teachers for alternate weeks. Today commuting is mostly done by helicopter, but in the old days it was different! A schoolteacher who worked in the two *bygdir* of Trøllanes and Mikladalur in Kalsoy before the tunnels came told hair-raising stories of how she journeyed from one place to another along the frightening path high up on a ledge through the snow and storm of winter, while securely roped between two of the toughest men in the island.

The national movement of the late nineteenth century emphasized the importance of knowing the Faroese language, history and general culture. An application to the teachers' college for these subjects to be included in their curriculum was turned down, and this made the two young teachers Símun av Skarði and Rasmus Rasmussen, who wrote under the name of Regin í Líð, start Føroya Fólkaháskúli, or Folk High School. Such schools, meant to be a school for life, had become popular in other Nordic countries. The school was run in Fagralíð west of Klaksvík for the first ten years but in 1909 was moved to Tórshavn. A boarding school with room for twenty-four students, it was meant to be apolitical, but was gradually drawn into the ongoing political debate. It came to be a strong supporter of the Sjálvstýrisflokkur or Home Rule Party, as it upheld the rights of the Faroese to their own language. The strength of the Faroese language today owes a great deal to the Fólkaháskúli and the ideas it stood for.

The educational system is based on the primary school of ten grades, where the first eight years are compulsory, and the next two are optional. In 1937 a gymnasium – a secondary school preparing students for academic studies – was opened in Tórshavn; later another was established in Gøta in Eysturoy. In some of the larger *bygdir* there has for a long time been vocational training through apprenticeships combined with technical schools. In Tórshavn further education is offered in a number of fields, from nursing to engineering. The wish to strengthen the position of the native language even further led to the establishment of Fróðskaparsetur Føroya, which began as Academia Færoensis in the 1960s and has now become Universitas Færoensis. The aim was to create a scientific environment for the study of Faroese language, literature and history so that these subjects could be taught and studied at a high level. Basic studies in physics, mathematics, chemistry and computer science as well as general history and theology have since been added to the list of subjects taught.

A visitor to the islands in the 1870s saw their capital as a small heap of houses, or rather boxes strewed helter-skelter on the ground, and 'a large white church, whose belfry is adorned with a gilt ball and a profusion of crosses. It has, however, a literary dean, and, better still, a library' (Richard F. Burton). The dean referred to is V. U. Hammershaimb, the cultural giant of nineteenth-century Faroe, and a public figure. The library in question was founded in 1828, and is today known as Føroya Landsbókasavn, the national library, with a stock of some 106,000 volumes. Its aim is to collect and store

Tórshavn, at the turn of the century. Photo: Føroya Fornminnissavn

all Faroese literature as well as any books written about the islands; it is also expected to serve as a scientific library. It has been run directly by the Landsstýrið since 1948.

Another important cultural institution is Føroya Landsskjalasavn – the national archives – which was founded in 1932 and now has some 4.5 kilometres of shelves. All extant documents relating to Faroese administration are stored here, beginning with the records of the Løgting from 1615. For a long time research work for the writing of the Faroese shipping history in several volumes was carried out at this institution. For the general public, however, the Føroya Fornminnissavn – the museum of antiquities – and the Føroya Náttúrugripasavn – the museum of natural history – will have more appeal. Both institutions have interesting collections that are well presented, as well as staff who do not mind being asked questions!

The Press

The first attempt to launch a newspaper was made by Niels Winther in 1852. The paper, which was written in Danish, was called *Færingetidende,* and only nine issues were ever published. Winther used his sharp pen to flay the officials of the Trade Monopoly and the Danish government at a time when the Faroese people were without an assembly, but he was too heavily fined for his headline 'Now the Trade Monopoly is carrying their swindle too far' to be able to go on. A Faroese version of the name, *Føringatíðindi,* was used for the paper published from 1890 to 1901 by the national movement Føringafelag. This was the first paper to be published in Faroese, and it became a forum for the new literature in the vernacular, but it turned out to be impossible to make a go of it financially.

In 1877 came *Dimmalætting,* which has the rather romantic meaning 'Dawn'. It was supported by well-to-do Tórshavn citizens and the Danish community. When the schism came in Faroese politics in 1906, *Dimmalætting* became the voice of the unionists, and has always strongly advocated the closest possible relationship with Denmark. It was a long time before any articles were written in Faroese, and even today the leader is usually in Danish. It is published three times a week, and is still the paper with the largest circulation, some 13,000 copies. As *Dimmalætting* has a large share of the advertising market, it is a sound business.

All the other seven papers that today are published in the islands are written only in Faroese. Five of them take a political stance: *Tingakrossur,* which was founded in 1906, represents the old Home Rule Party the Sjálvstýrisflokkur; *Dagblaðið* is the mouthpiece of the Fólkaflokkur, *Sosialurin* of the Social Democrats or Javnaðarflokkur, *Fríu Føroyar* of the Communists, and 14 *September,* which is named for the day of the referendum in 1946, voices the views of the Tjóðveldisflokkur. The *Oyggjatíðindi* is politically independent, and so is *Norðlýsið*, which is published in Klaksvík. As the name indicates, *Dagbladið* was briefly a daily paper at first, but is today published three times a week. Common to all these papers is their difficult, hand-to-mouth financial position.

It is difficult to publish magazines in such a small community, and over the years several have come and gone. But for some seventy years publication of the cultural magazine *Varðin* has been an almost invariable annual event. For a long time it was edited by the poet Rikard Long. It is published by the literary society Felagið Varðin, and has been a welcome platform for young writers. In addition to the magazine the society has also published a series of books and has thus been a focal point in all cultural life. Another magazine that has become very popular is *Mondul,* which is mostly about Faroese history. It is published by Føroya Fornminnissavn and has three issues a year. The newest and most ambitious magazine as far as illustrations are concerned is *Brá,* which is also rather outward-looking in its choice of subject-matter.

Radio and Television

Since 1957, when the Faroese radio station Útvarp Føroya first went on the air, the newspapers have had competition in the reporting of news. According to the rules set down by the Løgting all broadcasts are made in Faroese, and their aim is to cover as many aspects of Faroese life as possible. On average the Útvarp broadcasts ten hours a day, and all programmes sent out to its 17,000 paying listeners are produced in the islands. On its twenty-fifth anniversary the Útvarp received a splendid birthday gift: a new, well-equipped broadcasting house in Tórshavn, next door to the Nordic House. The new radio station has five studios for various purposes, as well as a large record collection. The Útvarp Føroya has had stereo coverage for all the islands since 1971, so Faroe was possibly the first country in the world to have total stereo coverage. It transmits in the medium wave band and the FM band, using a 200 kW transmitter, so as to reach the fishing fleet everywhere in the North Atlantic.

The public Faroese TV station Sjónvarp Føroya started transmitting in 1984, but private local TV associations had by then been transmitting for six years. Thus Faroe was probably the last country in Europe to get its own TV system. The average transmission time is six hours, five days a week, with Mondays and Wednesdays without any programmes. The Sjónvarp can help themselves to any programmes they want from the public Danish television network, and also get quite a few transmissions via satellite. Apart from children's programmes the Sjónvarp's own production consists mainly of news and topical magazine items. The news programme 'Dagur og Vika' –

The Day and the Week – is on the screen for half an hour three days a week, and 'A Synini' – Horizon – discusses current affairs. The Saturday magazine 'Grannar Okkara' – Our Neighbours – shows news items from the other Nordic countries, and is very popular.

The Theatre

So far the fear that television will destroy the old culture of participation seems unfounded. Amateur theatre groups and performances are more numerous and ambitious than ever. In the summer of 1990 a dancing group was invited to the Baltic states to give a performance of *Kópakonan* – The Seal Woman – based on the Kalsoy legend. Later that year Faroese actors gave beautiful and moving performances of *Antigone* at the Nordic House, directed by Ulla Ryum from the Royal Theatre of Copenhagen. Plays and play-acting have long been popular, and in many ways Faroese dancing is related to the theatre. The Faroese theatre was founded as early as 1889, at the same time as Føringafelag. It naturally became part of the national movement, and over the years many popular plays were written and enacted by and for the Faroese. In 1926 'Sjónleikarhúsið' was built in Tórshavn, and until 1985, when the theatre in Klaksvík was established, it remained the only theatre building.

In the years 1961 to 1978 most of the productions in Tórshavn were directed and produced by a professional Faroese actor, Eyðun Johannessen. During this period dramatists from Beckett to Shakespeare and Strindberg were represented in the programme, and there was a great interest in the theatre. In 1977 a small group of actors who called themselves Gríma appeared, with the aim of working professionally within the theatre. They have staged plays by Faroese writers both for adults and children, and have also been busy teaching amateur theatre groups as well as school children.

It is a tribute to Faroese theatrical circles in general that a film produced in the islands has been showered with prizes. During the Seventh Nordic Film Festival, which was held in Tórshavn in the spring of 1989, and later at a film festival in Lübeck in Germany the young Katrin Ottarsdóttir of Tórshavn won international acclaim for the first Faroese feature film *Atlantic Rhapsody*, of which the idea, script, direction and production were all her work. She spent a whole year's cultural budget of 1.7 million Faroese krónur on the film. *Atlantic Rhapsody* links fifty-two short stories in a chain, almost like the Faroese dance. Everyday life is at first described realistically, but gradually reality and dream merge. The critics found its freshness and spontaneity as refreshing as the Faroese weather. It is a wise, warm and funny picture of Tórshavn, a tribute to the smallest capital in northern Europe, as it was made for, by and with its inhabitants, and everyone appearing in the film is an amateur.

Music

The Faroese are a singing people. Today they sing in many choirs all over the islands, but in the old days they would sing over the day's work or while sitting together at the *kvøldseta*. Special songs were used for special occasions. The gannet catchers of Mykines would sing what they called their 'Súla Song' as they left at night for the bird stacks, and fishermen had their special hymns for rowing out as well as homecoming. 'Near the mouth of Klaksvík bay we meet a boat that is coming home from the fishing. We see nothing, but we hear the strokes of the oars and the sound of the hymn they sing at homecoming' (Severin Thomsen).

While most of the hymns were written by the Dane Thomas Kingo (1634–1703) or the Norwegian Petter Dass (1647–1708) and were thus part of the Lutheran heritage of Scandinavia, a way of singing them developed that was specially Faroese. Instruments were never used for the hymn singing, nor for the ballads, which formed another important part of the living tradition. For the large collection of ballads there is a wealth of tunes that can be found only in the Faroe Islands. Many of these obviously go a long way back, as they contain musical and stylistic elements of early medieval church music.

Instrumental music was almost unknown until the end of the nineteenth century, when organs were placed in some churches. And in the more culti-

Part of the exhibition area in Nordic House. Photo: Mette Bleken

vated circles of Tórshavn the violin had many followers. This was mainly thanks to the young baker Georg Caspar Hansen, who came from the island of Bornholm in Denmark to the Faroe Islands, where he spent the rest of his life. He was an enthusiastic musician, who could play practically any instrument, but preferred the violin. Soon he did nothing but teach music, and all kinds of enterprise grew up around him. He organized choir and chamber concerts and inspired a general interest in music that led to the founding of the Tórshavnar Musikkskúli.

The discovery of instrumental music and the delight taken in playing it by Georg Hansen's pupils have been described by William Heinesen in his novel *The Lost Musicians,* which in 1950 made him an internationally known writer. The story ranges in mood between farce and tragedy, between an infectious gaiety and a deep sadness. None of his musicians are really ready to cope with the demands of everyday life – they are happy amateurs in the art of living as well as music – and they are all unforgettable characters. Georg Hansen appears as Kaspar Boman, the old teacher who dies happy after having heard a symphony orchestra on its way to Iceland play in one of the Tórshavn warehouses.

Today the islands have a symphony orchestra of their own – Føroya Symfoniorkestur – with some forty-five active players. New symphonic pieces have also appeared, for example by Sunleif Rasmussen and Kristian Blak. Other young composers are Bjarni Restorff and Pauli í Sandagerði, who mostly write choral compositions. Pauli í Sandagerði has won acclaim for his settings of William Heinesen's poems; they are melodious with a restrained use of instruments.

There are also about ten brass bands, which give concerts all over the islands. These bands picked up a lot of technical skill from British soldiers during the Second World War, and some of them still keep in touch with their old teachers. Skills have also been learned from outdoor revivalist meetings, where brass music is much used. One of the bands is called GHM in memory of Georg Hansen. A Nordic Jazz, Folk, and Blues Festival is held every August in Tórshavn. It is supported by the Faroese authorities and the Nordic House and usually lasts for three to four days. The festival is a popular event and attracts many visitors. Kristian Blak has worked and taught in these fields too, especially in jazz, and is thought of as a modern Georg Hansen. The folk singer Hanus Johansen has become popular in the Nordic countries and at home, and the group Frændur sing their own songs, which are rapidly becoming part of the national heritage.

On the whole cultural life in the islands has an impressively broad base. The individual is very visible in such a small community, and this perhaps provides the challenge necessary for artistic development. At any rate fears that Faroese artistic activity might be crushed by foreign influences have proved unfounded; if anything, such influences have inspired independent work.

11
LITERATURE

The oldest known literature in the islands is the ballads, or *kvæði*, which have been preserved so faithfully because they were used, both for dancing and for evening entertainment. Some of these epic ballads can be found in other Nordic countries too, but most of the Faroese variants are longer and have also retained more of the old poetic expressions, the *kenningar*, which are used for woman and man, battle, sword and blood, sea and gold. Most of the ballads were made in the Middle Ages, some of them perhaps as early as in the reign of King Hákon Hákonsson, who died in Orkney in 1263. What saga literature was to Iceland , the *kvæði* became to the Faroe Islands – exciting, dramatic, romantic and bloodcurdling stories.

All through the nineteenth century the work of writing down the wealth of oral tradition went on. Much work was done by enthusiastic local people. Jóhannes í Króki (1794–1869) copied down some 900 pages of material from his native Sandoy, faithfully recording the name of each singer, and the farmer Hans Hansen collected the local tradition of Fugloy. In the 1870s most of the *kvæðir* were collected in *Corpus Carminum Færoensium*.

The collection of stories in prose went on at the same time, the main work being *Faroese Legends and Folk-Tales* by Dr Jakob Jakobsen. That such work required both mental and physical stamina is apparent from Dr Jakobsen's description of a trip to Mykines, in a letter to J. J. Haldane Burgess:

> In the most westerly of the islands I was fortunate enough to uncover a local legend which is a definite derivative of a Norse tale found in the *Jomsvikinga saga*. It was, however, a tough journey. The first time I was on my way to the island by boat, the crew had to turn back – there was no hope of being able to land. The second time it went almost as badly, but finally we found a place where we could land. To be sure I got a breaker over my head and was almost struck by another one, but fortunately there was a man ashore who got a rope round my waist, so there was no danger to my life. After that I had 10 kilometres to walk in this dripping state to reach the village and find shelter. I had to cross a high mountain in such a thick mist that one could hardly see a yard ahead. But I got good results in Mykines …

The first writer to break the anonymity of folk poetry is Páll Nólsoy (1766–1809), who used the satirical verse known as a *táttur* to perfection. Although his main work, *Fuglakvæði*, holds the merchants and officials up to ridicule, he also has it in for his own countrymen in *Jákup á Møn*. In this *táttur* he describes how the spoiled youngster Jákup goes courting, in a parody of such descriptions in the ballads. But in the *Fruntatáttur* he is writing merely for his own enjoyment, making fun of women's hairdos! The farmer Jens Christian Djurhuus (1773–1853) from Sjógv in Kollafjørður went on writing ballads in the traditional way, and only rarely does he depart from the old style. His favourite saga material was *Færeyinga Saga* and *Olav Tryggvason's Saga*. Every time the dancing season opened he would contribute a new ballad, and *Ormurin Langi* about King Olav's death in the battle of Svolder, the most popular dancing ballad of them all, was made by Sjóvarbóndin, as he was popularly known:

Viljið tær hoyra kvæði mítt,	Will you hear my song,
viljið tær orðum trúgva,	Will you believe my words,
um hann Olav Tryggvason,	about King Olav Tryggvason
hagar skal ríman snúgva.	this song will tell.

And the refrain:

Glymur dansur í høll,	The dancing sounds through the hall,
Dans sláið í ring!	So let us dance in a ring!
Glaðir ríða Noregsmenn	Happy ride the men of Norway
til Hildar ting.	to Hild's ting [into battle].

The first writing in Faroese was closely connected with the national movement, and began in the 1870s among students in Copenhagen, who wrote lyrically about the beauty of the islands they had left. The best known writer among them is Fríðrikur Petersen (1853–1917), who wrote the first Faroese national anthem. The young editor of *Føringatíðindi* and leader of the national movement, Rasmus Effersøe (1857–1916), also wrote popular poetry and plays. The poetry of the late nineteenth century was naively didactic, all written with the purpose of leading the Faroese back to their roots, especially to their own language. Nobody did so more plainly than Jóannes Patursson, and nobody could provoke and challenge to action as he did, and not just in words. When at a celebration in Tórshavn a toast was proposed to the 'mother country of Denmark', everybody rose but Patursson. To explain his action he wrote a poem saying that to him only the Faroe Islands could be *móðurland*, and he wanted only one – 'Eina móður vil eg eiga'.

After 1900 poetry becomes more free and less polemical; it is more personal and is meant to be read rather than sung or recited. In 1914 came *Yrkingar*, the first individual collection of poetry published in the Faroese language. It contained many beautiful lyrical poems and was written by

Sjóvarbóndin's great-grandson Jens Hendrik Oliver Djurhuus (1881–1948), popularly known as Janus Djurhuus. As a young man he became absorbed in a study of the classics, especially Plato, and his poetry also shows how well he knew the Icelandic sagas. But the German writer Heinrich Heine probably meant most to him. Djurhuus worked as a lawyer in Denmark for many years, but always wanted to come home, and the last ten years of his life were spent in his native Tórshavn, where his sharp intellect and biting sarcasm did not make him popular.

Djurhuus lifted Faroese poetry above the provincial level. He is a master at blending matter and form, but his poetry is often deeply pessimistic, full of doubt and cold despair.

Ver sterk mín sál á køldu náttarvakt	Be strong my soul in your cold nightwatch
har eingi altarljós til gudar brenna,	where no altar lights are burning for the gods,
har hvør ein vón av fannkava varð takt	where every hope is buried in the snowdrifts
og hjarta ongan hita meir kan kenna.	and the heart can feel no more warmth.
Ver stór mín sál sum rúmdar kalda tøgn,	Be as great my soul as the cold silence of space,
ið eina er, táið slóknar lívsins søgn!	which is all, when life's story fades away.

No one has been able to stretch the Faroese language as far as Djurhuus did to express the thoughts and feelings of the twentieth century. But he also added to its scope by translating poetry by Fröding, Ewald, Heine and Poe, as well as making prose versions of Homer's *Iliad* and Plato's *Symposium*. His importance to later writers can hardly be overstated.

Unlike his elder brother, Hans Andrias Djurhuus (1883–1951) chose to stay at home, and was for many years a schoolmaster in Tórshavn. His whole outlook was different; he preferred to see the positive side of things and writes about summer and the sun and the joy of life. He was a most productive and versatile, although uneven, writer, trying his hand at everything from drama to children's verse. In *Hildarljoð* (1916) and *Søgumál* (1922) his poetry is concerned with Faroese history, and in *Sjómannsrímur* (1925) he writes about life at sea. No other Faroese writer has been so much in accord with the people, nor has anybody been so popular, although many other poets, such as Mikkjal Danjalsson á Ryggi, Rikard Long, Poul F. Joensen and Christian Matras, contribute in very different ways to this golden period of Faroese poetry.

Apart from V. U. Hammershaimb's sketches from popular life and the tales collected by Dr Jakobsen there is no older prose. The first novel to be written in Faroese was *Babelstornið – The Tower of Babel –* 1909, by Rasmus Rasmussen (1871–1962) from Miðvágur in Vágar under his pen-name Regin í Líð. It describes a family through three generations in the latter half of the nineteenth century, and paints a dark political and social picture of a community where every reform is met with suspicion. Another prose pioneer is Sverri Patursson (1871–1960), a younger brother of Jóannes Bóndi. His main interest was ornithology, and in the years 1898–1902 he published a paper he called *Fuglaframi.* He wrote almost lyrical descriptions of bird life as well as sensitive short stories, such as his much praised *Ábal* about a mentally retarded boy. Mads Andrias Winther (1871–1923) wrote stories from his native Sandur. Another early regional writer is Hans Marius Eidesgaard (1887–1964), who describes life in Oyndarfjørður in Eysturoy.

In the early part of this century two closely related boys were growing up in Tórshavn, to become the best known Faroese writers outside the islands: Jørgen-Frantz Jacobsen and William Heinesen. Intimate friends, they shared a world of story and fable. Although their family background was bilingual, they both write in Danish, and this has set them apart, in a kind of no man's land, in spite of their writing about Faroese subjects in a way that only the native-born could do. When there were rumours that William Heinesen was about to receive the Nobel Prize for literature in 1981, he wrote to the Swedish Academy and renounced his candidacy. Later he explained why:

> The Faroese language was once held in little regard – indeed it was suppressed outright. In spite of this the Faroese language has created a great literature, and it would have been reasonable to give the Nobel Prize to an author who writes in Faroese. If it had been given to me, it would have gone to an author who writes in Danish, and in consequence Faroese efforts to create an independent culture would have been dealt a mean blow.

As a young boy Jørgen-Frantz Jacobsen (1900–38*)* was sent to Denmark to attend the prestigious Sorø Akademi, and later studied History and French at Copenhagen University, where he did well. He was only twenty-two when he first became aware of the symptoms of tuberculosis. For the remaining years of his life he was in and out of sanatoriums, in a brave but hopeless struggle against his illness. He worked for some time as a correspondent for the Copenhagen newspaper *Politiken,* then did historical research. In the winter of 1934–5 he started work on his historical novel *Barbara,* and worked on it until his death in Vejlefjord sanatorium in March 1938. The novel was not completed; he wrote about it in his last letter to William Heinesen: 'And so, my friend, there remain only the two-thirds of the Mykines chapter and the three final chapters. My poor heart beats. It is cold, but spring is in the air and in the light.'

The novel was hailed as a masterpiece by Danish critics, and became a bestseller overnight. It has been translated into thirteen languages, among them Faroese. The novel, which is set in the eighteenth century, is a love story based on the life of the legendary Beinta who married three ministers. The legend was taken down by Dr Jakobsen and had already been used by two other writers. The love affair that Jørgen-Frantz Jacobsen himself was involved in gave another dimension to the story, and especially to the woman at the centre of it. It is a colourful story, and he gives it vibrant life: '... it is not just a story I want to write, nor do I just want to give a picture of the Faroe Islands, but I want to express a deep feeling for life, yes, in the end I want to give thanks to life.'

The same wonder, joy and belief in life can be found in the work of William Heinesen, for example in this much quoted poem:

> Here among naked cliffs,
> scoured by frost and surf
> here under stern stars
> here I will sing threateningly
> of the power of light over darkness,
> of the indomitable strength of goodness,
> of the right that joy has on earth.

Through a long life William Heinesen (1900–91) tried his hand at many kinds of self-expression, and did well at them all. His paintings and collages are a popular part of the Tórshavn scene, and his love of music is evident throughout his books. Sent to Copenhagen to learn about commerce, he felt like 'a Gulliver fallen from the skies into Brobdingnag', and instead of going to school roamed the streets excitedly with a friend until 'it all ended when the venerable old headmaster Jacobsen confided, without rancour, that we were a menace to the discipline of the school, and suggested that we take the final step and withdraw entirely from the course of studies.' For some time he worked as a journalist, then came back to Faroe for good in 1932 and tried to work in the family business, but without much success.

Heinesen had his literary debut as a young man of twenty-one with a collection of poetry he called *Arctic Elegies,* and had published three more before he wrote his first novel *Blæsende Gry – Stormy Dawn –* in 1934. He would read every chapter as he finished it to the painter Sámal Joensen-Mikines, as he was worried that his Danish was not good enough. Whereas in his poetry Heinesen writes mostly in the abstract about the lonely landscapes of his native islands, his fiction is all about people. There are many characters and a confusing number of events in his first novel. It describes a community in the throes of violent change, where the position held by the Church is being taken over by various sects, but where there is also hope that economic expansion will bring about a better future – a new dawn.

William Heinesen
at home, at 90

His second novel *Noatun* (1938) is logically constructed and gets its political and social message across clearly: that solidarity is the basis of progress. It is the story of a small group of people building a pioneer community in high hopes. In Norse mythology Noatun was the home of Njorð, the god of fertility, riches and shipping. The next novel, *The Black Cauldron*, did not appear until eleven years later, and shows another world entirely. The war years had been extremely hard for most people in the islands, but there were those who made money from taking fish, at the expense of many Faroese lives, from Iceland to Britain. Heinesen shows up the war profiteers and the aftermath of decadent living and religious hysteria caused by them, but the novel is saved from gloom and the ever-lifted finger of morality by its effervescence, its humour and its wonderful characters. *The Lost Musicians* came out in 1950 but was actually written much earlier, as an exercise to escape from wartime pressure. In this book Heinesen leaves social realism altogether and lets the story-teller take over. The book is divided into four movements like a symphony, and a love of music is the bond between the characters, true innocents who muddle into situations that all seem to be variations on the same theme – an ecstatic experience of beauty.

The realist form was too confining for William Heinesen, and in *Mother Pleiades*, published in 1952 with the subtitle 'A story from the beginning of time', he gives free rein to his imagination in the description of a small boy who is the victim of a strict and insensitive upbringing. Through the boy's fantasies we meet the two kingdoms of heaven and hell, which are both doomed to destruction, leaving the kingdom of the earth to survive in the end. The shorter form of this novel seems to have appealed to Heinesen; soon afterwards he began writing short stories. Most of his stories and sketches were printed in the three collections, *The Enchanted Light, Gamaliel's Bewitchment* and *Cure Against Evil Spirits* (1969). In his novel *The Good Hope* (1964), the main character, Rev. Peder Børresen, is based on a historical person, Rev. Lucas Debes. As the story is told through his letters to a friend and colleague, Heinesen was faced with the difficult task of reproducing seventeenth-century Danish. He succeeded so well that this novel, which many consider his best work, was awarded the prize for literature of the Nordic Council. When asked how long it had taken him to write it, Heinesen answered, 'Forty years. But then I did other things in between.'

In Heinesen's writing there is always the contrast between darkness and light, between the destructive and the creative forces, and in this continuous struggle man is forced to take sides. How to do so, however, is not clearly defined, nor are the dividing lines always clear, as there is also a mysterious side to life. He says somewhere that 'life shall not despair, and death shall not rule', and perhaps Heinesen's fascination lies in this optimism, as well as in his acceptance of the fantastic and the irrational as part of life.

Whereas Tórshavn is the centre of the Heinesen world, the *bygdir* and the sea are natural subjects for Martin Joensen (1902–66) and Heðin Brú (1901–87), and to them Faroese is the natural medium; indeed they both add to the stature of the literary language. Paradoxically, Heðin Brú had his first novels translated into five languages while it was still against the law to teach Faroese in schools! Heðin Brú grew up in Skálávík in Sandoy, and his real name was Hans Jakob Jacobsen. By adopting a genuinely Faroese name he was in his quiet way taking sides in the cultural conflict.

As a young boy he went fishing off Iceland or worked on the family farm. After one year at the Føroya Fólkaháskúli in Tórshavn he studied agriculture in Copenhagen. His work as a farming expert took him to all the islands, where he walked from one farm to another. Whenever he had a free moment he would write down what he had heard and seen, and perhaps this is why his characters and his use of the language are so authentic. A recurrent theme in his six novels is the problems and conflicts arising in a society at a time of revolutionary change: from farming to fishing, from the Middle Ages into modern times. With great sensitivity he portrays communities still rooted in the old culture, and an expression often used is '*Teir gomlu vóru vanir at siga . . .*' – 'The old folks used to say. . .'. Whilst not a nationalist in the usual sense of the word, Heðin Brú is Faroese in his choice of subject matter and not least in his use of the language, his terse, ironic and often humorous style being extremely difficult to translate.

Even his first novel *Lognbrá – Mirage* – shows that Heðin Brú is a born story-teller. Drawing heavily on his own experience, he tells the story of the young boy Høgni and his life in a *bygd* at the beginning of the twentieth century. In *Fastatøkur – A Firm Grip* – he takes his story of Høgni further, giving the first realistic description of the work on board the smacks, the two-masted boats used for deep-sea fishing. The crew in the story know that the *Rúðan* is not seaworthy, but they do not protest, as they need the pay. On the way home they run into a terrible storm and barely make it; it is a life where Høgni has no choice but to grow up.

The short novel *Feðgar á ferð* (1940) – *The Old Man and his Sons* – is considered Heðin Brú's major work. Set in Vágar, it gives a humorous description of a *bygd* where the old and the new ways of life meet and clash. Old Ketil has rashly and totally against his ingrained caution bid too much for *grind* – whale-meat – at an auction, and, as there is no way he can pay and all attempts to raise money fail, he has to take the difficult decision to sell his only cow. It is a story both funny and touching, but on a deeper level it takes up the question of personal honour and morals. But Brú is no pastoral romantic; he also sees clearly the levelling tendencies of the old culture. In his short story 'Alone on Lítla Dímun' the dreamer, who never quite fits into the life of the *bygd,* is left behind on the island because the others believe he has been killed falling off a cliff. He exults in his freedom, and shouts in the direction of the *bygd,* 'I shan't light the beacon, I don't want to go back, I can't bear your scorn and your mockery!'

Among the next generation of Faroese writers Jens Pauli Heinesen (b. 1932) from Sandavágur in Vágar is almost the only one to express himself in prose, and the only one apart from William Heinesen to make a living from his writing. A productive writer, he published his first collection of stories in 1953, and recognition came with the trilogy *Tú Upphavsins Heimur* (1962–4) – *The World's Beginning.* In this social satire he describes an isolated *bygd* that is suddenly opened to the world when a tunnel is built. In his large novel *Frænir Eitur Ormurin – The Serpent is Named Frænir –* he uses the old conflict of the Sjurður-kvæði – the ballads of Sigurd who slays the dragon – only today's hero fights what he sees as today's monsters, the technocrats and capitalists. A realistic writer, Jens Pauli Heinesen does not hanker for a lost simplicity, but takes on the challenge of writing of life in the Faroe Islands of today, a society he sees as part of a complex modern world. In the same way his linguistic style is untraditional; he is not a purist and has no qualms about using modern words.

Among the many more modern prose writers Oddvør Johansen (b. 1941) has won acclaim for her novel *Livsins summar – The Summer of a Lifetime –* where the main character is a ten-year-old girl. Marianna Debes Dahl (b. 1947) and Steinbjørn B. Jacobsen (b. 1937) also write for and about children. Hanus Andreassen (b. 1942) is a popular short-story writer. Together they provide a rich and complex literary picture.

This is also true of poetry, where modernist influences led to a renaissance. Established writers like Karsten Hoydal (1912–90) and Regin Dahl (b. 1918), who both have a considerable output behind them, have experimented with the use of language, and have tried to teach the younger generation of poets to become more European in their outlook.

When Rói Patursson (b. 1947) won the Nordic Council award in 1986 for his collection of poetry called *Likasum – As if –* the jury considered the poems to be contemporary comments on texts by Marx and Freud and on the peace and disarmament debate, and found that the poet demonstrated the connection between a Faroese reality and modern existential questions with openness and

*Poet Rói Patursson
with daughter Lív*

lyrical power. Rói Patursson's life in many ways follows the pattern of Faroese writers before him. He went to sea at fifteen and twelve years later began studying philosophy at the University of Copenhagen. Today he is head of the Føroya Fólkaháskúli. He has sailed around the world, and this experience has left its mark on his poetry. He dislikes absolutes of any kind, and his poetry leaves the conclusions to the reader. He is an ironic writer in the modernist tradition, but he uses images drawn from the scenery around him – the rhythm of the sea and the race of the clouds. Rói Patursson may embrace the world, but there is no doubt that he does so from the Faroe Islands.

> Although it can often feel as though writing for this small nation is like shouting into an empty nothingness – no reply, no echo – it is still my life; I write every day, every moment is precious, every day is exciting, time never passes slowly, and the loneliness here does not feel oppressive.

This comment made by an ageing Heðin Brú reflects a problem faced by many writers in a community which is too small to form a literary milieu. And yet the lack of anonymity that makes it impossible for writers to isolate themselves in ivory towers must surely work positively. And to the reader this closeness is invaluable – after all, where else in the world is it possible to walk up to the writer of a book you are just reading and ask about its meaning? Faroese literature today is part of the people's life, and everything that is published is also read. Yet in spite of a large readership it is difficult to produce books because most writers not only have to edit their own books, but sometimes even have to do the marketing themselves. Even so some hundred titles are published every year, of which about half are translations and the rest original works.

12

DANCING – A JOURNEY IN TIME

> This half-darkened room, where the mild, yellow light of an oil-lamp falls on the weathered faces of men and the soft cheeks of girls, this wild chorus from straining throats, this is the Faroe Islands – the darkness, the surf, the storm. It is the violent as well as the strangely intimate, it is the powerful epic and the gentle poetry, which it has been the cultural achievement of the Faroese to preserve in an ancient form even to this day and age.
>
> *Jørgen-Frantz Jacobsen*

To watch or take part in the *'føroyskur dansur'* – the Faroese dance – is a strange and intriguing experience for a visitor to the islands. It is a manifestation of tradition preserved through the ages – Faroese dancing may not have changed much since medieval times. And even today people can dance the night through, living and enacting the drama of the ballad story through mime and movement. The Faroese think of this as dancing a ballad.

Although the dancing is part of popular culture it cannot really be defined as folk dancing. Faroese dancing is a part of European cultural history, as it is closely related to the chain dance that was popular all over Western Europe in the late Middle Ages, and was known in France at the time of the troubadours as the 'carole'. Its roots may go even further back, to classical Greece. Dancing to ballads was a popular custom in all the Nordic countries. For a long time it had the blessing of the Church, and there was often dancing after the service on Sundays. But in time, excesses on the part of the dancers put a stop to this practice, and the tradition died out and became more or less forgotten. In Orkney and Shetland the ballad dancing was still known at the end of the eighteenth century, but according to the minister George Low it had 'almost given entire way to the reel'. In the Faroes alone the dancing has flourished in an unbroken tradition to this day.

Although it probably had come to the Faroe Islands through Norway, there was little or no dancing tradition left in that country, so in 1902 the Norwegian folklore expert Hulda Garborg went to the Faroe Islands to learn about it and 'bring it home'. She saw that what went by the name of folk dancing in Norway at the time was only a pale reflection of what it could be. 'Such paganism I have never seen in dancing. Old weather-beaten men became quite wild and howled from happiness and joy of life.' She also came to realize what dancing could mean to a people socially and culturally. 'We saw the Faroese people in their historical isolation. Cut off and downtrodden they lived in their islands, confined by the darkness of winter. Then hand found hand. They found *each other*. They rose to sing and dance together, finding strength against the silence and their own helplessness.'

We find dancing mentioned as early as 1616, when the Icelander Jón Ólafsson Indíafari describes an evening spent with Mikkjal í Lamba in Eysturoy, but unfortunately he only says that there were 'round dances in the Faroese fashion with song and ballads'. Then in 1669 Thomas Tarnovius, the son of a Suðuroy minister, enumerates in his book on Faroe the seven different ways the people have of keeping physically fit, and as the last of these he mentions dancing, 'where one person holds the hand of another, so that at one time 12 or 14 may be dancing in a ring … then one of them sings ballads, and then they dance to that according to the mood of the ballad, sometimes fast, and sometimes slow, sometimes stamping the floor, sometimes lifting their legs high.'

The dancing went on throughout the year on all festive occasions. But the real dancing season was in the wintertime, when the men were not busy with fishing or bird-catching, from Boxing Day until the first Monday of Lent. During this period everybody – young and old – would meet every Sunday and holiday at the *dansistova* – the room that a family with space to spare had made available for the dancing season. This was often a *roykstova* with an earth-packed floor. The great dancing days were Boxing Day, New Year's Eve and the first Monday of Lent when the season was closed with a special ceremony. On nights like these the dancing often went on till the early morning.

There was no dancing during Lent, but otherwise people would dance whenever the opportunity offered. The men who had taken part in a *grindadráp* (the whale-slaughter) would afterwards dance the night through. This was how they expressed their satisfaction with a job well done and their joy in achieving a large catch, but it was also a way of keeping warm and drying out their wet clothing. At weddings there were dancing ceremonies with traditional parts played by the bride and groom. Sometimes the minister himself would take part in the wedding dance, but usually he did not dance at all. And on 29 July people would gather in Tórshavn for Ólavsvøka, where the dancing was an integral part of the festivities.

There are three elements in the dancing: the narrative ballad, the tune and the dance steps. Of these the ballad is the most important factor. The ballads are long epics known as *kvæði*. The stanzas have two or four lines, as does the refrain. Whereas the stanzas tell the story, the refrain may be purely lyrical, as in the ballad about Ásmundur Aðalsson:

| *Leikum fagurt á foldum* | Let us dance joyfully on earth, |
| *Eingin treður dansin undir moldum!* | No one does any dancing in the grave. |

Sometimes the refrain refers to the dancing itself:

Stígum fast á várt golv,	We step firmly on the floor,
Sparum ei vár sko,	We do not spare our shoes,
Gud man ráða, hvar vær drekkum	God may decide, where we will celebrate
Onnur jol.	The next Christmas.

This is the refrain of the *Olúva-kvæði*, which tells the poignant story of Queen Olúva, the sister of Carolus Magnus or Charlemagne. In the old days this ballad was often used to end the dancing season.

Many of the ballads are extremely old and belong to a common Nordic heritage, but nowhere else have they been preserved so faithfully or with so many stanzas. The story and strife of the *Edda* and the *Volsunga Saga* are brought to new life in the *Sjurðar-kvæði,* the ballads about Sigurd, or Sjurður, who slayed the dragon Fáfnir. This is traditional material common to all the Germanic peoples, and was used by the composer Richard Wagner in many of his operas. The narrative ballads about Sjurður all run to between 400 and 670 stanzas in length. Not all the ballads are as long as that, but a length somewhere between 100 and 200 stanzas is not uncommon.

Perhaps the most popular of the historical ballads is the *Margretu-kvæði,* the story about the little Margreta Eiriksdóttir, who is known as the Maid of Norway. She was also the heir to the Scottish throne, and in 1290, when she was just seven years old, she was sent to Scotland, but died en route in Orkney. Some ten years later a German woman appeared in Bergen, claiming to be Margreta. The king did not believe her, and she was burned as an impostor at Nordnes in Bergen. But the people of Bergen believed her and saw her as a martyr. The ballad must have been composed just after the events it describes, as it gives what is really a very graphic account of the political opinions of the day.

The ballad singing alternates between the dancers and the leader of the singing who is known as *skipari*. It is the *skipari* who sings the story as it unfolds in the narrative stanzas, and the dancers take up the refrain. Everybody should know the *kvæði* so well that they concentrate on acting out its story; this is what is meant by dancing the ballad. Nevertheless, for the dancing to go well everything depends on the *skipari*.

The *skipari* needs a powerful voice as well as physical stamina. He must also be something of an actor and have a sense of drama. It is up to the *skipari* to create a rhythm as well as a mood to match the story of the ballad. The

The Faroese dance   heavy steps should fall on the stressed syllables. A good memory was also essential, as the ballads were not written down, and he was expected to have a large repertoire; a good *skipari* did not make do with the same ballad twice in one winter. Even so, the role has been much sought after and to become chosen as *skipari* has been considered a great honour. Some of them excel so greatly as dramatic artists that both dancers and spectators get completely carried away. Such a *skipari* is known as a *kvæðakempa* – a great ballad singer.

It is difficult to say where the ballad melodies came from, but it has been suggested that they derive from the old Gregorian chants. Rhythmically they have much in common with English medieval ballad melodies, but there are also elements unknown in any other folk-songs. These rather suggest an early Norse, pre-Christian tradition. In the ballad singing it is always the refrain that carries the weight of the melody; and in some islands it has been customary for the *skipari* just to recite the stanzas in a forceful rhythm.

The dancing is done mostly in the form of a chain dance, and is very simple. It consists of a basic pattern of six steps: the left foot takes one step to the side, the right foot follows, the left takes another step to the side, the right foot follows, finally the right foot takes a step to the right or forward, and the left foot follows. This is usually done in a skipping way and can become quite fast, but is done slowly and ponderously during the serious parts of the ballad. During the main stanzas the chain hardly moves, but while the refrain is being sung the speed increases and the chain moves forward. Thus the steps are always the same, only their length and speed vary.

> Although just a simple basic rhythm, this continuous, monot-
> onous step has, in itself, the power to vary the dynamic tension in
> a way which can make the dance tremendously exciting. In a
> good Faroese dance, where narrative, step and chanting combine
> in a throbbing, billowing whole, you experience an intoxicating
> power which is superb. From their everyday existence, the
> dancers are drawn into a richer world of imagination, where the
> events of the well-known ballads of the Middle Ages are time and
> again recognized as new and exciting.
>
> *Ólavur Hátun*

The dancers fall under a strange spell; they are conscious of nothing but the ballad and the drama in which they are taking part.

The ballads kept the past alive, so that for many children the heroic characters of Sigmundur Brestisson, Tróndur í Gøtu and Magnus Heinason still walked among them. The dancing was entertainment to young and old alike, often the only entertainment there was, but it was also a very important cultural and educational influence. Through the ballads the young were taught the ideals and virtues of the Age of Chivalry: courage and loyalty, honest and seemly behaviour, as well as faithfulness in love and friendship.

In the ballads disgrace and dishonour would befall those who betrayed these ideals, and it was not uncommon for this to happen in real Faroe life too. The dancing circle would at times function as a kind of popular court where the accused was manoeuvred into the middle of the circle and made to listen to a satirical ballad composed about him. Satirical ballads or *tættir* are usually of a personal character and are aimed at local people or their affairs. The victim was expected to reply, straightaway if he was able to improvise, if not, at the next dance meeting. There are a vast number of these satirical ballads in the islands; this aspect of the ballad tradition, at least, has stayed innovative. It may be this tradition that is behind the rather cut-throat nature of Faroese politics, as satirical ballads have been used in politics until recently. The most successful political satire was the *Fuglakvæði*, which Nólsoyar-Páll wrote about the Danish officials at the beginning of the nineteenth century.

There are other dance variations as well. The *Bandadansur*, which is danced with garters, has been popular for a long time, and is even mentioned by Tarnovius: 'But among all the others none is as strange as one they call Bande Dans where five or six on each side dance with ribbons in their hands, holding them sometimes above their heads ...' In the Sandoy dance the participants dance in pairs and change partners for each refrain. At Velbastaður and Kirkjubøur it has been customary to dance almost on the spot during the stanza and move ahead during the refrain. The well-known Sumba dancers have an exceptionally powerful way of dancing that is all their own, achieved in part by including light extra twists in the step pattern. In 1977 the Sunnbiar Dansifelag of Sumba in Suðuroy won The Freiherr von Stein Award for European Folk Art for the Faroe Islands.

Dancing to instrumental music has, of course, not been unknown in the islands. As early as the 1780s J. C. Svabo writes that: 'At fashionable weddings and parties, especially in Tórshavn, Faroese dancing is not so much used any longer, instead minuets, Polish, English and Scottish reels and country-dances are becoming popular.' These new dances, which needed instrumental music and were mostly danced in pairs, were commonly referred to as 'English dancing'. They remained popular, especially in Tórshavn, and lived on side by side with the Faroese dance. In the *bygdir* the Faroese dance for a long time held its ground and had great social significance.

But conditions have changed in the *bygdir* too. Fishing caused the men to be away for long periods of time, and the affluence which it brought has changed the social structure. Modern houses were not suitable for dancing, so special houses had to be built for it. But these lacked the intimacy of the old *dansistova,* and the older people often stayed away, as they did not feel at home in them. The many puritanical sects that appeared in the early decades of the twentieth century called the dancing houses dens of sin and iniquity. The national movement on the other hand saw the dancing as a valuable tradition that must be continued, and included it in their political programme. A number of dance societies have been founded expressly to maintain the Faroese dance.

Through the centuries the rhythmic thumping of many feet when people danced the ballad has drowned even the pounding of the surf in the Faroese *bygdir.* And today the tradition of the dance shows no signs of dying, but as with all traditions it needs fresh life breathed into it if it is to continue.

13

ART

The Faroese have left little historical evidence of their artistic creativity. This may be because their energy was spent on the making of everyday things, such as a beautifully shaped boat or an intricately carved *grindaknívur*. The interiors of the churches suggest a wood-carving tradition, and the simple carvings in drift-wood that decorate the church in Skálavík in Sandoy were made by the local farmer Tróndur á Trøð (1846–1933), who was also the best *skipari* of his time. In the nineteenth century the eccentric Díðrikur á Skarvanesi painted real and imaginary birds. But in general the demands of day to day living were so heavy that any creative energy tended to be channelled into poetry, which after all could be composed while digging a ditch or fishing for saithe! The explosive development taking place in the visual arts during the last fifty years has therefore come as a surprise, although the visual impact of the islands in the ever-changing light cannot fail to appeal to the imagination of an artist. During the national revival towards the end of the nineteenth century poets painted their native islands in words; a few years later the first few Faroese painters repeated the exercise in oils. Even more so than the poets they were pioneers completely lacking any tradition on which to build.

In 1901 Elizabeth Taylor, an American woman from St Paul, Minnesota, spent the winter in Tórshavn at the house of T. Christian Bærentsen, the first and only Faroese *amtmaður* of the islands. She kept coming back to the islands, sending home to various magazines humorous and perceptive articles. Miss Taylor, or Mistela as she was affectionately known, collected folklore as well as flora, and was also an accomplished painter of water-colours. Unable to leave the islands when war broke out in 1914, she spent four years as a lodger in the attic of the Kruse family at Eiði in Eysturoy. During this period she taught and encouraged Niels Kruse (1871–1951) who became one of the first landscape painters of the islands. When in 1924 he had his seascape 'First Day of Autumn' accepted by a Danish gallery, he was the first Faroese painter to succeed outside the islands. He was completely self-taught, 'except for the good advice and valuable schooling for which I can thank Miss Taylor'. Kruse lived at Eiði almost all his life, trying to capture in oils the scenery of his native *bygd*. In muted tones of brown, grey and green his gentle and poetic pictures reflect the effects of light on the landscape in changing seasons. Niels Kruse was the first Faroese artist to live for and from his art alone, and it was often a hard, uphill struggle.

Like Kruse his two contemporaries Jógvan Waagstein (1879–1949) and Chr. Holm Isaksen (1877–1935), or Kristin í Geil as he was known in Faroe, were mainly landscape painters, and were also largely self-taught. Unlike Kruse they had many other interests and did not make their living from painting only: Waagstein was a teacher and composer, and Isaksen edited the newspaper *Tingakrossur*. The view of Hestur and Koltur from Streymoy was one of Waagstein's favourite subjects. Today Isaksen's drawings and paintings of his native Tórshavn are considered his best work.

These three pioneer painters took the first steps towards making the Faroese aware and appreciative of visual art. But it took thirty years before the next generation of artists appeared. The real history of Faroese art begins in 1927 with an exhibition held in Tórshavn by three young artists: William Heinesen, Jákup Olsen and Sámal Joensen-Mikines. William Heinesen was perhaps the leading and most inspiring artist of this group at the time, and though his writing was gradually to become his major interest, he remained a versatile artist, who painted naturalistic landscapes as well as humorous sketches of trolls and other folklore characters. His paper cutting has become famous. Jákup Olsen (1902–63) worked as a theatre painter and book illustrator, and won acclaim for his oil painting 'Snow-covered Islands'.

It was the youngest of the three exhibitors who was to achieve international attention and spark off the impulse to paint among many of his fellow countrymen. Sámal Joensen-Mikines (1906–79), who has been called the father of Faroese art, was born and grew up in Mykines, the most isolated of the islands. He received his first instruction from a Swedish artist, who had come to Mykines to paint birds. Then for six years he studied at the Royal Academy of Art in Copenhagen, and had his second debut there in 1931. Mikines acknowledged his indebtedness to the Norwegian artist Edvard Munch, as well as his admiration for El Greco and Delacroix.

Whereas his early paintings are quite naturalistic, and record his home surroundings in careful detail, Sámal Joensen-Mikines later became highly original in his use of colour and design, and the best of his paintings are psychologically very suggestive. His famous painting 'Home from the Funeral' evokes the inevitability and fatalism of a Greek tragedy; his characters are painted in dark, greenish colours with faces and hands accentuated. This picture won acclaim for its daring use of line and shape: the figures form a steep pyramid, in the eternal shape of Faroese mountains. In all his work Mikines turns to Faroe, and especially his native island of Mykines, for his themes. His life there had been difficult, as some of his closest family members died of tuberculosis while still quite young, and he himself suffered from ill-health. The doubt and depression that often overwhelmed him account for the deep pessimism and pathos in his pictures of the late 1930s.

Later Mikines painted a series of pictures portraying *grindadráp,* where men with spears do battle with whales in an orgy of blood and death. One of these paintings takes up much of one wall in the room where the Føroya Løgting convenes. These dramatic pictures seem to have represented a cathartic transition to a more peaceful, harmonious period during which he often portrays sunny summer landscapes. But whatever his motif, Mikines is never boring:

> There are no false tones, and his base is Faroese: the people, the land, the immense sea. Mikines is the painter of human life. We see the grief reflected in the faces of relatives on the voyage home from a funeral. We feel the salty sea and the salty tears in the heavily loaded boat. We see the blood-coloured sea when the *grind* is cut.
>
> *Högni Torfason*

Through his interpretation of life around him Mikines appealed to his countrymen, and their interest in visual art was born.

In 1941 Listafelag Føroya – The Faroese Art Society – was founded by Faroese students in Copenhagen, with the express goal of buying the best works of art by Faroese artists and building an art gallery in Tórshavn, where exhibitions could be held. As a consequence of this a permanent art collection, Føroya Listasavn, was established in Tórshavn, and is housed in the art gallery Listaskálin, opened in 1970. It receives annual support from the Løgting, and houses many interesting paintings by Faroese artists. The first major exhibition of the Listafelag was held at Ólavsvøka in 1948, when nineteen artists exhibited 169 works. Since then this has become an annual event, where the established artists as well as the more promising young talents hang their work side by side. There has been an ever-growing interest among the general public, to the extent that today the pictures of popular artists are sold during the first day of showing. Whereas all who wish to show their art are welcome to the Ólavsvøka exhibition at the Nordic House, recently there have also been exhibitions where the paintings have had to be selected by a committee.

The work of Sámal Joensen-Mikines may have inspired other painters but there seems to have been little imitation. Apart from the interest in nature, it is difficult to find anything in common between the numerous painters who have followed him. On the contrary, Faroese artists all seem to do their own thing, unaffected by any -isms, so that there is a great diversity.

Ruth Smith (1913–58) from Vágur in Suðuroy is considered to be one of the most talented of Faroese artists. Growing up in straitened circumstances, she held a variety of jobs both at home and in Denmark, while studying painting first at evening school, then at the Academy in Copenhagen. Later she came home and settled with her family in Nes, near Vágur in Suðuroy, where she could find the images she preferred – scenery and faces. Painfully shy and critical of her own work, any pictures for hanging at the annual Ólavsvøka exhibition had to be practically dragged from her grasp. She worked consciously with form and colour, and was a productive artist who returned to the same subjects time and again, always trying to see them from new angles. These subjects included herself. She painted several self-portraits over a period of twenty years; one of them has been held to be among the finest portraits in Scandinavian art. The drawings she made of her children are warm and sensitive, and count among the finest produced in the islands.

Frimod Joensen (b. 1914) from Sandur in Sandoy, who in his youth went deep-sea fishing in the North Atlantic, is one of the loners in Faroese art, having created his own naïf, extremely colourful style. He has won acclaim both as a figure and a landscape painter, but his landscapes in particular are now much sought after. The late Steffan Danielsen (1922–76) was also unaffected by modern trends, and achieved a style all his own. He was completely self-taught as an artist and in his youth worked in traditional fishing and farming in his native island of Nólsoy. His debut at the Ólavsvøka exhibition in 1952 created quite a stir; people just stood and stared at his work, while William Heinesen went around whistling happily – a new artist had arrived! What Mykines was to Sámal Joensen-Mikines, Nólsoy was to Danielsen, as practically all his paintings portray life and landscape in this island. His detailed images are usually clearly outlined against a framework of monumental hills, sea and sky, and thus his pictures create a feeling of space as well as a strange, melancholy clarity.

Elinborg Lützen (b. 1919) grew up in Klaksvík, and when quite young went to learn more about art in Copenhagen, where she was confined through the war years. She later studied graphic art under Poul Christensen in Bergen, and still works mostly with woodcuts and linocuts, in black and white prints. Her subject matter is sometimes townscapes of Tórshavn or Klaksvík. Perhaps her best-known picture is 'Neytakonur' – 'Milkmaids' – which was shown at a Scandinavian travelling exhibition in 1976. Her images are often taken from folklore and fairy tales and portrayed in a humorous and tongue-in-cheek style that is all her own, full of an imagination and gaiety that are somewhat reminiscent of the work of William Heinesen. She has been much in demand as an illustrator of books, and has illustrated a Norwegian edition of the novel *Barbara*. Another Klaksvík artist is Frida Zachariassen (b. 1912) – Frida í Grótinum – who has painted a number of pictures of life in her busy home town. She has worked out a technique of her own for composition and colour structure.

Hans Hansen (1920–70), also known as Hanus í Mikladali, and Hans Jacob Glerfoss (b. 1937) both come from Mikladalur in Kalsoy, a *bygd* with rich craft traditions. Whereas Hansen studied fresco painting in Copenhagen and the

Ingálvur av Reyni, one of the most important Scandinavian painters of today

technique of mosaic work in Ravenna, Glerfoss is a self-taught painter whose work is sometimes reminiscent of the dark period of Mikines. Hans Jacob Glerfoss is also a well-known poet. Hans Hansen is considered one of the finest portrait painters in Faroe.

Ingálvur av Reyni (b. 1920) attended the Academy in Copenhagen during the Second World War, and is a dedicated but also experimental artist. He has drawn many portraits, but in his painting colours are as important, or perhaps even more important, than his subject. His first landscapes were fairly naturalistic, although he even then experimented with strong colour contrasts. His pictures have become more and more abstract, so that in his landscapes only the main contours are discernible. Ingálvur av Reyni is an independent artist who goes his own way, and expresses in his work his musicality and deeply religious nature. He is considered by many critics to be one of the most important Scandinavian artists of today.

The generation of painters born in the years between the two world wars were also influenced by French artists. This is especially true of Bent Restorff (1922–76), whose pictures were uneven and often controversial. He was completely self-taught and liked to experiment with colour. So does Zacharias Heinesen (b. 1936), who at one time was perhaps the most experimental both in technique and style, but now concentrates on the intense power and expressiveness of colour, or what he himself terms the symphony of colours, best found at sunrise or sunset. He has time and again painted the dark cluster of houses at Tinganes, but he concentrates on landscape paintings from the *bygdir*, where the horizontal and vertical lines of his images are quite marked. Tummas Arge (1942–78) started out in the footsteps of Sámal Joensen-Mikines and Ingálvur av Reyni, but soon branched out on his own, choosing the wild, untamed and dangerous side of Faroese nature, and using a wide range of colours on a large canvas. With his early death Faroese art lost one of its finest and most promising talents.

The first Faroese sculptor, and thus along with Mikines a pioneer of Faroese art, is Janus Kamban (b. 1913), who was one of the founders of Listafelag Føroya in 1941, and was the director of Føroya Listasavn in Tórshavn from 1969 to '76. He uses both clay, bronze and Faroese basaltic rock for his sculptures, in a style ranging from the strictly naturalistic to the classically simple. His subject is almost exclusively people at work or play,

Sculptor Janus Kamban

portrayed with a serious simplicity that is very impressive. Among his best-known work is his 'Fisherman'. For his 'Adam and Eve' he has chosen a Faroese fishing couple. In his relief 'Søga' – 'History' – for the school at Gøta, he shows three generations, with the child standing tall in the centre. Its theme is taken from *Færeyinga Saga:* Tóra Sigmundardóttir has come to Tróndur í Gøtu, who fosters her son. Apart from the Creed, which she finds strange, Tóra is satisfied with what the boy has learned from Tróndur. Kamban also works as a graphic artist producing linocuts in particular. His work mostly portrays Faroese landscapes in a simple, almost austere style.

Another artist to follow up the craft traditions of Mikladalur is Fridtjof Joensen (1920–88) who lived from his drawings and wood-carving. He is concerned with people in most of his work, and is one of the first Faroese artists to show the naked human form. Among his most famous works is the altar relief of The Last Supper in Glyvrar church in Eysturoy.

Among the younger sculptors is Tróndur Patursson, who experiments both in style and material. His early training as a smith makes it natural for him to form reliefs in iron. He later studied painting in Oslo under Ståle Kyllingstad. As a painter he has more and more tended towards the abstract. His experiences as a crew member on Tim Severin's Brendan voyage to Newfoundland in 1976 have given him valuable inspiration. He later continued his travels as seaman-extraordinary by going on a scientific voyage in an Arab dhow across the Indian Ocean, and yet again by rowing like Jason in search of the Golden Fleece from Greece to the Black Sea. Tróndur Patursson paints in the summertime, both in oil and watercolour, so as to make use of the changing light, and works on sculpture and glass mosaic in the wintertime. Among his glass work is the reredos in the new church at Gøta in Eysturoy.

Another well-known work by Tróndur Patursson is his monumental stone sculpture close to the Nordic House in Tórshavn. There we also find the *grindadráp* sculpture in iron, the work of Hans Pauli Olsen (b. 1957), one of three Tórshavn brothers who have already left their mark on Faroese art. His younger brothers are Torbjørn and Marius Olsen, and they are only some of the names on a long list of established and up and coming artists, which also includes Olivur við Neyst, Amariel Norðoy, Eyvindur Mohr and Bárður Jákupsson.

The mainstream of Faroese art has been concerned with showing nature in all its manifestations. Today this field ranges from the strictly naturalistic to the experimentally abstract. Painting techniques have become more varied, and there is more scope in the choice of image. To an outsider the vitality of the art scene is astonishing. At the same time there can be no doubt that the interest shown by the authorities in the artistic decoration of schools and other public buildings, as well as the critical appreciation of the Faroese people in general, is an invaluable support.

14

FARMING

For centuries the Faroese have lived in *bygdir* or settlements, whose form has changed surprisingly little since the Viking age. The requirements of the original Norse settlers were easy access to the sea, fresh water, some cultivable land and large pastures for grazing. As only a small percentage of the Faroese landscape lends itself to cultivation, and climatic conditions are suitable for hardy crops only, agriculture could never be anything but marginal, especially when only manual tools were available. Instead additional food resources were sought and carefully husbanded, the utilization of all resources being controlled by the community as a whole.

Thus the old economy was highly diversified, and the working tasks varied with the seasons – egg-catching, fowling, peat-cutting and working on the land. The raising of some barley was perhaps the most labour-intensive part of the economy, but the keeping of sheep was by far the most important, as without the sheep life would not have been tenable through the centuries. There is no doubt that for a long time agriculture in all its aspects was the mainstay of the economy; thus Seyðabrævið of 1298 gives rules for the sharing of the *grind*, but does not mention fishing at all.

It was always necessary to import grain, but perhaps the most badly-needed import was timber for the building of houses and boats. In return the Faroese provided tallow, feathers and wool, which was increasingly sold in the form of knitted stockings. This trade was carried on through the Trade Monopoly, and no cash changed hands, as any income earned had to be spent on company goods, at fixed prices. This state of affairs prevailed until the 1870s, when fishing began to flourish and farming to decline. Although the old pattern of cultivation can still be seen in the landscape of many *bygdir*, the traditional farming society virtually disappeared around the beginning of the twentieth century. Whereas in 1801 some 80 per cent worked on the land, this figure had fallen to 18 per cent by 1911, and in 1977 it was down to 1.4 per cent. The income from farming now makes up about 1 per cent of the gross national product. Yet it is fair to say that the land still features strongly in the life of the islands.

Today the infield is used mostly for growing grass

The system of land ownership has not really changed since the sixteenth century. There are three different kinds of land: *kongsjørð* or king's land, *óðalsjørð* or private land, and *traðir*, which are more recently cultivated plots of land. Roughly half of all land was once Church property taken over by the Crown after the Reformation and then leased to hereditary copyholders – the *kongsbøndir* – for a nominal rent. From 1937 the income from this land was given to a Faroese fund, the Føroya Jarðargrunnur, to use for agricultural improvement, and in the 1950s the Løgting took over all the *kongsjørð*, so that the *kongsbøndir* are now their tenants.

There are some 300 *kongsgarðar*, or king's farms, and as they are indivisible, they have represented a stable factor in the *bygdir*. In a way the *kongsbøndir* have had the status of an aristocracy, and this may explain why the title of *bóndi* carries such weight. Recently the Løgting have perhaps been more willing to let the land be taken for house-building and industrial purposes than they should have been, so that some fine old farms have disappeared. The *kongsgarðar* are the only modern, commercially run farms in Faroe today.

The system of *óðalsjørð*, on the other hand, turned out to be an unfortunate form of land ownership in some ways, as the idea of keeping an *óðalsgarður* intact as a working unit seems to have been given up at an early stage. Every time an *óðalsbóndi* died, the land would be divided among his heirs, every field being divided into narrow strips so that the heirs could share and share alike. The reason for this division is not far to seek, for it is a natural consequence of the social conditions prevailing in the *bygdir*, where a landless person had no status and few rights. In the 1860s a law was passed prohibiting the division of the *óðalsjørð* into units smaller than one *gyllin* – a *gyllin* being one sixteenth of a *mørk*. The Faroe Islands have 2,400 *merkur* of land, the unit rating being complicated as it refers to the quality of the land and not the quantity. Another law from 1962 forbids any further division except in special circumstances, but whereas at one time anybody wanting to sell *óðalsjørð* had to offer it first to his family, the *óðal* right has now been given up and the land can be bought and sold without restrictions.

Today the *óðalsjørð* consists of private lots that are too small to be run on any kind of commercial basis. Ownership is sometimes ridiculously complicated, as one person may own anything up to a hundred tiny plots, sometimes even spread over several *bygdir*. Attempts have been made since the 1930s to exchange plots so that land holdings could become unified and workable. In some *bygdir* the land has been carefully exchanged to make larger units, only to be divided again among the next generation. Legislation by the Løgting to prevent such division has been opposed, as people feel that it would threaten their rights – they want to keep the right to give land to their children. At best the lots supply their owners with agricultural produce for their own use – mutton, potatoes and perhaps some milk. This land may have very little economic significance, but just as once it paved the way to an independent life, it still opens doors of fellowship and community and binds people to the *bygd* and each other. For the fishermen it means roots and a sense of belonging somewhere.

A plot that has been recently cultivated and made part of the *bøur is* called a *trøð,* and anybody renting it for farming is obliged to fence off the land and cultivate it for a period of at least twenty years. A *trøð* would usually be some three acres in size and have enough cultivable land to keep a cow and supply a family with potatoes. The farms that have ceded the land have a right to graze their animals on it in the winter or be paid for waiving this right. The *traðir* are not supposed to be divided. A *trøð* holder has no share in the *hagi* and therefore cannot keep sheep there, nor do any fowling. This system of landholding was very important in the years between the two world wars, when it was a way of eking out the income of a fisherman, who would be away at the fishing for only part of the year. After the war fishing became a full-time occupation, and the *traðir* lost their importance. There are, however, whole new farms, as in Norðradalur on Streymoy, which have been cleared on land once belonging to the outfields. These new farms have *trøð* status and therefore no rights in the *hagi.*

Pollen analyses have shown that cereals may have been cultivated in the Faroe Islands as far back as the seventh century. It was always difficult to grow cereals, and it is no wonder that at one time a farmer's skill was measured by the quality of his field of barley. An especially hardy kind of barley that could grow and ripen in the course of some 150 days was used, but even so it needed sunny, fairly protected places to thrive, and the yield was uncertain because of cool or wet summers. Cereal growing was therefore the first farming activity to be dropped when economic conditions no longer demanded it, so that it virtually disappeared in the early twentieth century. In Gásadalur in Vágar it lasted until the 1920s, and in 1986 cereal growing was revived there for one season, in order to record the methods of cultivation for posterity.

The soil in Faroe is thin and rich in humus, and therefore it cannot be exposed for any length of time as it will crumble and be carried away by wind and water. Over the centuries a technique was developed that was carefully adapted to conditions. It was not so very different from methods used in Orkney, Shetland, Western Norway and the Hebrides or other places with a climate similar to that of the Faroe Islands. Crops were rotated in a careful cycle so that a cereal crop could not be taken from the same field more often than every seventh year. Care had to be taken not to crumble the soil more than necessary, and the grass was kept to protect the soil when the barley was harvested. Thus the soil was turned in March and the grass not buried deep. The fields were small, perhaps 30 by 3 metres, and built up in terraces facing the sun. The Faroese had developed a special tool for this work. It is a long wooden spade known as a *haki,* which is individually made to the size of the user, and looks rather like a cricket bat.

Cereal growing was heavy work as everything was done manually, and no animals were ever used. When in 1774 a Norwegian farmer was sent by well-meaning Danish authorities to Sandavágur in Vágar, taking with him a plough and two horses, to show the farmers an easier way of doing things, this petition was sent to Copenhagen: 'One and all inhabitants of the sýsla beseech in humble obedience our most gracious authorities mercifully to free us from burdening ourselves with the plough.' This resistance to using a plough was due not to backwardness but to common sense: ploughing was too rough a method for the land. The *haki* might be time-consuming, but then time and labour were available. But the Norwegian farmer liked the islands so much that he settled for good.

The potato was introduced *c.* 1820 and soon became an important part of farming. A new method of potato cultivation evolved in Miðvágur in Vágar at the time of the First World War, when the growing of barley came to an end. This was the so-called *reinavelting*, which would soon become popular and take the place of cereal growing in the rotation of crops. With a spade the turf is cut into squares and lifted. Potatoes are put in the ground along with some manure, then the turf is replaced. In the autumn the turf is removed again, to reveal the potatoes lying as snugly as eggs in a nest. Like cereal growing *reinavelting* is labour-intensive, but it yields good crops, and is considered less harmful to the soil than the conventional growing methods. In general potatoes do well in Faroe, so that during the first part of the Second World War the islands were self-sufficient, but these days about half the potatoes have to be imported.

The first market garden was established at Kirkjubøur. Today a few vegetables are cultivated in private plots, but mostly they have to be imported, along with the potatoes. In the old days angelica, or *hvann,* was the most important source of vitamin C, and was also believed to prevent infection. The *hvanngarður,* a small fenced-off enclosure, could be seen close to many houses, and the remains of some survive even today. The first real gardens were those laid down by the farmer H. K. Joensen á Ryggi in Miðvágur in Vágar and in Dalur in Sandoy by the farmer Oli í KIæmintsstovu. By the turn of the century small private gardens had become more common, with rhubarb a popular plant.

Today the *bøur,* or infield, is used mostly for growing grass, which is needed as winter feed for the animals. The wet, cool climate is excellent for grass; the best pasturage is always found in meadows facing north. There is enough milk produced for direct consumption; the number of milch cows has been steadily rising, and there is a modern dairy in Tórshavn to receive the milk. As recently as the 1930s the cows were still milked in the *hagi,* and the milkmaids, or *neytakonur,* would make two trips daily with the milk pails strapped on their backs. They often had as much as a two hours' walk each morning and evening and were a familiar sight with their knitting in their hands.

Sometimes the milk had to be carried even further, and at the beginning of the century a legendary old woman named Rachel would come into Tórshavn every day carrying milk from the farm at Kirkjubøur:

> She has done so for many years, and in the course of her work has walked so far that she is often called 'the woman who has walked three times round the world'. Old Rachel appears to be half-witted, and the loss of her senses is believed, by herself as well as by others, to be due to the fact that when a little girl she was stolen by the trolls and spent ten days inside the fairy mount. After ten days' absence from home she was found lying on the top of an almost inaccessible cliff.
>
> *Nelson Annandale*

Although the horse was not in common use in all the islands – indeed there were none at all in the northern islands – there were some 700 of them in use at the turn of the century, and most of these were to be found in Streymoy. The old Faroese horse was small, with fuchsia-red hair covering most of its body, and it had a powerful head. It was believed to be a cross between the original Norse horse brought from Norway and other species introduced

Dalur, Sandoy. Milking cows being taken to the hills for grazing

later. It was never used as a draught animal, nor was it usually ridden, and it was not shod. Two large wooden baskets of the type known as *leypar* would sometimes be placed on its back, and thus it would serve as a pack horse, mostly for transporting manure and peat. When it was not used for work, the horse was let loose in the *hagi* where it had to fend for itself through most of the year. Thus it was usually a wild and uncouth animal: no power on earth could make a Faroese horse move when it did not want to.

The keeping of pigs must have been fairly common in the early Middle Ages, as some fifty place-names refer to this practice. It seems to have more or less stopped with the coming of the Reformation, probably because there was little to feed the pigs with, as cereal growing was difficult. Another reason appears in a document of 1709 which maintains that in many places pigs are not kept 'because fields and meadows are quite ruined by them'. Today a business in Froðba in Suðuroy raises pigs on a commercial basis.

Geese have become popular farm animals and can be seen in most *bygdir*, often grazing in flocks both in the *bøur* and the *hagi*. In Mykines a special species of cat has evolved, with hefty six-toed paws, perhaps the better to catch the specially large Mykines species of mice with! The Faroese sheep dog is highly skilled, and does the work of many men at sheep-gathering times. At one time it was forbidden to keep dogs of more than one sex in a *bygd*, so as not to distract them in their important work of minding the sheep. The new vicar of Sandoy did not know of this rule, and brought along a dainty miss to an otherwise strictly male territory, with the result that the next morning there was a riot outside the vicarage at Sandur! The legal regulation known as Hundabrævið from *c.* 1400 lists the number of dogs that could be kept in each *bygd*.

Sheep-breeding is carried on extensively; indeed it seems that no matter how high one gets in the mountains or how inaccessible the ledge, the Faroese sheep will still be there, hopping agilely on to the next outcrop of rock. In 1298 Seyðabrævið stipulated that 'the number of sheep to be kept in an area of pasture shall be the same as it was in previous times, unless men see that it can accommodate more.' This optimum figure was known as *skipan*, and expressed the permitted density of sheep within a defined area. The overall number of some 70,000 sheep is still considered suitable, as a too intensive use of the pastures would cause the thin soil to crumble and be blown away, and if anything the density is now diminished compared to what it was in the Middle Ages.

Every autumn some 40,000 sheep are slaughtered. Over the ages the remaining sheep have stayed in the *hagi* and have sometimes frozen to death in cold winters. In blizzards the sheep might be buried in snowdrifts, and a loss of some 10 per cent over the winter was considered normal. If more than a third of the flock perished in a bad winter, this was known as a *felli,* and in the old days people reckoned that such a *felli* occurred on average every fourteen years. One of the worst years on record was 1913, when some 20,000 sheep and lambs died. These days sheds have been built in the *hagi*, where the sheep can shelter and also find food. In addition the fences between the *hagi* and *bøur* are opened in the winter so that the sheep will have access to the cultivated fields as well.

The sheep are rounded up in the summer for their wool and driven into the sheep-folds. At that time they are wild and they take some catching. As the wool is then long and loose it is usually torn rather than shorn from the sheep by hand. The gathering of the wool is known as *royting*. 'Seyða ull er Føroya gull' ('the sheep wool is the gold of Faroe') is an old saying that is no longer true. In the eighteenth century wool and wool products alone made up 90 per cent of all exports, with 60,000 pairs of knitted woollen stockings being sent every year to Holland alone. The Faroese themselves used to wear wool from the skin out. Today the Snældan spinning and knitting mill is making Faroese sweaters and knitting wool at Strendur in Skálafjørður, but there is room for expansion in the wool industry.

In the autumn the sheep are rounded up once more, with the lambs, for the annual slaughter. This used to be undertaken with all the solemnity of an Old Testament rite, and was for the brotherhood of men only, as in this description from Trøllanes in Kalsoy.

> The men came down from the mountain, driving the sheep ahead of them into the fold, where a score of large rams were selected and had their feet tied. There were marvellous types among these men; one of them stood down in the muddy fold and tossed up the heavy rams; he had a red humorous face with inflamed eyes and his name was Absalon. We went home with him. In his dark roykstova everything was made ready for the slaughter, the rams were shut into the neighbouring, pitch dark room, lamps were lit and hung up under the rafters. The men picked and chose from among a number of sharpened knives on a bench and the slaughter began.
>
> *William Heinesen*

The old practice of hanging the meat in the *hjallur* to dry is still followed. The dried, unsalted mutton is known as *skerpikjøt* and is the favourite national food. Another popular dish is *skinsakjøt,* which is made when the meat is boiled, salted and then hung. The annual production of mutton is now some 500 tons, which amounts to about 40 per cent of the consumption. The rest is imported, mostly from Iceland.

Although the sheep are privately owned in some *bygdir,* the general practice is that the *hagi* and the sheep are owned and administered by the community as a whole, and that all work involved is shared. Generally speaking the number of sheep each farmer can have in the *hagi* depends on the size and value of his holding in the *bøur*, but there are many complex variations to this system.

Fowling rights in the cliffs are also held according to the same principles as sheep rearing. There are set rules for the number of birds that can be taken as well as when this should happen. Fowling has been extremely well organized, and was always controlled by the community. This was always considered necessary, as otherwise the bird cliffs would be ruined for generations to come by greedy fowlers. This happened at Gjógvin Stóra, north of Sandvík in Suðuroy, which was at one time an excellent breeding place until it was ruined by Vegarin, the son of Annika í Dímun, and at a *drangur* off the coast of Sumba, which has been shunned by the guillemot ever since a man who was permitted to take 900 birds there actually took 1,400. Guillemots are said never to breed in a place where they were once so heavily hunted.

Through the centuries sea-birds and eggs have provided a significant supplement to the Faroese diet. The meat of the puffin, guillemot and kittiwake was eaten both fresh, salted and dried. Eggs were popular too, and they were taken in large quantities; as many as 34,000 guillemot eggs might be taken in Skúvoy in a good year. Bird feathers also represented a valuable commodity, and at one time as much as two tons were exported annually. Birds nest on the south and west cliffs in order to get as much warmth as possible from the sun, and traditionally some of the best bird cliffs have been found in Mykines and on the west sides of Skúvoy.

There are three main fowling methods, *fygling*, *fleyging* and *omanfleyg*. *Fygling* was the method used mostly to catch the guillemots, which breed on high, steep cliffs facing the sea. The fowler is lowered at the end of a long rope over the upper edge of the cliff, to catch the guillemot by a long-handled net. For this method as many as twenty men might have to be on hand to get the fowler and his catch safely up again. *Fleyging is* the most important method of catching puffin. Just taking the birds in their nesting holes is now frowned upon, as too often it is the nesting birds that are killed. The fowler finds himself a strategic place (known as a *fleygingarsessur*) close to the puffin ledges, and then catches the birds in mid-flight by means of the long-handled net (known as *fleygastong*). It was necessary to have 'the eye of a cricketer and the wrists and shoulders of a wrestler to whip these birds from the air, for the pole must be heavy and stiff or the birds would bounce out. You must swing it fast while not taking your eye off the bird, and a good catcher can sometimes take two birds, altering the stroke to take a second puffin in the same sweep. The bird-catcher needs very swift reactions as the bird can come from any direction' (Tom Weir). *Omanfleyg* is a successful method when the sea is reasonably calm. As the young guillemots often sit on flat rocks they can be caught with nets from a boat as they launch themselves to head for the sea. But *omanfleyg* has not been practised for the last fifty years or more, and is today prohibited.

The fleygastengur,
the long-handled nets
for catching puffins

Fowling was at best a hazardous occupation. The Faroese were extremely bold when going to the bird cliffs, and the precarious art of fowling was to some extent regarded as a test of manhood. But when men left home to go to the cliffs they were sometimes mourned by their families as if they were already dead, and it is not surprising that they would kneel in prayer before going over the cliff. Today there are fewer birds in the cliffs, but this is not due to over-exploitation, as these days bird-catching is carried on mostly for sport, even though both eggs and birds, especially puffins, are still very popular food.

With the coming of large-scale commercial fishing a gradual retreat from the land began to take place. The men might be away at sea for the better part of the year, leaving the farming that for most families has little economic significance. In consequence much of the privately owned land lies more or less fallow or is used for grazing sheep. It is strange that the Faroese, who are so inventive and constructive where fishing is concerned, cannot get their agricultural act together. It seems hopeless to change the part-time nature of the *óðalsjørð* farming, but in the last few years a lot of new land has been cleared, as there are many large areas of moorland well suited for cultivation, such as Saksunardalur and Fossdalur in Streymoy. The goal is to have some 20 per cent of the land in the islands under cultivation, which might lead to more stable social conditions in the *bygdir* and keep people from moving away.

*Today's speciality,
puffins with game
sauce*

15

FISHING

The Faroese boat does not seem to have been built, but to have been created by the waves, born from the sea like Venus. It floats on the sea as naturally as a seagull or a drake, and glides across the surface as easily, softly, surely. It is the work of hands but it is not handicraft, nature rather than art, belonging to the scenery as do the mountains, the waves, the birds.

Sven Barthel

Until the end of the nineteenth century fishing was carried on in small open boats, mostly in the eight-man rowing-boat known as *áttamannafar,* but the ten-man *tíggjumannafar* was also used. These boats are remarkably seaworthy. The inshore fishing, known as *útróður* – rowing out – provided a necessary addition of fresh food to the diet, and also offered a living of sorts to the landless poor. It was a hard life, but as a school for seamanship there was nothing like it. Detailed knowledge of the currents and reefs around the islands was necessary, and an intuitive feeling for weather could mean the difference between life and death.

In many *bygdir* the landing place was extremely difficult and dangerous – perhaps just a cleft in the cliffs, without protection from the surf. Both the launching and the landing of the boats required practised skill and daring. The men knew they might not come back, and before setting off on the *útróður* to the fishing grounds they would sing an old Kingo hymn, 'Now I seek thy mercy and give myself in thy hands', and when they were back safely they would sing another hymn of thanksgiving. And yet the unequal struggle between the boat and the sea appealed to the men – like fowling it was a test of manhood. To the women it meant waiting, and when a storm blew up without warning while their men were still out at sea, they would rush to the landing-place, to look anxiously for a sign of the boats.

The Faroese fishing banks are fifty times larger than the islands themselves, and are rich in fish. Other nations discovered these riches as early as the sixteenth century, and even in 1615 the Løgting complained that:

a lot of English and Scottish ships have gathered here, more than there ever were, and they are fishing close to land, not out at sea as they do off Iceland, but they run their ships close to land and fish on our grounds and reefs and thus steal the meagre food and God's gift that we poor people could otherwise fish with our small boats.

This complaint prompted James I in 1618 to prohibit any fishing by the British closer than sixteen miles from the Faroese coasts, but such a regulation was difficult to uphold, and in any case the British were not alone in coming north to fish.

A handline was used for fishing from the small open boats. The catches were small and the Faroese could only watch helplessly as large quantities of fish were caught just off their coasts by Shetlanders, Belgians and Frenchmen using decked boats. Modernization was obviously needed, and in the summer of 1839 Governor Pløyen therefore arranged his famous trip to Shetland, Orkney and Scotland to study the fishing methods used there. He brought along three Faroese *kongsbøndir,* from respectively Eiði, Nólsoy and Hoyvík, who were greatly impressed by the intense fishing activity they witnessed in Shetland, but were none too pleased to see boats come in loaded with fish from the Faroe banks – 'while we sit by with our hands in our laps and complain that we do not fish'. The Faroese learned from the Shetlanders how to fish with a long line and how to make dried cod or stockfish, known in Faroe as *klippfiskur.*

When weather permitted it was usual for the *áttamannafar* to leave early

Both the launching and landing of the boats required practice and skill and daring. Photo: Føroya Fornminnissavn

in the morning and return in the late afternoon or evening. The new fishing line would be some 3,000 metres long with perhaps some 500 hooks, each fastened to a short sideline. The line would sink to the bottom, and the spot be marked with buoys. There it would stay until the current turned, and then be taken up again. When the fishing was good there might be a large cod on each hook! Thus the longline fishing yielded much larger catches than the old handline method. The catch would be divided into ten parts, one for each of the eight-man crew, one to pay for boat repairs and one for the line. To catch halibut it was necessary to use larger hooks and to fish in deeper waters. Longline fishing from small boats is still going on, and is important in *bygdir* like Fámjin and Hestur, but motors were installed in the boats long ago.

A small export of fish took place even in the eighteenth century, and by the 1840s the inshore fishing must have grown in importance, as by then dried and salted fish products constituted as much as 40 per cent of the total export. But the watershed in Faroese fishing history is the year 1872, when the three Haraldsen brothers from Tórshavn bought the 28-year-old sloop *Fox* in Scarborough, and thus began the modern industry. From 1880 onwards the Shetland cod fisheries declined, and before long the Faroese were going there to buy up the smacks. Development continued at accelerating speed, and by the end of the century the whole community had changed character. As the fishing industry began to attract capital investment, deep-sea fishing rapidly expanded, soon to become the mainstay of the Faroese economy.

On the Faroe banks nine out of every ten fish were taken by foreign boats, and because of overfishing there was little fish left. The Faroese smacks instead ventured to the grounds off Iceland, where they did well. Still it was a risky business, because of the frequent extreme changes of weather. For instance in 1920 the Faroese lost sixty-two men at sea – 2 per cent of the total number of fishermen. Two trips were made each year; seven months were spent at sea, with the men staying at home for the five winter months. The boats left for Iceland in late February and early March, and the parting was painful as rarely would they all come back. Then the boats would be back in May with their catches of cod. In June the men were off for their second trip, which lasted until October. The second trip was usually to Greenland, and after 1925 the Greenland fisheries became very important – in fact about half of the total catch would be taken there.

The men's short stay and their second farewell were very hard on the women. In the *bygdir* most of the men were gone; only some of the *kongs-bøndir* were left at home along with the very old or the very young. The women's workload and responsibilities were heavy; added to that were loneliness and anxiety. An additional worry was caused by the custom that the men of one family would as often as not sail together in the same boat. Just such a family crew was rescued in 1935. The skipper of the ship had three sons among a crew of twenty men. Three more sons worked on another ship,

which was skippered by one of them. The first ship was wrecked in a terrible storm just south of Greenland. By a strange coincidence the second ship was close by, and the skipper, along with his brothers and the rest of the men, succeeded in saving the whole crew, including his father and three brothers, just before the ship sank. But not all shipwrecks ended so happily, and only too often there was grief, as so poignantly portrayed by Sámal Joensen-Mikines in his early pictures.

The writer Heðin Brú went to sea in 1914 when he was quite a young boy, and spent four years working on the smacks.

> We had to stand there and fish the whole day if the weather allowed it. Then we had to clean the ship, and get the fish washed and salted into the hold. Off the south of Iceland it was at any rate a hard life – it was cold, mid winter and quite often there was ice on the deck. We had to climb the rigging with axes to remove the ice, the ship became too heavy, and we could not make the tackles work. But when we reached eastern Iceland it was summer, and it was not so cold. Then we had to stand there and fish all day and night if there was fish to be had, as the nights were so light. So we fished until we could take no more.

When Brú was working on the smacks they were still using sails, but from *c.* 1925 onwards most of the smacks had motors installed. By 1930 the ocean-going fishing fleet consisted of 180 vessels.

Much of the fish brought back was used to produce *klippfiskur,* which was exported mainly to the Mediterranean countries. The salted fish would be received at the wharf by the women. They would scrub it clean in big wooden tubs, and then spread it out to be dried in the sun – no mean feat in a country that on an average has only sixty days of sunshine a year. Air-drying the cod was a long and weary task that took up to two months. Old men, women and children watched lovingly over their fish; there would be acres of cod, spread out on rocky shores like shingles on a roof. Each community

> designates one old man as weather expert to scan the skies. When a squall threatens, he beats a gong and everybody who can use his legs rushes shoreward to pile the fish in stacks under canvas. No one is exempt, according to the custom of the country, from rescuing the cod from a rainstorm. Sometimes the fish are distributed and stacked seven times in a single day!
>
> *National Geographic*

As a result of all this trouble Faroese *klippfiskur* was the best in the market, both in vitamin content and looks.

You can still see today, on a smaller scale, the drying of fish

The economic crisis of the 1930s hit the Faroese fishing industry hard. In addition, the market for dried cod collapsed when the League of Nations called for economic sanctions against Italy, which was the main Faroese market, and Spain became racked by civil war. Nobody could live on what they made from fishing, so people who had no land were close to starving. It was during this period that the authorities tried to help by letting the fishermen have land for cultivation. The fishermen also wanted to extend the Greenland fisheries by establishing more fishing stations there than the one they already had: the port on the western Greenland coast known as Færingerhavn, which was equipped with a radio station, hospital and other facilities. The Danes wanted, on the other hand, to protect the Greenlanders, and a bitter conflict ensued in which feelings ran high.

The Faroe Islands got their first steam trawler in 1911. Just before the Second World War medium-sized trawlers were acquired from England, so that there were ten such ships in all. As fish prices on the world market were low, it was very hard to pay off the loans on the new trawlers. With the coming of the war the situation altered radically, and Faroese fishing acquired a new importance. For the duration of the war Britain bought every single fish the Faroese could produce. As British fishing vessels were mostly on naval duty, the Faroese together with the Icelanders had the fishing in the North Atlantic to themselves, and they were able to sell the fish at high prices.

But they were working in dangerous waters. The fishing boats were bombed from the air and torpedoed by U-boats while trying to avoid the mines. For a while so many boats were sunk and the danger was so great that the Icelanders refused to go to sea, but the Faroese sailed all through the war, and for a period of the war they supplied most of the fish that reached Britain. But the price was heavy: 132 fishermen and a third of the ships were lost.

When the war was over the Faroese spent much of their accumulated assets in Britain on ships for their depleted fishing fleet. But ships were scarce, so they had to take what they could get, and many of them turned out to be expensive-to-run coal-gobblers that soon had to be scrapped. A number of owners went bankrupt; even so by 1951 the fishing fleet had doubled its capacity and numbered thirty-seven trawlers and some 200 other vessels. Fishing had thus become the main source of income for most families.

But the end of hostilities also brought the foreign fishing boats back in force to the Faroe banks, and the Faroese themselves therefore went further afield, and took most of their catches far from home: around the coasts of Canada, Iceland and Greenland, as well as in the Barents Sea and more and more in the North Sea. In 1959 the six-mile fishing limit was set, in 1964 the limit was extended to twelve miles, but still this only affected the inshore line fishing. In 1961 a serious incident took place in Faroese waters, when a British trawler was seized for fishing too close to shore. A Danish prize crew was put on board to take the trawler to Tórshavn, when the trawler captain locked them in a cabin and ordered full speed ahead! The Danish coastal inspection ship opened fire to make him stop. The case was tried in an international court, which fined the British trawler captain and reprimanded the captain of the inspection ship for firing a gun.

Then in 1977 the fishing limit was extended yet again, to 200 nautical miles, which gave the Faroese a fishing zone of some 300,000 square kilometres. Although all political parties in Faroe agreed that this step was unavoidable, there were still many critical comments from those who felt that it meant a return to the period of the old Trade Monopoly, when regulations and prohibitions were the order of the day. Obviously there were also conflicting interests between trawler owners and inshore fishermen. There was, however, no real choice; when others fenced themselves in, the Faroese would be excluded from those waters where they had so far taken most of their catches, and would therefore have to protect their own rights.

As a consequence of the new fishing limits the Løgting decided that the Faroe Islands would not join the EEC along with Denmark. The EEC fishing policy was unacceptable, as it was based on free access for member countries to all Faroe waters outside the old 12-mile limit. Because their economy was almost exclusively based on fishing, the Faroe Islands could benefit little from the diversified industry of the EEC countries; they would be giving their fishing away and in return getting few rights that would be of any use. The Faroe Islands have for the same reason remained an independent customs area, which has full control of import and export regulations.

The extension of the fishing limits in the North Atlantic meant that the Faroese fishermen had to adjust to fishing in home waters, and in the last few years about half the total catches have been taken there. Among the species caught are cod, haddock, coalfish, ling and blue whiting, and most of the catches are landed fresh in Faroe. Throughout the islands are scattered some twenty factories, which process the fish into frozen fillets and salt fish. The Faroese share of international quotas is taken in distant waters by sophisticated ocean-going factory trawlers. The catches of cod and shrimp are mainly taken in the Barents Sea or around Canada and Greenland, and then processed on board. Fish taken in the North Sea or west of Britain may be landed in Faroe, and so is most of the fish caught off Iceland. The efficiency of the modern fishing fleet results in a higher ratio of fish caught per fisherman, but as the number of factories grows, a shifting of manpower from sea to shore has taken place.

The Faroese have recently specialized in producing technically advanced machinery and equipment designed for fishing, fish farming and fish processing. Computer systems for the monitoring of fish processing have become a popular export article. The fishing restrictions of the last decades have prompted the development of salmon farming. This industry has had an explosive growth, and there are a large number of salmon farms, with a total production of fish for export of some 10,000 tons a year so far.

Fish and fish products account for about 97 per cent of Faroese exports. Ever since the war the highly organized and technically sophisticated fishing industry has been productive enough to support one of the highest standards of living in northern Europe.

16

THE GRIND

It is two days since the grind and the waters of the bay are still thick and red. We long for strong winds and tides to bring in fresh seas and purify us again. People are still busy salting meat, cutting it in strips to dry in the salt-laden air, making oar straps from the hide of the back fins, tanning and blowing up stomachs to use as buoys for the fishing nets, and boiling whale heads to extract the prized oil they contain. Moreover, there is the refuse to be carried out to sea, for a wise law requires all to be removed within 72 hours.

Elizabeth Taylor

For hundreds of years the *grind* (schools of pilot whales) that were caught around the Faroe coasts meant for many people a sorely needed addition to a subsistence diet. The meat was a gift, a sign that the Lord provided for his people, and none of it was ever wasted.

The *grind* are a species of dolphin, *Globicephala melaena,* a comparatively small, toothed animal which roams the North Atlantic from Labrador and Greenland to Britain and Norway in large shoals of up to a thousand; they are to be found in the Mediterranean and the Pacific as well. They are known as blackfish along the New England coast, as caaing whales in Shetland, and are generally called pilot whales in English because of their habit of following a leader or pilot. In the Faroe Islands the word *grindhvalur is* used about one whale and *grind* about a school of them. The word *grind* means a gate. The whales will sometimes stop for a while in a dense school, and scholars believe the name may refer to the fact that a school has the appearance when pausing of a barred gate. It is also possible that the name simply refers to the old method of chasing the whales into a trap by closing some kind of gate behind them. The whole course of events from the moment the whales are sighted until they lie dead on the beach is also known as *grind;* more specifically *grindarakstur* is used about the hunt and *grindadráp* about the actual slaughter.

The torpedo-shaped *grind* can reach up to 5 or 6 metres in length. A type of squid that is especially plentiful around the Faroese coasts in the late summer seems to be their favourite food, and although schools have been known to come in at any time of the year, hay-making time in August seems to be the most likely time for their visits. The *grind* spout water into the air through blow-holes, and thus give themselves away, because that is how they are sometimes sighted. Although the pilot whale is not covered by the regulations of the International Whaling Commission, it is carefully monitored by both Faroese and international scientists, and is not threatened with extinction.

In the latter half of the ninth century the Norseman Ottar, who 'lived the furthest north of all Norwegians', came into the service of the English King Alfred the Great. He told the king that in Norway whales were driven into the fjords, trapped and killed. This method of trapping the whales by shutting off their way of escape with nets has been used till recently in Norway, and one of the largest catches on record was made in Austvågøy in the Lofoten islands in 1890, when some 1,100 whales were taken. In Vestmanna this method was long used, as the entrance to the bay could be shut off by nets. Rules for the ownership of whales found stranded or sighted off the coast of Faroe were set down as early as 1298 in articles 8 and 11 of Seyðabrævið. In 1832 came the first detailed regulations of pilot whaling. These did not prove sufficiently clear, as quarrels sometimes erupted over hunting methods and catch-sharing, so that in 1872 came the revised *grind* law which, with some changes, is still in force; the latest revisions were issued in 1986.

The first description of a Faroese *grindadráp* dates back to 1584, and statistics of the catches have been kept regularly since then, apart from the Gabel period of the years 1640 to 1709. In fact, for no other wild animals have catches been recorded so faithfully or for such a long time. Annual catches have varied between 0 and 4,325 animals, which, opportunely, were caught in 1941. Over the last 300 years the average annual catch has been some 600 whales. The largest shoal ever taken was over 2,000 whales, but mostly they are 150 to 200 in number. The best *grind* places are Miðvágur in Vágar, Klaksvík and Norðuri í Sundum, the sound between Hvalvík and Oyri. It can safely be said that the pilot whale hunt is traditional, and it is still carried on non-commercially for the sole purpose of supplying the islanders' need for whale meat and blubber.

Like fowling, the *grind* has provided the islanders with challenge and excitement. It is not as dangerous as balancing on bird ledges, but accidents can happen. From the moment the *grind* was first sighted, often from the top of a mountain, people were gripped with excitement. The call of 'Grindaboð' – literally, 'grind message' – was the signal for an intense, highly organized activity, in which everybody knew the part they had to play. Today the message is relayed by telephone and radio; in the old days it would echo through the *bygdir* with the authority of a mobilization order, and through a series of pre-arranged signals would in a short time reach most people. The different types of signals were: *grindaglaða* – a lit bonfire, *breiðsla* – sheets would be spread out, a method used in Úti á Bø to alert Skopun in Sandoy, *gonguboð* – men would run to the next *bygd*; then in some places the message could be shouted from one *bygd* to the next, and finally it could be brought by boat – the only way to reach Mykines.

The islands are divided into nine *grind* districts. Not all beaches and bays are considered suitable, so twenty-one places have been authorized for the beaching of the *grind*. In each of these areas a group of four men will be elected as *grindaformenn,* or leaders of the *grind,* to be responsible for the conduct of the proceedings. The *grindadráp* thus takes place under their authority, but the *sýslumaður* or chief police officer of the district is notified when a *grind* has been sighted, and will come to supervise the division of the catch.

There are many descriptions of the frenzy which took hold of the men at the magic call of '*Grindaboð!*' Young or old, *bóndi* or Løgting members in session, the men would drop whatever they were doing and run. For this too was a man's world from which *konufólkið,* the women, were banned. Their presence, especially if they were pregnant, could make the *grind* change course and get away. Clergymen were not welcome either. V. U. Hammershaimb, the grand old man of Faroese letters, wondered about 'the old story that a whale hunt would be unsuccessful if clergymen and women watched from the shore. Would that not be because the men were embarrassed by those people seeing their behaviour in the whale kill?'

With lightning speed the boats are manned and gather in a half-circle behind the whales, ready for the awesome play to begin. This has changed little over the centuries, as the description from 1673 by the Tórshavn minister Lucas Debes shows. His account was translated into English three years later for the Royal Society in London:

> … They drive the whales with great crying, noise, and casting of stones, driving them as fast as they can upon the sands … In the meantime some of the people lie in ambush on the land, till the whales are come on ground, and wade to them as deep as they can, and then kill them chiefly with their weapons, with such fury on both sides, that the water becometh as red as blood, whereby the whale is also blinded, so that it cannot see to run away, it is a strange thing, to see that these strong creatures make no resistance, but only plunge as well as they can before the boats, and people, till death cometh upon them, and then they strike terribly about with their tails, so that they beat sometimes the boats to pieces, and the men come in danger …

The boat that spotted the *grind* hoists any handy rag to signal the news as well as to show who is the finder. With their boats marked by Faroese flags flying at the stern, the *grindaformenn* take charge and organize the fleet of boats with the discipline of admirals ordering a navy to battle. They aim for the nearest authorized *grind* site which can still be quite some distance away, and the *grind* can therefore go on for hours. The shoal does not always allow itself to be led, but tries to escape. The important thing for the *grindaformenn* is to make sure that the whales do not panic; if they dive or increase speed, the boats cannot keep up with them. The whales could easily smash the boats to pieces, but they do not seem to realize their own strength, and generally go like lambs to the slaughter.

And a slaughter it is: terrifying and cathartic. When the *grind* are close to the shore, the animals at the back are harassed, the noise increases brutally, the pressure mounts until the pilot of the *grind* dashes ahead to become stranded high up on the shore. The others follow blindly and loyally in one rapid black flow. The climax is mercifully swift: eight minutes was all it took to kill 136 whales at a *grindadráp* in Leynar in Streymoy. The men leaping from their boats or waiting on the beach draw their beautifully-worked *grindaknívar* and with deep cuts across the heavy necks of the *grind* sever the main blood vessels so that the animals die within seconds. This is the most dangerous part of it all, as the thrashing of the tails is forceful enough to kill a man or splinter a boat. The agility and daring of the bullfighter is required of the *grindamaður,* as he stands unprotected up to his waist in bloodied water. No wonder that for a while he turns wild.

In the meantime the *sýslumaður* has arrived. His task is to measure and count the whales so as to distribute them fairly among all those who are entitled to a share, and it is all done according to an ancient and intricate system. The idea is to get the work done during the evening and night after

A fairly modern grindaknívur

the *grindadráp,* so as to be ready to hand out the shares in the morning. In the old days one tenth would be reserved for the Church and the Crown, and the owner of the land where the *grindadráp* took place also had certain rights, but these rules no longer apply. The rules vary somewhat from district to district, thus Suðuroy has introduced the principle of complete equality, the catch being shared equally among all inhabitants in the district, whether they have participated in the *grindadráp* or not.

In all districts the largest whale, the *finningarfiskur,* has traditionally gone to the boat that first sighted the *grind* or was the first to reach it, the head going to the person who actually was the one to see it. Then one whale is used to feed all the visitors, another whale is set aside to pay for the damage to the boats, the *sýslumaður* is entitled to 1/2 per cent of the *grind,* each of the four *grindaformenn* gets an eighth, and the rest is shared according to set rules, but everybody in the district has the right to a share. Socially this communal sharing has been important; economically it has been invaluable to the sick, the elderly and the poor.

It used to be that a *grindadráp* would be the occasion for great festivity with everyone sharing food, drink and hospitality. The women would start cooking when they knew for sure that the *grind* was on its way, and when the whales were killed they would be there with tubs to get the kidneys and the meat that could be freely taken to provide a good meal for the guests. The *grindadansur* would go on until morning, when it was time to get one's share of the *grind.* The *grindamenn* who had come some way did not want to go home in the meantime, but as they had come away in a hurry they only had the wet and often blood-stained clothes they stood up in, and the dancing was a good way of drying out. Happiness with the day's work is expressed in the old ballad that would open the dancing. Known as *Grindavísan,* it was written some time in the 1840s by Christian Pløyen, who was Danish governor of Faroe from 1837 to 1849, and it has remained popular ever since. Through more than fifty verses it tells the story of a *grindadráp,* with the rousing refrain *'Raske Drenge, Grind at dræbe, det er vor Lyst'* – 'Strong lads are we, to kill the *grind,* that is our joy'. Through the dancing and the ballad-singing all the excitement and drama of the drive is re-enacted, with growing intensity.

In no other country has the *grind* meant so much as in the Faroe Islands. There were times when the meat saved people from starvation; incredible riches were won from the sea, and a *grind* assumed the qualities of a miracle. As an old man once said about the *grind:* 'There is good food here for the winter. The Lord *has* provided flesh for His people.' The average weight of a whale is about 500 kilos, and in the old days when the population was smaller, an ordinary *grind* would mean the gift of the equivalent of a pig for every inhabitant.

The meat would be salted or cut into strips and hung on the walls to dry.

Thus cured it can keep for years, and blubber and grindameat served in various ways are favourite dishes in most Faroese homes. The meat is nourishing and even appeals to visitors, though they may perhaps sometimes have found it too much of a good thing:

> I am weary of whales. I have eaten whale boiled, fried, and minced; the liver, heart, brains, and kidneys of young whale; and best of all, head fin boiled, cut in thin slices when cold, and eaten with thin slices of dry bread. It has a firm white substance and a pleasant nutty flavour.
>
> *Elizabeth Taylor*

However, it has been proved that the *grind* has been good for the health of the people. The blubber, which over the years has been eaten with meat, fish or bread, is full of vitamin A, which has otherwise always been scarce in the islands.

In the mid-1980s the *grindadráp* came to the notice of environmental and animal welfare organizations, and a major publicity drive against the hunt was begun. The London newspaper the *Daily Express* published a large photograph of dead whales, with the headline, 'Shock front-line despatch from the islands where death is a way of life – Slaughter of the Innocents'. The public outcry was quick in coming, and the Faroese government was inundated with tens of thousands of pre-printed cards as well as personally written letters. Much of the protest was along the lines that since it now was possible for the Faroese to buy the meat and blubber of the *grind* whale in the shops, why should it then be necessary to kill it? Although they know that the *grindadráp* is no picnic, the Faroese consider much of the protest against the *grind* as hypocrisy, voiced by city-dwellers who have become strangers to the cycle of nature.

As the pilot whale is not an endangered species and the hunt is of a communal and non-commercial character, organizations like Greenpeace today take a pragmatic view of the *grindadráp*. On the other hand the methods of slaughter have been made more efficient and therefore more humane; the *grindadráp* is not cruel compared to most other forms of hunting. As part of this policy only the foremen carry spears, for emergency use only, and whales cannot be killed from a boat. In addition any of the nine whaling districts can be closed by government order when they are believed to be adequately supplied.

The *grind* even today represent an important source of food in the Faroe Islands, as whale meat accounts for about one quarter of the total meat consumption. The *grind* thus contributes perhaps more to the Faroese larder than all the sheep and cattle raised in the islands put together. The hunt is also an integral part of the Faroese culture and way of life.

17

KIRKJUBØUR

Throughout the Middle Ages Kirkjubøur was the centre of the Church in Faroe. This is where the bishop lived and where the divinity school for educating priests was established, so that culturally and socially this was the most important site in the islands.

Probably the history of Kirkjubøur goes much further back, perhaps to the early Viking Age, as a rune stone found at Kirkjubøur may date from *c.* 800. It is not surprising that Kirkjubøur was among the first sites to be settled by the Norsemen. The high and steep backdrop provided by Kirkjubøreyn and Kirkjubøkambur gives shelter from the east and north winds. At the time of settlement there was, however, more land than there is today. The small island of Kirkjubøhólmur was at that time joined to the shore, and the first farm seems to have been built close to it. The remains of a paved road leading from the old church towards the island are still visible. The wide bay thus formed was a natural trap for driftwood and seaweed, which could both be put to good use. But such a low-lying tongue of land was also exposed to the sea and natural erosion as well as to storms, and some time during the late Middle Ages the line of the shore became drastically altered.

Færeyinga Saga does not specifically mention the farm at Kirkjubøur, but it tells the story of the chieftain Tórhallur hin ríki and his wife, who was known as Streymoyar-Birna, and their main farm may have been here. Birna left the property divided among her three daughters, and, again according to tradition, the home farm at Kirkjubøur along with the whole southern part of Streymoy fell to the lot of Gæsa, the youngest one. It was a holding large enough for 200 cattle and 5,000 sheep.

Today only parts of the north wall are left of what may be the oldest church; the rest has been taken by the sea. There is no way of verifying the story about its being built in the late eleventh century, as no evidence has been found dating from that period. A Faroese type of mortar was used for constructing this church as well as the other stone buildings. This was known as *skilp* and made of shells and bones, as there is no lime in the islands. The church was later used for funerals and became known as *á Likhúsi* – the morgue.

The white-painted parish church is the oldest church still in use in Faroe. Dedicated to St Olav, it probably dates from the twelfth century but has been both rebuilt and restored since then. It has also been known as the Monks' Church. In the 1950s the church was excavated, along with the other more important historical buildings on the site, in a joint Danish, Norwegian and Faroese archaeological project, but so far the final report has not been presented. The original stone structure was 21.8 metres by 7.5 metres, which are roughly the same measurements as those of a Viking longhouse. No fewer than three different floor layers from the Middle Ages have been found in the church. The choir was at one point enlarged at the expense of the nave, probably to give space for the clergy working for the bishop: as the bishop's seat grew in importance, so did his duties. In the choir traces of a bishop's throne were found during excavation, and under the floor of the crypt was a bishop's grave containing a wooden crozier with a gilded head. A coin found in the church was minted in Canterbury between 1218 and 1235. The position of St Olav's church in relation to the bishop's palace shows that it must have been built as part of a planned complex, probably in the early days of the bishopric.

In 1874 the church underwent a thorough restoration, as the site was being eroded by the sea. A wooden floor was laid, the walls were raised, the choir and the nave became one room, and in the south wall six Gothic windows were installed. Most of the interior fittings and furnishings of the medieval church were stripped out before the restoration work started. A thirteenth-century madonna of exquisite quality is kept at Føroya Fornminnissavn in Tórshavn, but most of the other objects were sent to the National Museum in Copenhagen. Among these it is especially important for the Faroese to recover the fourteen famous bench ends, which are decorated with wood carving of the highest order and date from the first half of the fourteenth century. Also taken from the church at the same time was the only Faroese processional cross known to exist, probably dating from c. 1400. However, according to an agreement with the Danish government, these valuable museum pieces will be restored to the islands when the new Faroese national museum has been built.

In the next restoration, which was carried out in the 1960s, an attempt was made to undo some of the damage, in so far as the church was given more of a medieval appearance. The south wall was rebuilt entirely with natural stone instead of brick, and four plain rectangular windows were installed. The interior and exterior of the walls are today painted white, and all the furnishings are of natural wood. With the striking altar painting by Sámal Joensen-Mikines as the only touch of colour, the church today is stark but impressive in its simplicity.

Early in the twelfth century Faroe was made a bishopric under the archdiocese of Lund in Sweden. In 1152 it became one of the ten bishoprics that made up the archdiocese of Nidaros at Trondheim – four in Norway and six in Norse dominions around the North Sea, from Greenland to the Isle of

Man. This new church province was established in order to make it easier for the Pope to control effectively the more remote parts of the Church, and it was a turning point in the relationship of the Norse Church with the administration in Rome.

Cathedrals were built throughout the province, and at Kirkjubøur work started on the building that would probably have become one of the most beautiful Gothic buildings in Scandinavia. It is slightly smaller than the cathedral at Gardar in Greenland, built a century earlier. Opinions have been divided as to whether the cathedral was ever completed. The archaeologist Knud Krogh, who led the church excavations in Sandur, believes that the cathedral was not only consecrated but actually in use. Although it has suffered from exposure to the relentless weather, the Múrurin – the Walls – as the Faroese call the building, is still an impressive sight. According to the most likely account Bishop Erlendur (1269–1308) began to build it in an attempt to turn Kirkjubøur into a spiritual centre in the west, but the people rebelled against the financial burdens involved. There is a very dramatic story of how he tried to escape from the rebels but was run to earth in the cathedral by them and killed there. But it is well documented that Erlendur died in Bergen after having been ill for some time. The gist of the story may be true – there were simply not the resources for such work, as all the Nordic countries went into an economic decline in the fourteenth and fifteenth centuries. The Norse church province was also hard hit by the Black Death. Somehow time ran out for the Magnus Cathedral of Kirkjubøur.

Bishop Johannes Teutonicus, who worked to have Erlendur made patron saint of Faroe, reports that he had his grave opened and there found a lead tablet with a runic inscription in Latin which read, 'This man was the first to build houses of stone in the Bishop's Palace, but he also laid the foundation of a stone cathedral and brought the work so far that the walls, at least of the choir, were almost finished'.

The cathedral consists of a simple, rectangular nave. A small sacristy on the north side has traces of paving and altar foundations and was perhaps the only part of the building that was finished. A tower was also apparently planned. Only the walls of the church are standing, and from them plaster and ornament have long since disappeared, revealing the excellent craftsmanship of the builders. The worn tracery of the windows is Early English in style. Faint traces of dragons' heads rather like Norman work are still to be seen in the arch of the south porch. No traces have been found of a floor or an altar within the nave itself, nor has anyone been buried there. This seems to indicate that the church was never consecrated and that no mass was ever said there. A series of Maltese or consecration crosses therefore seems very puzzling, as these were usually installed as part of a consecration ceremony.

On the outside east wall, to the right of its only window, a sandstone slab marks a relic chamber. Part of the slab has been knocked off – a rumour of gold in the chamber reputedly made somebody want to break in early in the nineteenth century. The inscription is therefore partly obliterated, but the rest of it has been interpreted as follows: 'Here is the abode of the following holy relics: some of the cross of Our Lord, of the sacrificial lamb, see here the holy Virgin Mary … and the bones of the blessed Magnus Martyr … from the grave of the holy Torlacius'.

The Magnus Martyr referred to in the inscription is Magnus Erlendsson the Saint, who in the early twelfth century ruled Orkney jointly with his cousin Hákon. They fell out, and Magnus was killed on the small island of Egilsay. He was canonized in 1135, and two years later his nephew Rognvald Kolsson started building a cathedral to his memory at Kirkwall in Orkney. For a long time it was believed that the shrine with his remains had been lost at the time of the Reformation, but during restoration work on St Magnus Cathedral in 1919 a wooden casket was found. It had been walled up in a pillar of the choir. Some bones were found to be missing, as they had been given to the cathedral churches at Kirkjubøur and at Skálholt in Iceland. St Magnus became a popular saint in the Norse world, as is shown by all the churches dedicated to his name – there were ten of them in Iceland alone.

The other saint whose bones are buried in the cathedral wall is Torlákur Helgi, who was bishop of Skálholt from 1178 until he died in 1193. He was a student at the centre of learning at Oddi, and later studied in Paris and Lincoln. His shrine was the most costly in Iceland, and the story of his life and work is told in *Biskupa Sögur – Sagas of the Bishops* – which also tell of miraculous happenings in the Kirkjubøur cathedral.

The chamber was first opened in 1905, and ten objects were found wrapped in cloth and kept in a lead box. The Danish authorities wanted them transferred to the National Museum in Copenhagen for further examination, but this met with stubborn resistance among the Faroese, who remembered what had happened to the bench ends of the parish church. The relics were therefore put back in the chamber, but have since then been given a thorough scientific examination in connection with the archaeological excavations on the site.

It seems natural to ask why the cathedral has never been repaired and finished. It could be done – after all the Nidaros Cathedral in Trondheim was at one time practically a ruin too. Such plans have actually existed. In the 1860s drawings were made and funds collected, but for some reason the idea was dropped and the funds spent on the parish church instead. Considering the disastrous result of the work done on that building, we should perhaps be grateful that the cathedral was left alone. Lately it has been found that drastic measures have to be taken to preserve the ruin, as time and tourists are taking their toll. A decision has been taken to build protective walls around the building. Hopefully it can be done in such a way that its beauty and dignity will still be apparent.

During the 400 years of the bishopric the names of 34 bishops are recorded. Most of them were Norwegian, but very little is known about them. The last Catholic bishop was Ámund Olavsson, who was in office until 1538 when the land was confiscated and the divinity school closed down. According to tradition the first Evangelical bishop, Jens Riber, fled from Kirkjubøur in 1551 because of the many attacks by pirates – no less than four raids in three years. The legendary Heini Havreki took over his duties, and became the real Church reformer.

Over the centuries the Church had acquired considerable landed property until by the time of the Reformation it owned about half of all the land in Faroe. Thus Kirkjubøur probably was not only a religious and cultural centre but a sizeable business one as well. In size and splendour the site at Kirkjubøur compared favourably with most of the Norse bishoprics: some fifty buildings were scattered over an area of 2,000–2,500 square metres, which was drained through a system of rain-water culverts. The bishop's palace was placed in the centre of this complex.

Today the remains of the bishop's palace are perhaps the most puzzling part of the site. Excavations have shown that originally the bishop's palace consisted of two buildings, which formed two sides of a rectangular, paved court. The eastern wing was 24 metres long and 11 metres wide and forms the foundations of the present houses. The western wing was 47 metres long and 7 metres wide and seems to have consisted of five rooms. Both wings have had portals facing the central court. The west wing probably had stone-built foundations and an upper storey of timber. The walls of the east wing are very thick and were probably the base of a two-storeyed stone building. At some later date this wing was added to, with the main entrance facing the Magnus Cathedral. It seems likely that this was done around 1300, when the cathedral was built.

Excavation has shown that the north end of the west wing was at one time completely crushed by a land or rockslide from the hill above. In 1673 a source tells us that 'earlier there were many large stone houses which are now destroyed' (Lucas Debes). Probably the second storey was badly damaged, and for some reason it was replaced by timber houses: the *roykstova* and the so-called *stokkastovur,* or block-houses. Of these, the *roystova* seems almost unchanged; it has much in common with the thirteenth-century *Raulandstova,* the oldest building at the Bygdøy Folk Museum in Oslo. And according to tradition the *roykstova* originally stood in Sogn in West Norway; it was taken down and the logs numbered so as to make it easier to rebuild. It was then floated to Faroe but was somehow lost on the way, as the story goes that the timber drifted ashore in the bay at Kirkjubøur. This explains why the house fits the foundation so badly that it was necessary to support it with pillars. It may be the oldest wooden house in Europe still to be inhabited.

Very little is known of the divinity school that was once housed in the bishop's palace, but its most famous graduate is Sverri Sigurdsson the Priest who was king of Norway from 1177 to 1202, and is praised in the Norwegian national anthem as the man who 'spoke out against Rome'. His early life is surrounded by legend; this was perhaps to some extent encouraged by himself. Although the historical saga written about him by an Icelandic abbot implies that he was born in Norway and came to Kirkjubøur when he was five years old, there is a strong tradition in Faroe that Sverri was in fact born in Kirkjubøur to a young woman called Gunnhild, who had come to the islands from Norway, and that she tried as best she could to hide the child's existence by keeping him in a cave in the mountainside.

Sverri grew up in Kirkjubøur, studied there under Bishop Rói and probably married his daughter Astrid – at least they had four children together, and their son Hákon became king after his father. But when Sverri was twenty-four years old and his future seemed settled, his mother told him that he was destined for other things; he was the illegitimate son of Sigurd Munn, a former king. Sverri went to Norway, joined the group of rebels and outlaws known as the Birchlegs, and eventually became their leader. Although Sverri was no soldier, he proved to be a master of military strategy, and won battle after battle. In the end his most formidable enemy was in fact the Catholic Church. Sverri was crowned king in 1190, but soon afterwards the bishops left the country and he was excommunicated. In 1198 all of Norway was interdicted. He had provoked the fury of the Church, but he fought back. In his brilliant 'Speech against the bishops', meant to be read in churches and at assembled Tings, Sverri anticipates Luther by more than 300 years in the way he flays the priests for their abuse of power and defends the authority of the king over the national Church. His learning shows how excellent an education he must have received at the school at Kirkjubøur.

For better or worse Sverri changed the course of Norwegian history. He introduced a strongly centralized system of government, with much power in the hands of the king. He has remained controversial; historians still disagree about his importance as well as his right to the throne. The first part of the saga about him was written more or less to his dictation and there are many gaps in the story. Few historians think that Sverri was a king's son; the interesting question is what he himself believed. There is no doubt that he must have been an extraordinary man.

Sverri founded a royal dynasty, which reigned in Norway and the Norse dominions for more than a century and a half. His motto was 'Suerus rex Magnus, ferus ut leo, mitis ut agnus' – 'King Sverri Magnus, fierce as a lion, gentle as a lamb' – and the story of his life shows us a peace-loving man who was forever fighting. Looked at objectively, without the trappings of romance, it is the story of a young Faroese priest whose claim to royal birth rested on his own unsupported assertion and whose success depended on his own gift of leadership. It is also as a Faroese that he likes to describe himself, perhaps in a wish to distance himself from the ongoing struggle: 'I am not fit to rule, I am a man who has grown up on an outskerry far from other lands.' The writer Hans E. Kinck even sees him as a second Tróndur í Gøtu, 'tough and indomitable, cunning and deep, with endless tricks and not shrinking from the use of any methods'. He points out that Sverri grew up among strong-willed men, 'who act and do not talk, from weatherbeaten, dangerous coasts. And in our own times we have had great politicians from there, who are altogether chips off the old block.'

One of the politicians thus referred to was Jóannes Patursson (1866–1946), also known as Bóndin – the farmer – and the grand old man of Faroese politics. Like King Sverri he grew up in Kirkjubøur. He came of the same mould as Nólsoyar-Páll, his great-grandfather. He studied agriculture in Norway and was influenced by the ideas of national freedom and independence that were then strong in that country. He founded the first Home Rule Party in Faroe and was one of the men behind the newspaper *Tingakrossur.* In the conflict between Denmark and Norway over Greenland in the 1930s, Bóndin openly sided with Norway, so that the Danes believed that he wanted to see Faroe back with Norway. The story goes that when King Christian X and Queen Alexandrine of Denmark were being shown around at Kirkjubøur, the queen noticed the Norwegian coat-of-arms above the door of the Bishop's Palace. 'Come and see the Norwegian lion', she told the king, who was still inside the building. But King Christian smiled at Jóannes Patursson and said, 'No, the Norwegian lion is right here.'

Actually, what Jóannes Patursson worked for all his life was to see his native islands become completely independent, but he died before the results of the 1946 referendum were known. He was also known for his poetry and his political writings; sometimes the two became one and the same. Thus the opening words of the poem he wrote for the 'Christmas meeting' on 22 December 1888 have become part of the Faroese heritage: *'Nu er tann stundin komin …'* – 'now the moment has come …' The memory of Jóannes Bóndi has inspired other poets as well:

Tú kveikti eld í faðir mín,	You lit a fire in my father,
tú kveikti eld í meg,	you lit a fire in me,
tú gekkst sum mikil ljósberi,	you walked as a great torch-bearer,
lýsti okkum øllum veg.	and showed us all the way.

Regin Dahl

When the land was taken from the Church after the Reformation it was given to the royal bailiff to administer. The lawman was the highest official of the country, chairman of the Løgting and chief judge. One of the lawmen, Petur Jakúpsson, is known today as the owner of Seyðabrævið, the Faroese lawbook. His daughter married into the famous Laðangarður family of

Sumba in Suðuroy, and their descendants have run the Kirkjubøur farm ever since, so that the present *kongsbóndi* Páll Patursson represents the sixteenth generation of his family on the farm. They are a gifted family, who have left their mark on many aspects of Faroese life. They have also taken seriously their task as guardians of the principal historical site in the islands.

Although the authorities early in the nineteenth century took some of the farming land for other purposes, this is still the largest farm in Faroe. It is also one of the best-run farms, with modern buildings and machinery. A generation or two ago there were thirty servants to do the work now done mainly by machines. Annually the farm sends some 100,000 litres of milk to the dairy in Tórshavn. Perhaps this is the best thing about Kirkjubøur – that it not only evokes the past so beautifully, but is very much alive today.

Cows head home at milking time to Kirkjubøur, the largest farm in Faroe

TOP
A wedding in Kirkjubøur. The farmhouse may be the oldest inhabited wooden house in Europe.
BOTTOM
St Magnus cathedral, Kirkjubøur.

TOP LEFT
Kirkjubøur: interior of the old farmhouse.
TOP RIGHT
St Olav's church, Kirkjubøur, with the altar painting by Sámal Joensen-Mikines.
BOTTOM
Distant view of St Olav's church, Kirkjubøur, with the islands of Hestur and Koltur across the sound.

One of the most beautiful of Nordic manuscripts, the 'Sheep letter', pagina 132b in Lundarbókin.
By kind permission: Føroya Landsskjalasavn and Lund University Library.
*On the flat rocks of Tinganes, in Tórshavn harbour, the main assembly or Ting met every summer,
probably from the early days of the Norse settlement.*

TOP
Tórshavn harbour, Vestaravág.
BOTTOM LEFT
At the Ólavsvøka festival even the youngest wear national costume.
BOTTOM RIGHT
A couple in national dress at the Ólavsvøka.

TOP LEFT
Tórshavn harbour: reflections.
TOP RIGHT
Mikladalur is the largest bygd *on Kalsoy.*
BOTTOM
Viðareiði has been called the queen of the Faroese bygdir. *In the foreground is a* hjallur, *used for drying meat.*

TOP
Djúpadalur on Kolsoy, looking out towards Kunoy.
BOTTOM
Klaksvík, the capital of the northern islands.

TOP
16. The people of Skarð would cross the tremendous cleft of Skarðgjøgv to go to church in the bygd of Kunoy.
BOTTOM
The bygd of Gjógv on the island of Eysturoy.

TOP LEFT
A couple working with hay in Gjógv, Eysturoy.
TOP RIGHT
The Snældan spinning and knitting mill at Strendur, Eysturoy.
BOTTOM
Eiði is a large and prosperous bygd on Eysturoy.

TOP
Beautifully-made Faroese boats lie idle in a shed.
BOTTOM
*The river cascades down through Kvívík, on Streymoy –
one of the most charming bygdir in the islands.*

TOP
The excavated houses at Kvívík show that this is an ancient Viking settlement.
BOTTOM
The dramatic scenery of Saksun on Streymoy.

TOP
Funningur. Like a handful of colourful toy bricks the bygd *clusters close to the river Stórá.*
BOTTOM
Nólsoy. A striking feature of the harbour is the archway made from the jaw-bone of a sperm whale.

Puffins on Mykines and gannets on Mykineshólmur.

A painting (1966) by Sámal Joensen-Mykines. Born on Mykines in 1906,
he was the first Faroese artist to receive international attention.
Potatoes growing on Mykines.

TOP
Grindadráp in Fámjin, Suðuroy. The climax is mercifully swift: it took just ten minutes to kill these ninety pilot whales.
BOTTOM
A fish farm in Haraldssund.

TOP
Sandvatn on Sandoy is rich in trout and a resting-place for whooper swans on their way to Iceland.
BOTTOM
Sandoy has impressive bird-cliffs on the western coast and scenery rather like that of Orkney and Shetland.

TOP LEFT
The first Faroese flag – the Merkið – hangs inside the church at Fámjin, Suðuroy.
TOP RIGHT
Høgubjørg, Suðuroy. Awesome scenery greets walkers everywhere in the islands.
BOTTOM
The old whaling station at Lopra in Suðuroy.

18

TÓRSHAVN

Tórshavn does not excel through visual beauty, a unique location or unusual achievements. It is only a small town between sea, mountain and moor. But this spot is not just the capital of a tiny island country; it is really also the navel of the world! Here it was that the sun and the moon first appeared, this is the place where night and day were created, here still exists the stormy primeval darkness from which all things arose and unfolded wondrously. From an attic window in the old Tórshavn you first exchanged glances with the Pleiades and felt the kiss of eternity on your brow.

William Heinesen

In this personal and poetic way William Heinesen, Tórshavn's most famous citizen, pays tribute to the town where he spent most of his life. As he points out, it is natural to see one's home town as the centre of the world, but surely any Tórshavner may be forgiven for thinking along these lines, with Tórshavn the only major port in a large Atlantic area and Reykjavik, Lerwick and Bergen hundreds of miles away?

To the islands themselves Tórshavn is the undisputed centre. All roads may at one time have led to Rome; in the Faroe Islands they all lead to Tórshavn, as practically all domestic and foreign communications naturally begin and end here. It is the administrative, economic and cultural centre, with all the bureaucracy this involves. The town necessarily has the functions of a capital, as the many foreign consulates confirm.

The town is spread out over a large area, as it would have to be when every family has its own house. Personal taste reigns supreme, and there are houses in all sizes, colours and materials, although the era of concrete seems to be over, as many houses are now built in the traditional tarred timber style that suits the bare landscape so well, and some of them even have turfed roofs. The town expands faster than the authorities can build roads, so that there is always a Klondyke area or two somewhere. Tórshavn is prosperous, and is full of activity and bustle. Because of all the young people everywhere and all the houses being built the town has a youthful, modern look to it. This impression is deceptive: Tórshavn may belong to the new rich but is no upstart; on the contrary it may with justice be called the oldest capital in Northern Europe.

On the flat rocks of Tinganes, the promontory that divides the harbour into Eystaravág and Vestaravág, the main assembly or Ting would meet every summer, probably from the early days of the Norse settlement. It was also a place of cultic importance, probably the site of the main *hof* or place of worship for the god Tór. The choice of this site shows systematic organization; it was the most central spot in relation to the other islands. *Færeyinga Saga* tells us that 'the tingstead of the Faroese was on Streymoy, and there is the harbour that is called Tórshavn.' It was on the rocks of Tinganes that Sigmundur Brestisson in the year 999 first tried to make the assembled men accept Christianity, but failed. And it was here that almost thirty years later the tax collector sent by King Olav Haraldsson the Saint was killed during the meeting of the Ting.

The Faroese usually refer to their capital as Havn or Havnin – the harbour. And as a harbour it has been important, although today it is difficult to explain why this should be so, as it is not naturally protected but is wide open to storms from the south-east. But back in Norse times this would not have mattered to the same extent, as the boats could be beached during the meetings of the Ting. These gatherings fostered a flourishing trade that in time became permanent. During the twelfth century all trade between Norway and her tributary countries in the west became centralized in Bergen, and according to a document from 1271 two ships would go regularly to Tórshavn from Bergen with cargoes of timber, cereal and salt. Probably warehouses were built for the merchants at Tinganes and on the higher slope behind it, which is known as Uti á Reyni. Some of the merchants would also have had accommodation built for their employees. But all through the Middle Ages this narrow promontory jutting out into the sea made up the main part of Tórshavn. It belonged to the *hagi* or outfield of the two king's farms of Eystari and Vestari Húsagarður. The third king's farm in the area was Sandagerði, which became a vicarage.

When pirate attacks began in earnest in Faroese waters it became necessary to protect the town and its trade. A small fort known as Skansin was built *c.* 1580 at the north end of the harbour, probably at the initiative of the legendary adventurer Magnus Heinason (1548–89), the younger son of Heini Havreki. He was the only Faroese ever to acquire the sole right to all trade in the islands, and he was also given the authority to capture pirates as well as any ship that tried to sail to Russia along the northern coast of Norway in order to get out of paying toll in Øresund. His exploits were spectacular and he became the favourite of King Frederik II, but fell out with his officials, as he was not too particular about keeping within the letter of the law. When the king died, Heinason was arrested, and after a short trial in Copenhagen he was beheaded. Later he was given a full pardon.

The character of Magnus Heinason has always fascinated the Faroese, and for a long time this fascination was shared by the playwright Henrik Ibsen, who during his stay in Italy in the 1860s toyed with the idea of writing a play about the Faroese sailor, having collected historical material on him and his times. Ibsen was at the time obsessed with the idea of the individual struggling for freedom within the constraints of society and, although he recognized the dark side to Magnus Heinason's character and called him a scoundrel, he still saw him as a free spirit, whose life at sea made him follow other laws than those acceptable to a narrow-minded bureaucracy. The play about Magnus Heinason was never written, but Ibsen used the same idea of a rebel against society in his *Emperor and Galilean* about Julian the Apostate, the play that the writer himself considered his masterpiece.

Small fortifications were later built at Tinganes as well, but nothing could stop the French from taking the town in 1677. When their demand for 100 oxen, 200 sheep, 500 pairs of gloves, 1,200 pairs of stockings and 60 nightshirts could not be met within the stipulated twelve hours, the fort was sacked and the town plundered. During the cold winters that followed, the townspeople suffered greatly. In 1808, during the Napoleonic Wars, nothing could prevent the British from repeating the French exercise. The story goes that the English brig *Clio* anchored outside Tórshavn and the commandant sent an *áttamannafar* out to the ship to inquire what they might want. The boat crew did not return, so he sent another. Then the English attacked, using the two Faroese crews as a shield. In April of 1940 the British returned to Skansin, and for five years it flew the Union Jack and served as headquarters for the occupying army. The fort has since been restored.

In 1584 Tórshavn had 101 inhabitants, among them the three king's farmers with their families and servants, a few trade and government officials and about a dozen people who owned no land or much else. Workers were needed for the construction and upkeep of Skansin and other buildings, and the landless proletariat of the *bygdir* now came to Tórshavn to find work, but there were no easy riches. Guard duty at Skansin was imposed on them without pay, and while they had the right to take peat for fuel, they had no land and were therefore unable to keep sheep. For clothing and food they depended on the bounty of the farmers, and Tórshavn people were therefore contemptuously referred to as 'woolbeggars' and considered of no account both by their own countrymen and by the powers that be, who gave them their begging passes. Fishing became their livelihood. Still the population grew, and the town became more congested than ever, so that there was no defence against small-pox when it struck in 1709–10: three-quarters of the population were wiped out, leaving mostly children and young people.

In 1673 a store of gunpowder kept in the old fort at Tinganes blew up, and in the fire that followed many of the old buildings went up in flames. There was another large fire in 1951. Among the buildings that survived both fires is Munkastovan. Before the Reformation this building was used to store tribute received by Munkeliv monastery in Bergen from its landed property in Faroe, especially in the Northern Islands, and this may explain the name. Another old building is Leigubúðin, which was used to store the king's tribute, which was also paid in kind. The vicarage of Reynagarður dates from *c.* 1630, but only a part of it survives. The first known church for the population of Tórshavn was built in 1609; before that they would have had to walk across the bare, bleak Kirkjubøreyn and go to church in Kirkjubøur. The timber for the church came as a gift from King Christian IV, but it became too small and was torn down in 1789 to make room for the present white-painted church, which can accommodate some 600 people. From its tower bells chime out some of the favourite Faroese hymns.

In the seventeenth century the importance of the port grew and foreign ships called regularly to load and unload goods. This was the period of the harsh Trade Monopoly, which was in foreign hands and not designed for the needs of the Faroese people. The country people would bring their products into town and have to be satisfied with whatever price they were given. Their choice of imported goods in return was extremely limited and expensive. The rule of the von Gabel family (1655–1708) is known as Gablatíðin and is the darkest chapter in the history of Tórshavn. The walls of the house known as Myrkastovan – the dark house – can still be seen; it served as a dungeon. A part of Tórshavn is still known as á Kák; here stood the post or *kákur* where the punishment of public lashing took place.

When the trade became a royal monopoly in the early eighteenth century conditions improved. For a short spell of twenty years from 1768 the enterprising Niels Ryberg was allowed to carry on an entrepôt trade, which to a great extent was based on smuggling to England. In the ongoing French–British conflict there was room for profitable manoeuvring, and in Tórshavn the warehouses built by Ryberg filled up with goods. He was the first to realize that for the Faroe Islands the future lay in fishing, and he experimented with dried cod and salted herring, but at the time nothing much could be done about it.

When the Løgting settled the long-lasting boundary conflict between the townspeople and the farms of Húsagarður, it became to some extent possible for the town to develop more freely. But its area was still fairly small, and with some fifty houses built helter-skelter all over Úti á Reyni there was no space left for the new church, which therefore had to be built outside the town boundary in what was then a new quarter known as 'north of the town'. With the coming of free trade in the middle of the nineteenth century Tórshavn forged ahead, and the farming land was rented out to the townspeople, who could later buy it if they so wished. The *traðir*, as these small plots of land are called, eased their existence considerably, as they were then able to keep a cow or a few sheep. Today the memory of these plots is retained in such street names as Haraldstrøð and Lutzenstrøð.

Free trade meant opening up the islands to the world and the transformation of a barter economy into a money economy. It also meant that Tórshavn was no longer the only market, but had competition from Tvøroyri and later Klaksvík. In 1801 there were 554 inhabitants in Tórshavn, and this represented a tenth of the total Faroe population. Today roughly a third of the people live in the capital. Of course the Tórshavn area has been much enlarged: in 1974 the neighbouring *bygdir* of Hoyvík and Kaldbak were made part of the town area.

But for a long time Tórshavn remained to all intents and purposes a large

Tórshavn is prosperous and full of activity but the quaint little town the foreign visitors saw, at the turn of the century, has not changed around the harbour areas

village. Foreign visitors around the turn of the century saw it as a quaint little town. There were no horses disturbing the peace in Tórshavn streets and ducks would sleep peacefully in the middle of them, while hens hopped from roof to roof to scratch among the tall grasses growing there.

> Never have I seen poultry – hens, ducks, geese – be a part of the scene the way they are here; these animals are living in the streets, every single family seems to have its own flocks that almost take over the street, especially in the old part of the town where they will not be disturbed by carriages.
>
> *C. Gulbranson*

As late as 1952 there were some 2,000 hens and 1,500 chickens registered within the town area.

There were always complaints about Tórshavn harbour, but they became louder as the sailing ships were replaced by steamers. There were no quays of any size, and unloading had to be done by lighters. In rough weather ships of some size had to seek a safer harbour. The standing joke was that Tórshavn was the port without a harbour. Today this has all been changed. Long, very expensive piers and jetties have been built, and the harbour area is perhaps

Pensioner out for a morning's fishing, selling haddock in Tórshavn

the most exciting part of the town, where there is activity around the clock, with ferries and freighters coming and going.

One of the busiest shopping streets is named after Niels R. Finsen, who in 1903 was the third scientist to be awarded the Nobel Prize in medicine. He was born and grew up in Tórshavn while his Icelandic father was governor of the islands. He is considered the founder of radiotherapy, and received the prize for discovering the healing effect of light on a tubercular skin disease called lupus. Another main street is called Jónas Broncks gøta. Jónas Bronck was the son of a Tórshavn minister and originally set out to follow his father's vocation. He was enrolled at the University of Copenhagen under the name of Johannes Martini Farinsulanum, but left his studies to go to sea and ended up as one of the founding fathers of what was then the Dutch colonial town of Nieuw Amsterdam, later New York. He bought land in what is today Manhattan, and when he died in 1643 he was a highly respected citizen. For a long time it was believed that the part of New York known as the Bronx was named after him, but this has now been proved to be a myth.

All kinds of cultural activities are based in Tórshavn. Newspapers and books are published here, radio and television have their headquarters in the town, painters exhibit their latest work, and there are plays and concerts. There is a variety of schools. The national library houses a Faroese book collection of 12,000 volumes, and there are more bookshops than in most towns many times the size. The Nordic House is another addition to the cultural life of the capital. It was built at the initiative of the Nordic Council, who hoped that it would serve as a forum for cultural life in the islands and bring them into closer contact with the other Nordic countries. It is all a joint effort; the architects were the Norwegian Ola Steen and the Icelandic Kollbrún Ragnarsdóttir; the woodwork is Swedish, the tiles are Norwegian slate, the glass is Danish, the roof Icelandic and the furniture Finnish. The work was done by Faroese craftsmen. Since it was finished in 1983, the Nordic House has become an indispensable part of Tórshavn.

For a few days in late July the town comes to hectic life. The Olai or Ólavsvøka has been celebrated for a long time. King Olav Haraldsson introduced Christianity into Norway by brutal means; he was defeated and died in the battle of Stiklestad near Trondheim on 29 July 1030. Although he was never canonized by the Pope, St Olav became the main saint of the Nordic countries. He had a powerful appeal to the popular imagination and long after the Reformation farmers would speak of 'King Olav's law' as the ultimate authority. King Olav was the protector of all land produce, just as the god Tór was before him. It is therefore rather significant that, apart from the saint's own town of Trondheim, Ólavsvøka has nowhere else been as important as in Tórshavn.

Ólavsvøka is a national holiday for all the islands, but the celebrations are held in Tórshavn. Visitors to the festivities begin coming in from the *bygdir* the day before, and soon hotels and private houses are filled to capacity. The word *vøka* means wake, and the festivities begin the day before. They go on for three days or more, and Tórshavn does not usually get back to normal until perhaps 31 July. The official part of the celebration is the opening of the Løgting, as it has been for 900 years and more. This begins with a service held in Havnar kirkja, and all the Løgting members as well as civil and church officials walk to the church in a procession. The ministers of the thirteen parishes take turns giving the sermon at Ólavsvøka.

After the service the procession returns to the Løgting for a short opening ceremony. Today the official programme ends there, but this was not always the case. In his description of the way of life in Faroe in the 1670s the minister Lucas Debes tells us how both officials and clergy would continue the celebrations with a tremendous party, where every conceivable toast would be proposed and drunk. Before each toast one of the ministers would intone a Latin hymn, and they all sang with him. Then the president of the Løgting would rise and propose another toast, every time concluding with the stock phrase, 'He will be dearest to God, who drinks the most and spares the least.'

Many islanders have taken this admonition seriously, but the Faroese never turn obnoxious when drunk. The celebration of Ólavsvøka has many facets, and that is as it should be. People in national costume take part in the dancing, listen to a pop singer or to a Salvation Army preacher. It is a great social occasion, when people who otherwise do not see each other very often get together. There are sports competitions of all kinds; perhaps the most popular of these is the rowing race in the harbour, where boats from the various islands compete while local patriots and family and friends urge them on. Organizations take the opportunity of having their annual meetings as everybody is in town anyway. The story goes that all the ministers were once gathered for a meeting in the old vicarage of Reynagarður when a drunk stumbled onto the scene, saw all the people in vestments and exclaimed, *'Her hevdi hin versti kent seg lítlan!'* – 'Here the Devil himself would have felt small!'

There is activity and change, almost to the point of chaos, in Tórshavn. And yet there is a feeling of permanence too. Walking through Gongin we can still vividly see Jørgen-Frantz Jacobsen's Barbara walking towards us, as well as imagine her first meeting with Peder Arrheboe. And the Restorff cream cakes can make us just as rapturous today as they made the English and German writers of travel books in the nineteenth century. So who would disagree with William Heinesen when he says that to be born and bred in such a place is a privilege?

19

THE NORTHERN ISLANDS

The six northern islands make up one administrative area, and have done so since Norse times. In many ways they are a world apart, with the south-western sides of Kalsoy and Borðoy showing a bare rock front to the other islands. In this north-eastern part of Faroe the land seems scarcer and the outfields smaller. The volcanic appearance of the mountains is more pronounced than further south, and from afar they look like a row of dark pyramids rising out of the sea.

Fugloy

Like Foula in Shetland this is a bird island. In Hattarvík the *lundi* (puffin) even nests in the infields. The 45-metre-high stack of Stapi is the most easterly point of Faroe, and teems with bird life. According to tradition Fugloy was from the beginning a floating island. It was difficult to find, for most of the time it was hidden in a magic mist. Men would sometimes row there and throw steel on to the shore, but there were trolls around the island, and they would throw everything straight back. Then all the ministers in Faroe were called in to make the island lie still. By throwing a Bible ashore they turned all the trolls into stacks; the coast of Fugloy used to be full of such stacks, but the surf has since taken many of them.

The sea is hard on these coasts and has hollowed out many caves. During the autumn storms of 1844 a strong tidal wave coming in from the north took the so-called Løgmannssker, a skerry that used to rise twelve feet above the water at low tide on the north-western coast. It was there that Jógvan Justinussen, who was lawman of Faroe from 1628 to 1654, was once marooned while out catching birds. He was saved through the quickwittedness of his servant. He was a *kongsbóndi* in Fugloy and *sýslamaður* for the northern islands, and it is said that he became the lawman because he had once rescued a boat crew down by the landing-place in Hattarvík.

There are two *bygdir* on Fugloy – Hattarvík and Kirkja – and as there is no natural harbour landing conditions are difficult in both of them. Kirkja lies on a steep slope in the southern part of Fugloy, with a lovely view of Svínoy and Viðoy. The name Kallanes for the point directly opposite tells us that

Kirkja is within shouting distance of Svínoy. The Fugloy people used to go across to Yvir á Dal in Svínoy to take peat. This necessitated many boat trips, and they would call from Kallanes for the boat when they were ready for it. Fugloy was settled early, and even in the Middle Ages there was a church in Kirkja, until it was moved to Hattarvík early in the eighteenth century. The present church dates back to 1933; the altar painting by Sámal Joensen-Mikines is of Christ walking on water. This is a recurrent theme in Faroese religious painting, and there is no need to wonder why – it uses a symbolic language wholly relevant to the life of the people.

Today a modern road connects the two *bygdir*. Further down, the old path ran along the cliff; it was steep, and there were those who never walked it. A woman living in Kirkja had turned seventy by the time she made her first visit along the path to Hattarvík. She had never been anywhere else in the world, and her dearest wish was to see at least the next *bygd* before she died. Although Hattarvík has more arable land than Kirkja, it was always the smaller *bygd*. It is shaped like an amphitheatre with the open sea as a stage; its terraced slopes are sheltered from all but the east wind, and it is not surprising that at one time corn was grown here quite successfully. Hattarvík may seem the more isolated of the two *bygdir*, but when the storms come, there is little to choose between them. A group of dancers from Fugloy went across to visit friends in Svínoy one Christmas, but it was two weeks before they could think of getting back!

During the last war there were forty inhabited houses in Fugloy. Now only fifteen houses are in everyday use for a population of fifty-two. Few of these are children. Because of the uncertain communications many people move away to places like Klaksvík or Tórshavn, although for a few hectic weeks in the summer many of them return.

Svínoy

Once upon a time Svínoy was also a floating island, and it was made stationary in no less an ingenuous way than its neighbour. People knew that the island was full of *svín* or pigs, but whenever they tried to throw steel at it, the island would disappear in the mist. In Viðoy there was only one pig, but it would mysteriously have a litter of piglets every year. It turned out that once a year it would swim across to the floating island. A woman who knew about such things then tied a bunch of keys to the pig's tail when next it went to the island, and since then Svínoy has never moved at all.

Only a low piece of land between high, rocky areas prevents Svínoy from turning into two islands. The valley of Svínoyareiði is about a mile across and nowhere more than 34 metres above the sea. Although there is no natural harbour in Svínoy either, it is fortunate in having access to sea both in the

west and the east, and when the weather permits it the daily boat connection will go along the eastern coast and into the bay where we find the *bygd* of Svínoy. As the nearest land is the west coast of Norway, nothing can break the force of the storm, and here too houses and land have been known to disappear overnight.

Unloading provisions on the island of Svínoy

In a strong east wind the landing-place on the west side known as Lendingin is used. In the old days there was yet another small landing-place, called Havnin. This lay at the point closest to Viðoy, where a cleft in the rock gave just enough room for a rowing-boat. Havnin must at one time have been important, as Havnartindur, the highest mountain in the island, is named after it. The path along the cliff can still be seen. The two other paths in the island take us either to Yvir í Dal or Yvir á Dal!

Svínoy has been inhabited since early Norse times. *Færeyinga Saga* tells us about the chieftain Svínoyar-Bjarni, who was closely related to Tróndur í Gøtu. He ruled the northern islands from Svínoy and seemed most of all to want to live in peace and stay out of all strife among the other chieftains.

When in 1828 the old church in Svínoy was torn down an old gravestone was found underneath the floor. A cross was carved on it, but there was no inscription. It is distinctly similar to the Sigmundarsteinur and the other cross-stones found in Skúvoy, and most probably this stone at one time was used to mark the grave of Svínoyar-Bjarni. People in the island knew that the stone existed and spoke of it as Bjarnasteinur.

Víðoy

The island is named for the fjordlike bay of Viðvík. *Viður* means timber or wood, and for some reason this bay, like the bay at Kirkjubøur, is a veritable trap for driftwood.

> The whole foreshore of this bay is piled high with drift-wood, and from the big trunks I infer that there is some specially strong current which brings them from the rivers of Norway and Arctic Siberia, for some of the trunks often bear the private mark of Russian and Norwegian owners. Why the current favours this one little bay almost exclusively is more than I can tell.
> *Joseph Jeaffreson*

In treeless islands so much driftwood would be riches indeed, and distinctive enough to give an island its name. In Víðoy itself the name Inni í Vík is today a more commonly used name for this bay.

Whereas the western coastline is fairly even, the eastern side has several large *botnar*. The mountains are high. The very distinctive Malinsfjall has the shape of a pyramid, and is most easily climbed from Dalar. Villingadalsfjall is at 844 metres the third highest mountain in Faroe. The best route to the top of Villingadalsfjall is from the south-west – it is steep but not difficult. On a clear day all the northern islands can be seen from here. Trøllanes in Kalsoy is seen as just a shelf in the rock face. This bird's-eye view shows clearly how wild the mountains are in the northern islands and that it is indeed only in the clefts in the rock that there is any room for man.

The top flattens out and it is possible to walk along the ridge to Enniberg, the highest headland in the world, and the most northerly point in Faroe. The word *enni* means a pan, and this is a plateau with an almost sheer drop of 700 metres. This is one of the best places for catching *lundi*; in fact the record of 1,200 birds for one man in a day was set here. In the old days the men might stay until the bird-catching came to an end. The many stacks below make this coastline an awesome sight. It is possible to descend through Ormadalur on the west side and return by a path along the coast.

Villing is a word used about a sheep that has strayed. But at one time there were other *villingar* in the mountain north of Viðareiði. Two little boys were left to their own resources when both their parents died, and nobody took much notice when they disappeared. Food would be taken from the *hjallar,* or outside storehouses, but at first nobody took much notice of that either. As things got worse people tried in vain to find out who was behind the theft of food. Then after many years two troll-like men were sighted on Villingadalsfjall. It was the two boys, who had lived like wild sheep. People talked to them gently, and after some time they were induced to come down to the *bygd* again. The two brothers had been living in a gully on the west side of the mountain, and this is still named Jóanisgjógv after one of them.

There are two *bygdir* in Viðoy – Viðareiði and Hvannasund – and for some years now they have been connected by road. Earlier Viðareiði could be cut off for weeks at a time in the winter. Although it is possible to land both from the west and the east, both landing-places are difficult, as even when they are safe from the wind there may still be a high swell. Some time in the sixteenth century the Danish minister Hans Jørgensen Fynbo saw his four sons drown in front of his eyes when they were caught by the swell in Eiðsvík. And in the

Viðareiði, Viðoy. Above the church and vicarage, Villingadalsfjall, the third-highest mountain in Faroe

late eighteenth century the sea swept away the church in the western bay in a storm; the new church was built further away from the shore. Today there is a pier further south at Leitið, where it is possible to land in most weather.

The wide fertile valley between the two high mountains is very striking, and Viðareiði has been called the queen of the Faroese *bygdir*. It used to be very strongly in favour of home rule, perhaps more so than any other *bygd* in Faroe. In spite of the uncertain landing conditions Viðareiði was for a long time the centre of the northern islands, until Klaksvík became all-important around the middle of this century. Today there are two parishes, but at one time a single minister was responsible for all the six islands. Only strong men could survive in such a parish, and over the centuries there have been many exceptional ministers. Stories were told of Klement Jensen, known as 'The Wise Priest', who stayed all of sixty years, from 1706 to 1766. Reputedly he knew 'more than the Lord's Prayer', as it was said of those suspected of knowing the Black Art.

It has not always been easy for the minister's family either. The last boat of the year would call in November, and after that they were virtually cut off from the outside world. Once the minister was detained in Svínoy for six weeks because he did not want to hurt an old woman's feelings. She wanted to give him some hot soup before he left, and in spite of his boat crew's protests he accepted. By the time he had managed to drink it, the weather had deteriorated and it was too late. At Viðareiði his family must have worried about his safety. The minister lives in the little vicarage called Onagerði, right next to the church. Tarred and turfed, it is built in the traditional style.

The *bygd* of Hvannasund has flourished since the causeway which links Viðoy with Borðoy was constructed. The fishermen objected to it at first, as the passage between the islands is now blocked. Although sheltered from the strong winds that at times sweep through Viðareiði, Hvannasund is vulnerable to the steep mountain behind it, and was once badly damaged by an avalanche of stones.

Borðoy

This is the largest of the northern islands. The fjords of Borðoyarvík and Árnafjørður give Borðoy the shape of a large fork, and when seen from the south-east it looks like three separate islands. Close to the north end, at Múlagjógv, is a large cave, which can be entered in a calm sea:

> Through a high portal we enter a long cave about 150 metres long, where colours play in shades of blue, green and brown. The silence is broken only by the splashing of the oars and by the water dripping from the vaulted loft, which is supported by

mighty columns, thus dividing the cave into side wings. We cannot help feeling as if we have been transported to a wonderful old vaulted church with soft coloured lights.

Valdemar Hansen

In the old *bygd* of Múli the houses are built close together, as the custom was. The 8-kilometre road from Norðdepil came too late to stop most of the people from moving away. Only a generation ago this was a thriving community of 30 people, of whom 18 were children. The men were often away for long periods, and the women had to cope with the farming. Every Sunday when weather permitted they would go to church at Viðareiði. Landing conditions were always difficult, so they kept their boats some distance south of the *bygd*.

Múli is known from old lore. Guttormur í Múla is the hero of many of

Looking across to Múli in Borðoy, from Viðareiði

these vividly-told stories. He lived in the seventeenth century and was the grandson of Magnus Heinason. His father started a family aged 90, and Guttormur, the youngest child, was born when Rasmus Magnusson was 103. He was seven when his wise old father died. They were both noted for their knowledge of the Black Art; Guttormur reputedly learned most of it from books he acquired from a Viðareiði minister! But they were both trustworthy men, who used their powers only for the good of their fellows. Thus Jonas Jonassen, who was the minister of Viðareiði from 1688 to 1700, had to have Guttormur's help to get rid of the ghost of his first wife. His reputation for sorcery also came to the ears of Barbara of Sumba, in distant Suðuroy, and according to tradition she came north to see which of them had the greatest powers. Barbara was once tried as a witch, but the judge acquitted her because she was 'too beautiful to be tarred'.

Guttormur's boat was one of the few to come back one summer, when a terrible storm suddenly struck in Djúpini and some fifty boats sank. In 1690 he was among those chosen at the Ting to go to Copenhagen to complain about the tyranny and oppression of the von Gabel rule in the islands, but he was not well enough to go. Guttormur evidently enjoyed great respect, but whether this is because or in spite of his reputed powers is difficult to say.

The abandoned *bygd* of Fossá was bought by the Norðoya Fornminnissavn in Klaksvík in 1969. The largest *bygd* on the east side of Borðoy is Norðdepil, which has almost merged with Hvannasund on the other side of the bridge. It was important in whaling days, and has now got a fish factory. Skálatoftir and Strond on the west coast are both ghost villages; the soil was poor and there was little of it. Even so Skálatoftir could man a *seksmannafar* at one time, but when that was no longer possible life became untenable for those left behind. According to written sources Skálatoftir existed as early as 1500, but oral tradition has it that the *bygd* was even older. It was abandoned in 1910, but because of centuries of cultivation the infield is still plainly visible. The electric power station at Strond is served by an artificial reservoir, which has been created 300 metres above sea level from the river Storá.

In the old days the only land route between west and east was a tremendous climb across the mountains, from Ánir to Norðtoftir. According to an old Danish guide-book these climbs 'can be quite difficult for strangers and ladies are advised against them'. The path crosses two steep mountain passes, and is narrow with abysses on both sides. This used to be the postman's route. But times have changed. Today two long tunnels have made Klaksvík easily accessible to people living on the east side and in Viðoy. Árnafjørður has now become the *bygd* between the tunnels. In the old days the Ting for the northern islands was held near by, at í Køtlum, close to Áarskarð. During the Second World War a German bomber was wrecked in this area when it flew into a mountainside after bombing Klaksvík harbour. The climb to Myrkjanoyrarfjall is strenuous but gives a view of many islands.

There is such a view up here, as I shall never see again; small ribbons of water everywhere between wild cliffs, everything spread before me in a bird's-eye view. Here one can look down through the narrow Haraldssund, along the coast of Kunoy, out towards the open sea; there one looks down at Pollur, where three English trawlers have taken shelter from the storm, and on the other side of this anchorage I can see the sharp, jagged contours of Kalsoy; further back is Klaksvík with a schooner and the whole *bygd* far down below. If I take a few steps back, I can see Borðoyarvík and the open water.

Severin Thomsen

The south-western part of Borðoy is steep and inhospitable, but this peninsula gave good cover against the many attacks of *fransar,* as the pirates were called. The first minister after the Reformation was killed falling down a cliff above Uppsalir in 1550, while fleeing from a pirate attack. The lowest point of the ridge between Klakkur and Hálgafelli is still known as Vektin – the look-out – where people took turns watching the sea. A hiding place was prepared in Ritudalur, well hidden from sight and inaccessible from below. The way there from Klaksvík crosses Brúnaskarð and then goes south along the steep cliff face of Háfjall. It is a very difficult path, yet even pregnant women climbed it and a future *kongsbóndi* of Vágur was born there.

Norðoyri is the southernmost *bygd* in Borðoy. Here Nólsoyar Páll, through his marriage, became the *kongsbóndi* at the farm of Uppistova. But he felt like a fish out of water so far from the harbour, and was able to swap farms so that he could move to Biskopsstøð instead. There he spent his last years in Faroe, and much of his famous *Fuglakvæði* was composed there.

Some distance further south there are remains of old houses, a *roykstova,* a boathouse and a shed. The place is known as Íslendingatoftir, and is believed to have been used by Icelanders on their way to or from Norway.

Klaksvík

With its wonderfully protected harbour it seems natural that Klaksvík has taken over from Viðareiði as the capital of the northern islands and even become the second largest centre in Faroe. In 1838 a monopoly store was established here, but even so it remained on the whole a farming district. An Englishman visiting here in 1898 was quite charmed:

Pursuing our course, we soon entered the narrow sound which led to our destination of Klaksvig, the capital of the North. The lonely little settlement came into view on turning the abrupt arm of the fjord here, and it was a sight well worth all the trouble of the journey. This settlement ... really consists of three small villages, all within a stone's throw of each other ... The villages are the neatest and tidiest that I saw in all the Islands, and by far the cleanest and most sanitary.

Joseph Jeaffreson

Until the Reformation much of the land here belonged to Munkeliv monastery at Nordnes in Bergen, and was for a long time afterwards known as *kleysturland.* It was one of the richest monasteries in Norway, founded by King Eystein Magnusson some time before 1110. The first settlers are believed to have come from Kunoy. There were four main clusters of farms known as *býlingar:* Vágur, Uppsalir, Myrkjanoyri and Gerðar. Of these Vágur was the oldest. People in Uppsalir were believed to live long because they got their water from such a wonderful spring. Myrkjanoyri is also known as Biskopsstøð. Gerðar was closer to Borðoyarvik, and had, as it happened, a very exposed position. Twice the farm was struck by an avalanche: on 12 March 1745 four people were killed and some houses ruined; then on the same date twenty years later all the buildings were destroyed and of the twenty-six people living there at the time, twenty were killed.

Originally the *bygd* was called Vágur, the name of Klaksvík being used only for the Trade Monopoly outlet and the area around it. But as the fisheries and fishing industry grew, so did Klaksvík, until the farming land was all but taken over for housing. Now there are factories of different kinds, not all of them related to the fishing industry. The brewery Føroya Bjór produces most of the beer drunk in Faroe. The founder was a younger son of the Vágur *kongsbóndi* who started his business in a small building which has now become a kind of museum – the large new brewery building is built above and around the old one.

The church in Klaksvík dates from 1963 and is built of wood and natural stone as a modern version of a traditional church. Inside, the church is dominated by the large fresco on the wall behind the altar depicting 'The Last Supper', which was originally painted in 1901 for Viborg Cathedral in Denmark by Joakim Skovgaard. The traditional wooden boat hanging under the rafters was once used by the minister when going around the parish. The old building of the Trade Monopoly dating from 1838 has been taken over by Norðoya Fornminnissavn and turned into a local museum.

Traditionally the northern islands have been a nationalist stronghold. In the 1946 referendum the votes were 954 to 398 in favour of home rule. In well-to-do Klaksvík especially it must be difficult to see why they should defer to foreign rulers. In 1953 protests began against the appointment of a doctor in the local hospital. The conflict lasted for two years and made the name of Klaksvík known all over Europe. The confrontation finally developed into

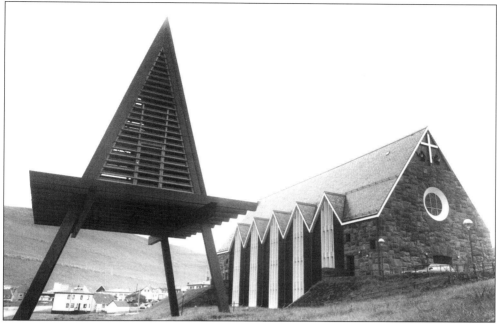

The church in Klaksvík dates from 1963

open revolt against the Danish authorities, who retaliated by sending a ship with 100 policemen with dogs. The Klaksvík people mined the harbour and warned that 'the dog ship' would be met by men armed with rifles. Feelings ran high, and the subsequent court proceedings were bitter.

Kunoy

The long narrow central mountain ridge of Kunoy has an average height of 790 metres, and five of its peaks are more than 800 metres. To the north Kunoyarnakkur falls steeply into the sea from a height of 828 metres. Kunoy appears as a series of *botnar* or rounded valleys, and these are especially striking in the north-east. Streaked with rivers and cataracts the valleys are picturesque but also barren, and most of them have therefore never been inhabited.

Today a road across a stone barrier between Strond and Haraldssund connects the islands of Kunoy and Borðoy. The barrier blocks off all traffic through Haraldssund, but then there are no *bygdir* in this fjord any more. There is now a kilometre-long tunnel through the mountain across to the *bygd* of Kunoy. Before the coming of the tunnel this *bygd* was threatened by depopulation, and the tunnel has saved it. It is a very attractive *bygd,* sheltered on three sides by high mountains. Beyond the cultivated fields, in the lee of the mountain, is a small plantation of mixed conifer and deciduous trees.

The path across the mountain ridge to Skarð is difficult, perhaps only slightly less so than the path between Trøllanes and Mikladalur in Kalsoy.

> You can see the line of the pathway as your boat comes in to Kunoyarbygd, climbing the long hillside behind Norður í Húsi, at one point traversing an almost perpendicular cliff-face, and finally vanishing in the entrance of a tremendous cleft. This is Skarðsgjógv, separating Middagsfjall and the great rocky pyramid of Kúvingafjall, both of which tower to a height of over 2,500 feet, and on our visit were still streaked with white where drifts of snow had lain under their summits since the spring.
>
> *Kenneth Williamson*

A green patch with ruined walls indicates where the *bygd* of Skarð used to be. The day before Christmas 1913 the boat crew, which consisted of all the seven able-bodied men of the *bygd*, went fishing. A storm sprang up, and the boat never came back. An old man, women and children were left to cope, and for some time they tried to go on as before. But Skarð was always a marginal *bygd* agriculturally, and the fishing was essential to its people to make a living. In 1919 they finally gave up and moved away from Skarð for good.

Six times a year the people of Skarð would cross the Skarðsgjógv to go to church in Kunoy. The well-known politician and writer Símun av Skarði came from Skarð. The story has it that he had an unusually strong voice, and once when *grind* was first sighted in Haraldssund Símun was sent up into Skarðsgjógv with *grindaboð* to the Kunoy people. But the acoustics in the *gjógv* are so fantastic that his shout of '*Grindaboð*' made people in Leirvík in Eysturoy, seven miles away, also set out in answer to the call.

According to tradition there was at one time a small Dutch settlement just south of Haraldssund. It is known as Hálendabúðir or just Búðirnar. The *buð* is a booth, and there may perhaps have been some kind of trade carried on here. There are ruined walls of houses as well as traces of cultivation, and a place known as Hálendinga gravir probably denotes the burial ground of the settlers.

Kalsoy

The long and narrow Kalsoy is the most westerly of the Northern Islands. The long rugged cliff of the west coast is steep and inhospitable. Only in the south-west is there a green patch – where the *bygd* of Blankskáli used to be. Because of its favourable position this used to be one of the best places in all of Faroe for growing corn. In the spring of 1809 an avalanche struck some of the houses, and the four families living there became afraid that it might happen again. They therefore moved to the east side of the island and founded the *bygd* of Syðradalur, but they went on using the land in Blankskáli for growing hay.

The east coast of Kalsoy has several characteristic *botnar*. There is no natural harbour, and the four *bygdir* of Tróllanes, Mikladalur, Húsar and Syðradalur have therefore at times been cut off for long periods. The most isolated has been Tróllanes, as in bad weather the mountain path from Mikladalur would have been impassable to all but the most intrepid – it was difficult enough on a good day.

In his young days William Heinesen once accompanied his friend Carli, the local veterinary surgeon, on a trip to the Northern Islands, and the account he wrote of his experiences for Jørgen-Frantz Jacobsen is really his first work in prose.

> The road to Tróllanes is difficult and impressive, first up a mountain pasture, then along a steep and high slope, and then through a *skora* which is famous for the danger involved in going through it. Under us lay a green gorge, Djúpadalur; through its bottom ran a large stony river. In several places Carli would stop and point while he told me about the men who had been killed by avalanches or falling stones.

And then later in Tróllanes he

> met the old crofter Rosenmeyer Wolles, a pleasant grey-bearded man, who had four times fallen down the cliffs in Djúpadalur and still walked around in his old age on sound legs in spite of once having nearly bled to death.

In the winter-time the swell of the sea would make it impossible to take out a boat at all in Tróllanes. Now a modern road runs the whole length of Kalsoy; four tunnels have made this possible. A side tunnel leads out into the wild Djúpadalur, so as to make it easier for the farmers to get to the sheep grazing there. The deep ravine of Djúpadalsgjógv is perhaps the most impressive of its kind in Faroe, as is the view of the Kunoy coast. Walking or sailing between Tróllanes and Mikladalur provides a unique experience of wild and beautiful scenery.

The name of Mikladalur means the large valley, and for centuries this has been the largest *bygd* in Kalsoy. At the beginning of the twentieth century there were some 200 people living here, with 40 children in the school. Today there is a population of 76 people. According to tradition there was at some time in the distant past a battle here between the local people and Norwegians come to collect taxes. Perhaps this shows that although Húsar

Kalsoy. Landing
diesel at Húsar

was settled first, Mikladalur was the more important *bygd*. It is also a significant fact that all over the islands the Mikladalsmen alone were referred to as
Kalsingar. The centre of the bygd has been quite well preserved and is
charming; the old mill on the river is constructed so as to need very little
water in order to turn the wheel. Landing conditions in Mikladalur were only
slightly less difficult than in Trøllanes, but a lot of effort and expense were
invested in building a safer landing place. Today this is no longer used, as all
traffic to and from the island goes through Húsar.

The contract given by King Frederik II in 1570 to Nils Henriksson for land
in Mikladalur is one of the oldest documents of its kind still extant. The king
admonishes his *bóndi* to look after the land and in all ways behave the way a
loyal subject should. Years later Mikladalur became the scene of a strange
drama when in 1656 Páll Jóannesson was accused of having killed his father
by sorcery. A servant girl, who felt herself betrayed by him, had told the tale
at the Ting for the northern islands. Páll was arrested but escaped three times
and fled home to Kalsoy. Part of the time he hid in the mountains north of
Trøllanes, where a cave in the mountainside is still known as Páll's loft. But
he was captured in Árnafjørður in Borðoy and taken to Denmark in irons;
after that his fate is not known. He has taken on the status of a legendary
figure under the name Páll Fangi – the Captive – and has always retained the
sympathy of people in Kalsoy.

20

EYSTUROY

> When we got to the top of the ridge and had Mikladalur below us, we saw to the south-west all the mountain tops of Eysturoy covered in snow; it was a sight for the gods! Highest up Slættaratindur with its shoulders, then a scale of peaks, sharp-pointed as well as more even ones, representing all variations on the theme of Faroese mountains; all resembling each other, and yet not two of them alike.
>
> *William Heinesen*

Eysturoy is the second largest island both in size and number of inhabitants. It has always been important; in a survey made in the first half of the seventeenth century there were 103 tax-paying farms in Eysturoy, 84 in Suðuroy and 80 in Streymoy.

The long fjords of Skálafjørður and Funningsfjørður divide Eysturoy almost into two islands, and the land between them is really a 7 kilometre-long and rather low isthmus. The narrow channel of Sundini that separates Eysturoy from Streymoy is difficult to navigate as there are many rocks and skerries as well as a swift current. The bridge across Sundini has brought a great improvement in communications; until it was built it could take half a day to get from Tórshavn to Eiði.

Towards the north there are majestic mountains, which give this part of the island a brooding grandeur. By contrast the southern part of Eysturoy seems idyllic, with sheltered valleys and rich pastures, and it is not surprising that the population of the Skálafjørður area has increased dramatically in recent years. Towards the east the sea has worn down the land to form several large bays, with room for prosperous *bygdir*. In 1800 there were twenty *bygdir* in Eysturoy; today there are thirty-three of them. A network of roads connects the *bygdir;* one more stretch of road between Oyri and Selatrað would place them all within easy reach of each other.

The large *bygd* of Eiði in the north-west lies on a narrow isthmus between Sundini and the sea. In the nineteenth century it had a good income from fishing and was second only to Tórshavn in size. The houses were spacious and well-built, and the streets were paved with basalt flagstones, which made the *bygd* look clean and prosperous. The church was one of the largest and nicest in Faroe.

The sun, which is denied the Tjørnuvík people, shines down on the people of Eiði. Their fields are easily cultivated, give excellent corn and good grass. The fishing is rather profitable and there is a great growth in population because of these circumstances.

Th. Sørensen

The building of new houses over the last few years has made the *bygd* spread towards Lake Tjørnin. The lake is 4 metres above sea level, but a long dyke of up-tossed boulders, known as Mølin, keeps it from flowing into the sea.

The striking promontory of Kollur slopes towards Eiði and is easily climbed. At the top of Kollur one is confronted by the open sea to the west and the north; in the old days the people manning what is now the ruins of a watch-house would have been happy to see the sea empty of ships. Close to the precipitous cliffs stand the famous landmarks of Risin and Kellingin – The Giant and his Wife. The sea has worn a hole through Kellingin, so that she has two feet to stand on. The couple had come to tow the Faroe Islands home to Iceland. The giant stood in the sea while his wife went to the top of Eiðiskollur to fasten the rope for him to pull. At the first attempt the Kollur cracked – the crack can still be seen – so she tried again, but in vain; the islands did not budge and the day was already breaking. So she hurried down to the sea to her husband, but then the sun rose and they both turned to stone, the way giants do if they are not careful. Even today Risin and Kellingin are looking longingly towards Iceland, which they will never reach.

The view to the east is of some of the highest mountains in the islands: Slættaratindur (882 m), Gráfelli (857 m) and Svartbakstindur (803 m). Slættaratindur is well worth climbing, although the summit is often wrapped in fog. *Slættur* means flat, and indeed the summit is smooth enough for Faroese dancing! The easiest route is from Eiðisskarð, which is so high above the sea that the climb to the top is cut by half. The vegetation in this altitude is distinctly alpine, with *Ranunculus glacialis* (Alpine buttercup) being fairly common.

A wide, green valley slopes down to the village of Gjógv, which has become a popular subject for tourist posters and postcards, because when it is seen from a special angle the *bygd* seems to cling to the edge of a chasm, or deep, narrow cleft in the rocky coastline. This is the *gjógv*, from which the *bygd* takes its name. Reefs and skerries serve as breakwaters so that the sea inside the cleft is relatively smooth, but it is still necessary to winch the boats up a steep track. The coast is exposed here, and sometimes waves from three different directions break violently on the same skerry. This coastline has taken its toll; in 1870 Gjógv lost seventeen men when in a storm two *áttaman-nafar* capsized in the surf. This was half the adult male population.

The houses of the village are built in clusters on both sides of the river Dalá, which forms a small pond before it falls into the sea. Down by the shore

stands the white-painted church built in 1929; it represents a milestone in the *Kollur, Eiði, with its* struggle for cultural freedom, being the first church to have its consecration *famous landmark of* ceremony in the Faroese language. The altar painting of Christ walking on *Risin and Kellingin* the water is the work of Niels Kruse of Eiði, one of the first Faroese painters. The village school dates back to 1884, and the two general stores are not much younger. Their range of goods may have changed, but their interiors are still in the original state. Gjógv is surrounded by high mountains and is therefore a popular base for climbers. The valley of Ambadalur not far from Gjógv is beautiful, with a striking view of Búgvin, at 188 metres the highest vertical *Overleaf:* stack in Faroe. It has large colonies of guillemots and kittiwakes, and was *Tróndur Patursson –* therefore often climbed by the bird-catchers. *Gøtuskeggjar in*

According to tradition Funningur is the oldest *bygd* in Faroe. About a mile *Skúvoy.*

One of Gjógv's general stores, dating back to the last century

before the point of Múlin we find the name Føroyaklettur, and this is the place where Grímur Kamban and his group of settlers are believed to have gone ashore. At any rate the place-names indicate that Funningur is older than Eiði and Gjógv. The mountain passes above Funningur are called Eiðisskarð and Gjáarskarð, and according to Norse practice this means that they were named from Funningur. At one time Funningsfjørður was regarded as the best fishing place in Faroe, at certain times of the year even better than the open sea, so that many boats used to gather there.

Today the *bygd* of Funningur is connected with the outside world by road in two directions, but once it was as isolated as Gjógv, as even on a calm day the surf thunders against the shore and landing is difficult. The old houses are built close together around the river Stórá. At the mouth of the river lies the fine old church with its beautifully carved interior in natural wood.

As in Funningur the river in Elduvík is called Stórá, and the houses form separate clusters on either side of it. The shore is exposed, so the boats had to land in the large cleft in the cliff west of the *bygd;* they would then be winched across the face of the cliff, rather as in Gjógv. The road was late in coming to Elduvík, and by the time it was completed many people had left the community. Several of the old houses are used as second homes and the owners take care to keep them as they were, thereby helping to give parts of Elduvík an air of earlier times.

The track from Elduvík eastwards to Oyndarfjørður is notorious. Running about 50 metres above the sea, it was always considered dangerous in wintertime. On a nice summer's day it is an interesting experience to walk along this track; it is not difficult, but care should nevertheless be taken. A narrow, green ledge circles the mountain. It is a fantastic sight to see people walking along it; from a distance they seem to be suspended, walking in an almost vertical landscape. From the track we see Funningur as a blot of bright colour against the intense green, and Slættaratindur capped with snow is a striking backdrop. The sea appears frighteningly close. Until their own church was built in 1951, the Elduvík people would walk this way most Sundays. Sometimes they would carry a baby for christening; at other times it might be a coffin for burial. And before the road was built in 1974 the postman's route was Fuglafjørður–Hellur–Oyndafjørður–Elduvík–Funningsbotnur and back to Fuglafjørður!

The name of Oyndarfjørður has been printed on Danish maps as Andefjord, in the mistaken belief that Oyndar is the same as the Danish word *and,* which means duck. The most probable explanation is that it derives from the man's name Eyvindr in the genitive form, and thus originally meant Eyvind's fjord. The farm of Garðshorn in Oyndarfjørður was given by King Christian III to Heini Havreki as part of his living when he became the first Protestant próstur of all the islands. Heini stayed in Eysturoy for more than twenty years, until he decided to return to Norway, and his son Magnus Heinason was born there in 1545. The church dates back to 1838 and has a rather unusual interior. Close by is Henriette Høgnesen's private museum with collections of furniture and old farming tools. Another tourist attraction in Oyndarfjørður is the Rinkusteinar – two boulders by the shore that move with the sea.

Across the bay is the tiny *bygd* of Hellur, named for the striking flagstones that were scoured flat by the ice. This *bygd is* part of Fuglafjørður, and a steep mountain track connects them. The mountains around Fuglafjørður are steep bare pyramids rather like those of the northern islands. At the edge of the eastern edge lies Borgin – the Castle – so called because at a distance this squarish block looks rather like a fortress. Fuglafjørður has one of the best natural harbours in Faroe; it is so shut in by mountains that it gives the appearance of being a lake.

Fuglafjørður was settled early, as is shown by the Viking Age farm found on the beach at Heimi á Oyrini by the mouth of the river Gjógvará. Excavation has shown that it was rather similar to the farm in Kvívík. The walls were 1.5 metres thick, and the house was about 17 metres long, but the southern part of it has been taken by the sea. This hall was inhabited in the Middle Ages as well; the walls were the same, but the floor was higher. On top of this were four more layers of ruins; evidently the site was continuously inhabited until quite recently. According to tradition a man named Rádni oman Lon who lived by the Gjógvará was the last Faroese to go to Norway before the Black Death to buy and sell goods. Originally there were four separate *bylingar* in Fuglafjørður, and gradually they merged as new houses were built between them. Since the end of the Trade Monopoly the *bygd* has prospered, as enterprising people set up in business to buy fish, liver-oil and knitted goods locally to sell abroad.

South of Fuglafjørður, by the side of the old Leirvík road, is a warm spring – Varmakelda – which has a temperature of 18 to 20°C, and was believed in the old days to have healing qualities. It was an old custom to meet here on Midsummer Eve and dance the night through on the flat rocks near by. The custom came to an end when fishing took the men away at this time of the year, but recently an attempt has been made to revive the tradition.

The road to Leirvík was considered dangerous because of the many rock slides, and a tunnel was therefore built instead. Because Leirvík is the key port on the road to the northern islands, with almost continuous ferry traffic, the tunnel is much used. Norse remains have been found and excavated in Leirvík as well. There used to be a *bønhús* or chapel here, which was closed down at the Reformation, and the ruins of this as well as the churchyard and dyke are well preserved. Leirvík was badly hit by a smallpox epidemic in 1725, said to have been caused by contact with foreign smugglers.

The wide bay of Gøtuvík may have seemed to the Norse settlers like a *gøta* – a street. Today there are three *bygdir* in Gøta; Norðragøta, Gøtugjógv and Syðrugøta. This is the classic territory of *Færeyinga Saga* as well as of Snorri Sturluson's *Heimskringla*. In the cellar of an old house in Norðragøta a stone can still be seen from Tróndur's hall; in the hill above Gøtugjógv was his look-out. Tróndur converted to Christianity at the point of a sword; according to his own code of honour his oath of faith was binding even though taken under duress. Tróndur is said to have built the second church in Faroe; the first was Sigmundur Brestisson's church in Skúvoy. This is believed to have been in Syðragøta, but was later moved to the site in Norðragøta where the church stands today. Remains of early settlement have been found by Mannuvegurin, the old track across to Ánir, and down by the beach in Norðragøta.

The beautiful church at Norðragøta dates from 1833. Thanks to the efforts of Gøtu Fornminnisfelag, or Antiquarian Society, and especially Arnleyg and Thomas Jacobsen of Norðragøta, whose life's work this museum is, the church is today the centre of a cluster of six well-preserved houses in the old Faroese style. The king's farm of Blásastova was built in 1835, just after the church, and consists of a barn and a farmhouse. The interior has been faithfully restored down to the smallest detail both in furniture and tools, and gives a superb insight into the way of life on a Faroese farm a century ago. Among the many interesting details the door handles and the double stoves should be noted.

The *bygd* of Søldarfjørður was, according to tradition, one of the oldest

Gøtu Museum is Arnleyg and Thomas Jacobsen's life's work

bygdir in Eysturoy, as it was first built by the two brothers Skeggi and Sólmundur, and was named after the latter. They were the sons of the Faroese chieftain Tróndur Tóralvsson and his wife Olúva, the granddaughter of Olaf the White, who in 853 became King of Dublin. Skeggi was the elder and thus the heir to the family property; the Gøtuskeggjar of Gøta descended from him. The brothers fell out and Skeggi was thrown off the cliff of Skeggjanøv by his younger brother, who was outlawed and had to leave the islands.

The fertile land of Lambi was probably cultivated from the earliest times. Until the Reformation there was a chapel here, and the old bell can be seen at Føroya Fornminnissavn. For a long time there was just one large king's farm here. Jón Heinason, the elder son of Heini Havreki and *Løgmaður* of Faroe from 1572 to '83, settled on the farm when he married the daughter of the king's farmer. Their son Mikkjal í Lamba, who took over after his father, was also a striking character, a quarrelsome man who often appears in Faroese court records of the early seventeenth century. But in the old stories it is really his servant Oli who plays the star part. He is nicknamed Jadnheysur – Iron-skull – because he is strong, hardy and quick-thinking. The farm stayed in the family for a long time, as did the king's farm at Søldarfjørður.

On the south side of Gøtavík a long ridge ends in Mjóvanes, which means the narrow promontory. In an onshore wind and a rip-tide, waves as high as houses get up, so Mjóvanes has proved fatal to many ships. It was in the bay of Lambavík that the ship *Norske Løve,* belonging to the Dansk-Ostindisk Kompagni, foundered and sank on New Year's Eve in 1707. The ship's bell along with a model of the ship hangs in Havnar Kirkja in Tórshavn. There have been various plans for salvaging the ship, but as it is buried under a rock slide, any such operation would be extremely difficult.

The *bygdir* of the south-eastern peninsula have grown and almost merged into one large town-like area, some 13 kilometres long. Runavík is now the largest *bygd* in Eysturoy, with some 2,500 inhabitants. Until Fuglafjørður

A good example of the expansion of the bygdir *in the south-eastern peninsula of Eysturoy is the church at Glyvrar*

became a separate living in 1929, the minister for all of Eysturoy lived in the fertile *bygd* of Nes. The Nes glebe was good land, but the lovely farm of Torkilsheyggjar also went with the living, so the minister's household was large: in 1800 it was made up of some forty people. It was a living much sought after, usually having attached to it the position of *próstur* of Faroe, and some outstanding ministers have held it. The best known of the ministers of Nes are V. U. Hammershaimb (1867–78), the creator of the Faroese literary language, and the poet and politician Fríðrikur Petersen (1900–17), who represented the Faroe Islands in the Danish Folketing. He wrote the first national anthem *'Eg oyggjar veit'* – 'I islands know'. But as Petersen became an influential unionist, his song became less popular. Today *'Tú alfagra land mitt'*– 'My beautiful country'– by Símun av Skarði, nationalist and founder of the Folk High School, has become the official anthem.

In the sacristy of the church at Nes there is an epitaph dated 1774 to the memory of the two wives of Andreas Djurhuus, who at that time was his father's curate but later took over the living from him. Both wives died in childbirth within a year of their marriage. Andreas Djurhuus was a kind man who was loved by his parishioners, and must also have had a way with the ladies. On his way home from university in Copenhagen he became shipwrecked on the south coast of Norway, and spent long enough in the small seaside town of Lillesand to turn the head of Maria Rønning, who went home to Nes with him. When his father pointed out that Andreas was betrothed, she married his older brother, who ran the Nes farm. They founded the Djurhuus dynasty of poets, of whom the first was their son Jens Christian Djurhuus, popularly known as Sjóvarbóndin, who composed the 'Ormurin Langi', still popular with Faroese dancers. In 1778 Maria Rønning

Carved panel in door, inside Nes church, Eysturoy

Djurhuus was given a medal by the Royal Agrarian Society in Copenhagen for teaching Faroese women how to use a new type of loom. A well-known museum piece is her silver vinaigrette, for smelling salts. Andreas married four times in all and had ten sons and six daughters.

In the idyllic lake, Toftavatn, there are two small holms where eider duck would breed 'if only they could be left in peace by poachers' (Landt). And it is full of trout:

> Having reached the lake, I found that the extreme end of it, which formed a circular pool about 600 yards across and divided from the main lake by a narrow stone bridge, was simply alive with fish, the whole surface of the water being rippled with their rises, and luckily I found that the water was deep enough to fish right up to the banks. For an hour and a half the fun was fast and furious.
>
> *Joseph Jeaffreson*

The main *bygdir* in the south-western part of Eysturoy today are Skáli and Strendur. Skáli has an important shipyard which, until it was bought by a Klaksvík firm in 1941, was known as Kongshavn; this name was also sometimes used for the whole area. The church as it stands today dates back to 1940. But in the Middle Ages there used to be a church in Skáli, at the point known as á Prestodda. According to tradition many people were at church one Sunday in winter when the thaw suddenly set in and the river flooded. One member of the congregation was embarrassed to notice his dog walking up the aisle towards him, and he got up to take it out. At that moment the church was swept into the sea by the flood, and he was the only survivor.

It is said that the *lestrarfjøl,* the lectern used by the *deknur* or parish clerk when he reads the sermon on the Sundays when there is no minister, drifted ashore further down the fjord, at Við Sjógv. There the new church was built, and for a long time this was the only church in the peninsula. The villagers of Selatrað had the longest walk. There was a church here in the Middle Ages but the present one was built in 1927 and has an altar painting of Jesus quietening the storm, by Niels Kruse. This *bygd* seems to have been subject to many pirate attacks, as the local place-names tell us of numerous hide-outs: Fransahol, Fransaklettur and Fransahús.

Tradition tells us that Selatrað was once a Ting site. Near Æduvík a flat rock is known as Tinghella, and is popularly connected with Ting meetings. Perhaps these were both sites of local Tings, but it seems logical that Stevnuválur, which is centrally located in the valley known as Millum Fjarða, was the main Ting site for Eysturoy. *Stevna* is an old word for meeting. The most dramatic story connected with Stevnuválur tells of how the *flokksmenn* or rebels of Fugloy try to gain control over the rest of the islands. They write to the king, asking for swords, but are told that the Faroese are peaceful people, and do not need weapons. They write a second time saying that the people are defenceless against the attacks of pirates, and this time they get the swords. They force a fourth man, Sjúrður of Gellingará in Hattarvík, to go with them. They seal their friendship with blood according to custom, but Sjúrður's blood will not blend with the blood of the others. They gain support, especially in Suðuroy, among men who want to get rid of the foreign officials. The rebels decide to meet in Gøta. As he leaves Hattarvík behind Sjúrður says, '*Frítt er Eystfedli frá at fara*' – 'Now I'm leaving I see how beautiful the eastern mountain is.' One of the others replies that the whole of the Faroes is even more beautiful. 'When you have them!' says Sjúrður. His words are, of course, prophetic, and the rising fails. Their violent behaviour loses them support, and they are betrayed: at Gøta the much-hated authorities are waiting for them. They flee to Svínoy and seek refuge in the church. But as the church has not been consecrated, their pursuers break in and capture them. They are brought back to Eysturoy where sentence has already been passed against them to the effect that all four rebels are to be thrown from the mountain of Valaknúkur, the ancient place of execution. Sjúrður is pardoned at the last moment at the behest of the people, but chooses to die with the others.

> The *flokksmenn* were then taken to the top of Valaknúkur, thrown from the mountain and buried underneath it. Their graves can be seen even today; the graves of three of them are black and ugly, with stones and coarse sand, but the grave where Sjúrður rests is beautiful; it is always covered in green grass.

There are no historical records of such a rising, but apart from some standard tricks of the narrative trade this is a story that rings true. It may have taken place sometime in the fifteenth century. The choice of Gøta as the site of a rebel meeting is certainly plausible.

21

STREYMOY

Streymoy is the largest of the Faroe Islands, and because of its central position it is also the principal island. As the channels separating Streymoy from Vágar and Eysturoy are narrow, these three islands often appear as a continuous land mass, a kind of mainland. With the bridge across Sundini connecting Streymoy with Eysturoy, and the planned tunnel under Vestmannasund to Vágar, the islands will to all intents and purposes become one area.

There are some 20,000 people in Streymoy, but as many as 16,000 of them live in the Tórshavn area. Large parts of the island are therefore sparsely populated. Together with Nólsoy, Koltur and Hestur, Streymoy makes up one sýsla, but three parishes. The two ministers of North Streymoy parish live in Kvívík and Vestmanna, with the original South Streymoy now being divided into a western and an eastern parish, with both ministers living in Tórshavn. The bishop's residence is there too.

The southernmost part of the island is relatively low-lying, but the mountains of Streymoy are mostly rather high. For a long time Skælingsfjall (763 m) was believed to be the highest mountain in Faroe, until a geographical survey established that both Melin (764 m) and Koppenni (790 m) in Streymoy are in fact higher. Both these mountains are part of the dramatic scenery to be found in the north-western part of the island, where high promontories fall almost perpendicularly into the sea and sea-birds are numerous.

There are good roads in Streymoy. The old island thoroughfare that went along the backbone of the islands from Tórshavn to Kollfjarðardalur was known as Eftir Oynni – along the island. In 1966 the present road, which is known as Oyggjarvegur, perhaps the most important road in Faroe, was opened. It quickly proved inadequate, mainly because of the dense fog that so often covers it and makes driving difficult, but also because in the winter it is so often icy. A tunnel, the tenth of its kind to be built in Faroe, was therefore planned between Kaldbaksbotnur and Oyrareingir.

The Oyggjarvegur passes through Mjørkadalur – the foggy valley – where a Nato base clings to the mountainside. A turfed roof large enough to provide grazing for a cow or two helps make the building blend with the scenery, and whether the motive for adopting this roofing material was camouflage or concern for the environment, the result is pleasing and shows how well the traditional style suits large buildings as well; both the Nordic House and Hotel Borg in Tórshavn are built in roughly the same style. The base has been something of a thorn in the flesh of the Faroese, as it was built in 1961 without their consent; the Løgting protested most loudly against it at the time. A side road leads up to the summit of Sornfelli (749 m), which is dominated by the large characteristic dishes of a radar station belonging to the North Atlantic surveillance system. Following this road up the hill towards Skeiðsskarð makes the ascent of Skælingsfjall less steep. The view of the islands from the top of the mountain is breathtaking, and in the old days Tórshavn people would gather here on Midsummer Eve if the weather was clear, to watch the sun rise.

Far below the Kaldbaksfjørður shines like a long silvery ribbon. It was here in the valley around the river Fjarðará that, according to an old story recorded by V. U. Hammershaimb, a veritable battle was once fought between the northerners and the southerners. The cause of the conflict seems to have been the taxes levied by Bishop Erlendur for building the Magnus Cathedral in Kirkjubøur, probably at the very beginning of the fourteenth century. The northern men rallied to the bishop; against them came the men of South Streymoy, Sandoy, Skúvoy and Suðuroy, and they met and clashed in the valley that has since been named Mannafalsdalur, because men fell there in battle. Grave mounds were said to have been visible for a long time, with the grass growing red because of the blood shed there. To the north of the valley where the battle was fought there used to be a large stone, which has now been broken in two, known as *Brynjumanna borð* – the table of the warriors. The name may refer to the feast held by the northerners after the battle, to celebrate their victory over the southerners.

The Oyggjarvegur, or Route 10, goes on to Eysturoy. At Hvalvík a road branches off to the north-west through the long Saksunardalur, where land is now being reclaimed. It is surrounded by high mountains with a number of waterfalls. The small *bygd* of Saksun is a romantic place, which draws many visitors and is pictured in practically every tourist brochure. It is shut in by towering mountain peaks that give to Saksun a certain mystery, a feeling of remoteness that is difficult to define.

The entrance to Saksun is known as Sakshøvn and is very narrow. Through the narrow inlet called Ósin we reach the round pool known as Pollur, which is so shallow that, when the tide is out, it is possible to walk dryshod across it in places. Probably Ósin was once a *gjógv* that became broken up by the surf. Sakshøvn was regarded as a safe and protected anchorage, until the whole bay filled up with sand. This is said to have happened in a terrible storm during *Kyndilsmessan harda* – the hard Candlemas – that is on 2 February, some time in the second half of the seventeenth century. During another storm in 1828 a ship loaded with 800 wooden beams from Pomerania tried to reach harbour in Sakshøvn, but it was wrecked and came drifting into Pollur. When shortly afterwards the old church in Hvalvík was ruined by another storm, the Pomeranian timber was put to good use. Today it is only possible to reach Pollur with a small boat at high tide. It is here that salmon and sea trout can be caught before they start on the last strenuous stage of their journey to Saksunarvatn, which is famous for its fish. Saksun is therefore a popular place for anglers.

There are three old king's farms in Saksun: Kvíggjahamar, Svartá and Dúvugarður, where the old farmhouse today belongs to Føroya Fornminnissavn, and has become a museum. The farmhouse is probably some 300 years old, and was lived in until the 1940s by up to twenty people. It gives a good idea of what life was like on an old farm. Towards the end of the nineteenth century Elizabeth Taylor visited it:

> Saksun I found to be a three-house hamlet. The house where I stayed had its peculiarities. There was a rooster who crowed every two minutes after midnight; a cow homesick for the 'outfields', and a calf whose lamentations had no beginning and no end; and all three lived directly under my bed, with only an open flooring between.

There was a chapel in Saksun in the Middle Ages, but since the Reformation people have had to go to church in Tjørnuvík, across the mountains. As Jørgen Landt pointed out in 1800, this was a difficult path at the best of times, but

> imagine then, how toilsome it must be to carry a dead body to the grave along such a route! Quite often the corpse has to be tied to a board and carried on someone's back. Would it not be better for such *bygdir* to have a small fenced graveyard, where the dead could be quietly and comfortably laid to rest, without all this trouble and inconvenience for the living?

In 1858 the old church in Tjørnuvík was dismantled and carried piece by piece across the mountain to Saksun, where it still stands.

The coastline south of Saksun is famous for its high mountain peaks and steep birdcliffs studded with *gjáir* and caves where seals used to breed. Numerous *drangar*, the highest being Heygadrangur (144 m), stand watch over the all but inaccessible coast, and demonstrate how forcefully the elements erode it. A boat trip along the narrow channel between the *drangar* and the coast is a fascinating and unforgettable experience. The current can sometimes make it difficult to round the promontory of Múlin into Vestmannasund.

Vestmanna has some 1,300 inhabitants and is thus, after the Tórshavn area, the most densely populated *bygd* in Streymoy. Its amphitheatrical position around one of the best natural harbours in the islands is exceptionally beautiful. Ships enter through a narrow but rather deep channel into a circular basin, several square kilometres in extent, which is deep enough for ships of ten metres draught. It is a perfectly enclosed and protected haven, which has served as a winter anchorage for fishing boats and has also been well placed for vessels seeking refuge from gales in the Atlantic.

Vestmanna was also a good place for farming, as it faces south. The old farm of Heygargarður passed from father to son in a direct line for nearly four centuries. Now much of the *bøur* has been taken over for housing, and only two of the original eight king's farms still exist. The sea has long been the crucial factor in the economic life of Vestmanna, which from the beginning took a lead in the fishing industry. Among the pioneers were the *kongsbóndi* Olavur á Heygum, who also set up as a shipowner, and Jógvan í Innistovu – or Vestmanna-Jógvan as he was popularly known – a well-known trawler skipper who learned the techniques of trawling in Grimsby, where he was known as Faroe-Jack.

Kvívík, on the other hand, has no natural harbour, but is exposed to the full force of the waves. Even so, it was an ancient settlement, as the excavated farmhouses on the beach show. When a house was being built near the shore in 1877, the first artefacts were found, and then in 1941, when the house was added to, further finds were made. Excavation followed. The site has been referred to as Niðri í Toft, but no local tradition of houses on the beach existed. The southern parts of the houses have been lost to the sea, indicating that the land has sunk or been eroded by the sea over the centuries; in fact the site may have been abandoned because of the encroachment of the sea.

The minister of North Streymoy has traditionally lived in Kvívík, in the lovely old vicarage which is known as Kirkjuteig. An annex farm at Kjalnes in Kollafjørður has been part of the living. The vicarage was moved to Kvívík in 1667, but the present house was built in the nineteenth century. The garden was for long a showplace: 'Beneath lies the village, its gloom only brightened by the green grass on its house-tops and by a solitary patch of colour – the pastor's garden, in which a border of yellow flag-flowers, a rare exotic in the Faroes, are now in their prime' (Nelson Annandale). The minister Jørgen Landt planted a lot of trees during his period in residence, but these were cut down by one of his successors, who wanted them for firewood!

A fairly broad river runs through Kvívík. Further up the slope, where the river falls in cascades, there once stood several water mills. One of these has been preserved; it is a Norse-type mill where the wheel revolves horizontally and turns the stone direct. The vicarage stood on the eastern side of the river. High up on the slope, at á Hellu, lived the one king's farmer. The main part of the *bygd,* however, was west of the river. Large stones, placed at intervals in the river, made it possible to cross from one part of the *bygd* to another.

Occasionally the river flooded while people were at church, and they had to wait in the vicarage for it to fall enough for them to cross. Today there are bridges across the river, and a lot of house-building has taken place, as the population has grown in the last decades. But many of the old houses have been preserved and help to make Kvívík one of the most charming *bygdir* in the islands.

In the old days the path southwards from Kvívík was the notorious Klivagøta – the climbing path – which was replaced many years ago by a wide modern road. At Stykkið above the road a cluster of modern houses has one of the most panoramic views in Faroe. Stykkið has also been known as Solitude, as this was the name given by a Kvívík minister to the house he built himself there some time in the early nineteenth century.

The *bygd* of Leynar has one of the few sandy beaches in Faroe; formerly it was much used for ferrying people across to Vágar even though the heavy surf often made the launching of a boat very difficult. Leynar lies at the end of the long valley of Kollfjarðardalur, which goes right across Streymoy and has therefore always been an important route. Leynavatn is a good place for salmon fishing, and in the 1970s ladders were built in the river Leynará to help the salmon ascend into the lake. The *bygd* is snugly placed along the canyon-like river, at the foot of the 621-metres-high Sátan, so named because its rounded top has a certain resemblance to a haystack. Small houses used by the Leynar people when pirates threatened can still be seen on Sátan.

The small *bygd* of Skælingur seems to have had an early settlement, as the remains of houses have been found. As yet these have not been excavated. In 1706 the *bygd* was the site of a grim incident: a brother and a sister were beheaded because of their incestuous relationship. This was the first and only time that a sentence of death was passed and carried out in all the long period when the old Norwegian law applied in the islands; no pardon was ever given for such a sin. The *bygd* lies on a green slope at the foot of Skælingsfjall, which rises above dramatic buttresses of basalt. The path along the coast to Úti á Fløtum passes many strange basaltic formations, so it is especially rewarding from a geological point of view.

A large smolt farm has grown up in Úti á Fløtum in the course of the last few years, using the river water to generate electricity for daily operations. Norðradalur is a large plain surrounded by high grass-covered mountains on three sides. The landing conditions are at best difficult and for a large part of the year impossible. One of the king's farms was for many years part of the stipend of the South Streymoy minister, and was reserved for ministers' widows. In the 1930s work started on the clearing of a *traðir* farm, that is a farm with no rights in the *hagi*, high up on the northern slope. At that time there was nothing but a bridle-path winding its way down the mountain. The modern farm, with a byre for forty head of cattle, was built in stone taken from the nearby mountain Núgvan, a back-breaking effort with an impressive result.

Jens N. Reinert manages the big smolt farm in Norðadalur, Streymoy

The old bygd of Velbastaður has well-run farms

The farm in Syðradalur was also church property for a long time; the first ministers after the Reformation are known to have lived there. A walk from Tórshavn to Syðradalur offers a beautiful view of Koltur and Vágar. The old *bygd* of Velbastaður boasts well-run farms. The story of the Velbastaður brothers belongs to the beginning of the eighteenth century. There were eight of them, good fishermen who excelled in a *grind*. When their boat was stuck in the boat-house and they could not move it no matter how much they pushed and pulled, they sent for the wise Guttormur í Múla, who understood some of life's mysteries. His advice to the brothers was not to try too hard, as if the boat did not budge it was because the *huldufólk* had left their boat there too. There was no point in going out anyway as it would be a stormy day – the *huldufólk* knew everything about the weather.

Rounding the Kirkjubønes has often been hard going, and passing along the eastern coast of Tórshavn has not been much easier. Hoyvíkshólmur is a famous breeding place for thousands of Arctic terns. The cliffs of Kyrberg are almost perpendicular and formed of basaltic columns. At Sund there used to be one of the most beautiful and historic old farms in Faroe, but it was wantonly ruined for an industrial development that never really materialized. The *bygd* of Kaldbak has so far escaped too much change, with the houses scattered in *býlingar* inside the *bøur* dyke. The church is one of the oldest of the traditional churches, and its ornamented wooden interior is lovely. Kaldbak has been isolated, and a way of getting messages through from other *bygdir* was to stand on the opposite side of the fjord and call across, so the place where people would call from is called Kallanes.

According to a nineteenth-century writer Kjalnes in Kollafjørður, with its lovely view of the fjord and of Eysturoy, is one of the most wonderful places to live in the Faroe Islands. The many original *býlingar* have become one large *bygd* known as Kollafjørður, this being originally the name of just the area around the church. One of the routes up Skælingsfjall begins at Oyrareingir.

At the farm of Niðri í Heyggi in Hósvík there was, according to tradition, a small fortification with a *hof* or pagan place of worship. When Christianity was introduced the *hof* was replaced with a church, which was in use for some time after the Reformation. An older name for Hósvík was Tórsvík, and it seems reasonable to connect this name with the *hof*. At við Áir the former whaling station, which was in operation until the 1960s, is now a government-run research station for fish farming. Apart from smolt breeding, experiments are carried out with the farming of halibut and with putting marked salmon into the open sea.

Hvalvík has probably got its name because the bay has been a good place for beaching whales. The *bygd* is separated from Streymnes by the estuary of the river Storá, the largest in the islands and a good place for salmon fishing. The church in Hvalvík was built in 1829, and is thus the oldest of the traditional wooden churches. The pulpit is believed to date from 1609, and origi-

nally came from the old Tórshavn church, which French pirates broke into *The octagonal church* and plundered in 1677. Scars in the woodwork are said to have been made by *in Haldarsvík is the* their swords. From Hvalvík an interesting route crosses the hills to *only one of its kind* Leynavatn, and both the strange mountain Sneis (745 m) and Ørvisfelli (784 *in Faroe* m) with its panoramic view make interesting climbs.

At the narrowest point in Sundini, the narrow flood-like sound between Streymoy and Eysturoy, is the bridge known as Brúgvin um Streymin, which transformed communications in central Faroe when it was first built. The small *bygd* of Langasandur was first settled in 1839 with public support, by people from Hvalvík who originally named it Nybo. The road passes the lovely, 140-metre-high waterfall Fossá, which tumbles over several *hamrar* before it falls into Sundini.

The *bygd* of Haldarsvík, or just Vík, lies at the foot of a rather steep *bøur* built up in terraces along the side of the hill. The houses cluster around the bay, which is a good anchorage, and right in the middle of the *bygd* the river Kluftá forms a small waterfall. The octagonal church is the only one of its kind in Faroe, and dates from 1856. The altar painting portrays the

Annunciation to the Virgin Mary, and was painted by Niels Kruse of Eiði in 1932. Close to the church stands a memorial to all those who have perished at sea. It was made by the sculptor Fridtjof Joensen; such memorials can be seen in many *bygdir* and bear witness to how close the islanders have always been to sudden death.

Today a road with a view towards Risin and Kellingin takes us around the coast to Tjørnuvík. It mainly follows the old track. 'The path over land to Tjørnuvík is in some places to the north very difficult, as it lies on the edges or on the slope of a high cliff facing the sea, and in some places it is so slippery that it is difficult to gain a foothold and to stumble will cost you your life' (Jørgen Landt). Until the coming of the modern road the *bygd* of Tjørnuvík was a world apart. Surrounded by high mountains and facing the Atlantic, the sound of the surf would drown any other sound.

Twice, in 1633 and again in 1868, the *bygd* was virtually ruined by rockslides. The steep slope behind the houses has been fenced in by stone dykes and produces good crops of turnips and potatoes. Indeed Tjørnuvík has been known for its good soil for a long time, as excavations and pollen analyses have shown settlement in the Viking Age, and possibly even earlier. It is also a good place for fishing, even though in an onshore wind the heavy surf makes landing dangerous. As the *bygd* was isolated but had good fishing in the vicinity, Tjørnuvík was used in the eighteenth century as a place of exile for women sentenced for immoral behaviour according to paragraph 6-13-13 of Christian V's Norwegian law of 1687.

The coastline around Tjørnuvík is full of caves. Tradition will have us believe that halfway to Haldarsvík a deep cave goes right through the mountains all the way to Saksun. Off Streymoy's most northerly point just west of Tjørnuvík is a strangely-shaped cliff known as Stakkur (133 m), on which a few sheep are grazed. Close by lies the small bay of Sjeyndir, where all those who fail to marry are said to end up, 'in total isolation and a towering landscape' in the words of Jørgen-Frantz Jacobsen, who spent a happy day there during his last visit to his native islands. In *The Farthest Shore,* written just before his death, he describes this little-known part of Streymoy:

> Down from the mountain edge comes the river. Its clear water forms an unbroken drop of some 1,800 feet down the valley's grass-grown slope, singing a great song which weaves itself into the solitude. It is the pulse of the place, making Sjeyndir live. From the sea its gliding ribbon of water is apparent. One wants to drink from its fresh water and rest in the sweet grass by its bank. And one reflects that perhaps the unmarried are not always so joyless.

22
NÓLSOY

The tall lighthouse at the southern end of Nólsoy is usually the first landmark to greet the marine traveller to the Faroe Islands. Its long white flashes are meant for ships in the open sea. Built in 1893, it is the largest and most powerful lighthouse in the islands, but by no means the oldest, as even in 1782 the Royal Trade Monopoly had one built on Stongin, the northern part of Nólsoy. Another, smaller light at Borðan helps guide the ships up the Nólsoyarfjørður to the capital. There the sea becomes smoother, as Nólsoy serves effectively as a breakwater, protecting Tórshavn from the worst of the easterly wind.

The long and narrow island of Nólsoy is very much a part of the view from Tórshavn. Although not in itself dramatic, Nólsoy provides the inhabitants of the capital with a stage on which all the natural lights and colours can play.

> Sunrise on a winter's morn, with high, bloodshot cumulus or feathery fronds of cirrus heaped above the low isthmus; moonrise on a winter's night, a scarlet lantern poised above the village, and the island's snowgleaming satin form clearer than during the light of day … But of all occasions, perhaps the most memorable were those long, light summer evenings when, by some trick of slanting light as the sun slipped at last behind Kirkjubøreyn, the whole length of the island's rocky face changed in a trice from the drab grey-brown of the basalt to a delicate rosy pink.
>
> *Kenneth Williamson*

The only *bygd* is situated on an isthmus that is only about 50 metres wide, and so low that during the winter and autumn gales the sea sometimes foams right across it. Thus the stream through the *bygd* changes direction with the flow of the tide. The land on both sides of the isthmus is cultivated, but the soil is peaty and rather thin. The northern part of Stongin is low and rounded, and almost completely under cultivation.

A striking feature in the harbour is the archway made from the jaw-bones of a sperm-whale found drifting in the sea and then towed in to Nólsoy. Behind this archway a bench with a ringside view of the harbour is known as

Nólsoy. The meeting place of the men of the bygd *with a ringside view of the harbour*

the meeting place of the men of the *bygd*. Close by is the row of houses built together that is known as Niðasta Lon. For several generations these houses, which individually are called Búð, Nyggjastova, Magnúsarstova and Gortrastova, have, along with the seat where the men's parliament gathers, been characteristic of the harbour area and have added to its charm. Around this part of the *bygd* the houses are built close together, and the streets are narrow. Today some of these houses are used only as second homes, and the Nólsoy people have built new houses. The fillet factory was built in 1979 as a joint venture in which almost every household in the island owns shares, and the fish is bought from two Nólsoy vessels.

In Korndalur, in the southern infields of the *bygd*, is a cluster of old foundations, believed to be the remains of houses that were left when for some reason the *bygd* was moved northwards to the bay. The houses lie close together; they are made of earth and stone and are relatively well preserved. So far only one site has been examined, without much result. According to tradition this village was built after the Black Death. The most striking of the ruins is known as the Princess's House, where the spring that was once led through it can still be seen. The princess referred to was said to be the daughter of a king of Scotland; according to local tradition James II (1437–60), but this seems impossible. The princess fell out with her father and fled with her husband and child to Faroe, where she settled in Korndalur on Nólsoy. Once her father came to see her, landing by the boat-houses in Hálgutoftir. She went to meet him, held the child out to him and told him to kill her and the child before he harmed her husband. This placated the king, and they are said to have become reconciled before he left Nólsoy again. Many Nólsoy families claimed descent from the princess, and it is said that there were those who gave themselves airs on that account.

The highest point in Nólsoy is Eggjarklettur (371 m), which is very steep on the east side but slopes more gently in the west and is easily climbed. Attempts have been made to make industrial use of the copper found in the horizontal tuff layers. Nólsoy is considered an interesting island by geologists, because most rocks and minerals characteristic of the Faroe Islands can be found here. The long slope of Eggjarklettur ends in a marshy area which stretches southwards for several miles. The southern end of Nólsoy is green and quite fertile. Close by the large rock of Hellan is the famous cave of Borðholið, which tunnels through the island and can be negotiated by a boat in calm weather.

At the site known as í Kassunum, on the green eastern slope of Tjørnunes about 100 metres above sea level, can be seen the remains of a Viking settlement. The houses lie on a plateau that seems to have been cultivated; the site is fenced in by stone dykes. One of the houses, consisting of one large and one small room, has been excavated and several clay utensils were found. The main entrance faces Nólsoyarfjørður. On the whole the site does not differ much from other settlements of the same period, but it is uncertain whether this was a summer farm or worked the whole year round. Scholars seem to consider this to be a permanent settlement, which suggests that the pattern of the compact *bygdir* is a later development.

The steeply sloping scree of Urðin on the east side is a favourite haunt of sea-birds, among them Manx shearwaters and storm petrels. Puffins have their hollows here, and at one time big catches of them were made every year. The fulmar colony has increased here as everywhere else, and just north of Urðin lives a fine colony of rock-doves. Nólsoy is a natural place for birds, and it is not surprising that it should also be the home of ornithologists. Around 1900 the fisherman and bird specialist Peter F. Petersen also set up as a taxidermist, and later his son Niels Fr. Petersen, better known as Niels á Botni, took over from him. Today the business is carried on by Jens-Kjeld Jensen.

'The inhabitants of this island are distinguished by their industry; the careful tending of their sheep, and the neat and proper handling of their peat

Taxidermist, Jens-Kjeld Jensen, in his workroom on Nólsoy

moors are unusual in the Faroe Islands.' This was written by Jørgen Landt in his description of Faroe in 1800. Though peat is no longer used, the islanders' ways of owning, herding, breeding, shearing and slaughtering sheep have hardly changed at all since Landt's days, nor has the number of sheep – the total flock still consists of 900 animals. The pasture has always been intensively used, even to the extent of lowering sheep by rope on to the ledges of the steep sides of Skúvafjall.

Nólsoyar-Páll, or Poul Poulsen Nolsøe as he was called in Danish, is the best-known and perhaps the most extraordinary man to have come from Nólsoy. Born in 1766 into a large and gifted family, he initiated the struggle against the stultifying Trade Monopoly, and had to fight two battles: one against the power of corrupt officials and the other against the passivity and lack of initiative among his own countrymen.

Of formal education he had little, but when he was quite young he began his training at the bailiff's office in Tórshavn. One day when he was home in Nólsoy his brother Jákup asked him how he was doing, and Páll complained that he would rather be at sea or in the bird cliffs than doing sums in an office, 'but one thing is for sure,' he said, 'one day they will know that Páll has learned to write.' He went away to America and worked as master on board ships there, and on his return found the girl he had left behind married to his younger brother Jógvan. He married another Nólsoy girl, who died after only two years of marriage. At that time he was working as a captain on board Monopoly ships. He got married again, to Marin Malena Ziska from Borðoy, and left the sea to become a king's farmer. It seems that no matter what Páll put his hand to, he was successful; he ran their farm at Myrkjanoyri in Klaksvík so well that he received a medal from the Royal Agricultural Society.

Still Páll could not altogether give up the sea. He bought the wreck of a ship that had beached at Hvalba in Suðuroy, and in 1802, together with others, he built the forty-ton schooner *Royndin Fríða* – the *Good Endeavour* – which is considered to be the first Faroese vessel. His years in America had made him into a seasoned man with the courage to oppose the petty tyranny of the Danish officials. He also saw clearly that as long as the Monopoly forbade the Faroese to own ships or go abroad on their own, they would be doomed to economic bondage. He told the officials, who grew nervous when they saw his ship, that it would only be used for inshore fishing, but a year later he took a cargo of coal from Hvalba to Bergen, and the officials were quick to complain to Copenhagen.

But Nólsoyar-Páll was quicker still; he went to Copenhagen himself and complained to Crown Prince Frederik about the misrule in Faroe. For a time everything went his way; there was even hope that the Monopoly might be abolished, but then Denmark-Norway became involved in the Napoleonic Wars. Against all obstacles Nólsoyar-Páll kept on carrying vital cargoes of corn to the Faroe Islands, until his ship and crew disappeared at sea in 1809, when he was still only forty-two years old. Nobody knows what happened, but Faroe people have always been convinced that somehow the officials got the better of him.

Nólsoyar-Páll lived close to the old Norse ideals; he was a man of action but he also excelled as a satirical poet. His verse is the weapon of the politically oppressed, and in it reading between the lines becomes a fine art. His best-known work is *Fuglakvæði,* where he compares the officials to birds of prey. It is cast in the form of the old ballads, and it is said that he walked back and forth for a whole night composing the verse and dictating it to his brother Jákup. A servant girl was listening, and she sang what she remembered of the ballad at the next dance-meeting. It spread like wildfire, and also reached the ears of those who were caricatured. Most of them were easily recognized: the commandant of the Skansin fort in Tórshavn was presented as a falcon and the *sýslamaður* of Streymoy as a crow.

Fuglin í fjøruni	The bird on the beach
við sínum nevi reyða,	with its red beak,
mangt eitt djór og høviskan fugl	many an animal and courteous bird
hevir hann greitt frá deyða,	has he saved from death,
fuglin í fjøruni.	the bird on the beach.

This is the refrain, as 'the bird on the beach with his red beak' regularly comes to the rescue of others. He is the *tjaldur,* or oyster catcher, and probably Nólsoyar-Páll saw himself in this role.

Nólsoy kept up its shipbuilding tradition for a long time and just before the end of the Monopoly a fifty-ton sloop, till then the largest ship in Faroe, was built and owned by *nólsingar.* Thus Nólsoy has left its mark on the maritime history of the islands.

23

HESTUR AND KOLTUR

The small islands of Hestur and Koltur form an almost straight line that runs parallel to the south-western coast of Streymoy, thus serving to protect the *bygdir* of Kirkjubøur, Velbastaður and Syðradalur from the worst onslaught of the sea. The rocky coasts are natural barriers, but waves from the west have occasionally flooded the lower part of Koltur.

Administratively these islands have for some time belonged together. In 1920 they were made a separate parish under Streymoy *sýsla*. The minister lives in Tórshavn, and preaches in the Hestur church once a month. In Koltur there are the remains of an old chapel, which was closed down after the Reformation. Later the Koltur people had to cross turbulent waters to go to church in Hestur, or perhaps at Kirkjubøur.

The story of the Koltur boy Magnus who swam to Hestur illustrates how strong the current is in Kolturssund as well as how the islanders have learned over the ages to make the best of it. Magnus was courting a girl in Hestur against her father's will, so they would meet secretly in a small cove at the northern point. Very cleverly making use of the tidal current, Magnus would swim south on the ebb tide, which would take him directly to Hestsboði. Then he would swim back to Kolturstangi six hours later on the flood tide. This went on for some time until her father found out and waited for him with an axe, saying he would kill him if he came ashore. Magnus had to turn back and swim against the current. He was never heard of again.

Rasmus Effersøe, who wrote the first Faroese plays, based his play *Magnus* on this story. A true romantic, Effersøe felt sorry for the young couple and let the young lover be saved. Magnus manages to hold on to a drifting log for a while, until he is picked up by pirates. However, a Danish frigate soon puts paid to them, and Magnus comes home to get his girl in a gloriously happy ending.

Hestur

The inhospitable west coast of Hestur with its deep *gjáir* and high stacks is one long bird cliff, with large colonies of many species, but especially guillemot. Bird-catching used to be important here and in some places relatively easy, but about two hundred years ago the best cliffs fell into the sea. The erosion is great, so that the ledges are not safe, and from time to time rock falls still occur. It is difficult to climb the cliffs from below because of the strong surf. The western rocks were the haunt of the great auk; in Hestur the last of this now extinct species was caught in about 1800.

Hestur is a small island, some five kilometres long and one kilometre wide, but the scenery is varied. The east side slopes steeply down to the coast, and it is necessary to know the paths to get to the *heyggjur,* or high area. Reaching the top of the cliff, we find a wonderland awaiting us. To the north rise the twin tops of Eggjarrók and Múlin, which are both 421 metres high, and to the south an intensely green plateau slopes down to an area of marshland and little lakes, full of trout. One of these lakes is called Fagradalsvatn – the lake in the lovely valley. In Hælur open fertile land slopes down almost to the sea. Conditions seem excellent for farming, and it comes as no surprise that there was once a settlement here. It was abandoned so long ago that there is no tradition in the island to tell us when and why it happened; probably the only harbour of Lendingargjógv proved impossible to rely on.

The *bygd* of Hestur has a better harbour and is also more protected from the sea. It is long and narrow because of the steep slope behind it; set at an angle of between 20 and 30 degrees the land is difficult to cultivate. For several months during the winter the sun never rises above the mountain. Nevertheless the *bygd* has seen prosperous times. As so often happened, the land declined in importance as the men began going away on fishing boats for long periods at a time. But in Hestur the local fishing has also been important. In Hestfjørður some saithe can be caught, but most of the fishing is done on the west side, where there are usually large catches of cod to be made. But these are dangerous waters, and in 1919 two boats were lost; their crews represented a third of the male population of Hestur.

> On our way we called at Hestur. Nearly all had lost their men either on the cliffs, which are particularly dangerous at Hestur, or in a calamity which happened a short time ago. A boat of the village coming back in rough weather was missing with five men on board. She was supposed to be overladen. Another boat with seven men went in search of them, but they too never returned. Every house in Hestur is a house in mourning. The dignity, the tragedy, and the heroism of labour are nowhere better to be seen than in the Faroes.
>
> *G. H. Harris*

Led by Johan W. Niclasen, who has been the mayor of Hestur for more than thirty years, the people of the *bygd* are trying to ward off depopulation, the blight of small islands. The swimming hall was built in 1974 with the help of international youth organizations. For people who have their daily work at sea learning to swim is important. Another project is the new harbour, which has taken thirteen years to plan. Combined with the new ferry harbour between Kirkjubøur and Velbastaður a modern pier and breakwater will make it possible to fillet and freeze the fish in Hestur. This will provide work for the girls too, and make it possible for them to stay in their home island.

Koltur

The beautiful and strikingly-shaped Koltur is the second smallest of the islands that have been under cultivation; only Stóra Dímun with its one farm is smaller. Its highest point is the monumental cone-shaped peak of Kolturshamar (478 m). Rising steeply and intensely green out of the sea, it dominates any view of the island. The west side of Koltur is one precipitous cliff wall running the whole length of the island. At the foot of Kolturshamar the island narrows into a low isthmus of fertile farmland above a sandy beach. The southern part is rocky, with the gently-rounded hill of Fjallið rising to 101 metres.

There is of course a story to explain how Koltur got its characteristic profile. There was once a giant who thought it a shame that many of the Faroe islands were so small, so he took it upon himself to do something about it. He had finished with Suðuroy, Sandoy, Vágar, and Eysturoy, and set about making Koltur part of Streymoy. The giant took hold of the north end but Koltur refused to budge. He pulled and pushed but the only result was a big hump in the north end. That is how it came about that a stubborn person used to be known as a *koltur.* It seems that Koltur people have also had a reputation for being rather aloof, just as people who sat whispering among themselves were sometimes rebuked for being *koltursmenn.*

The *bygd* of Koltur lies along the east side, where the island is at its lowest. There are two *býlingar,* each of which has two farms. The southern *býlingur* is Heimi í Húsi and the northern one is Norðuri í Gerði, and they are connected by a paved path. The southern *býlingur* has an old-fashioned appearance because of the many small buildings used for a variety of purposes, and is therefore of great cultural interest. All around the buildings and the *bøur* runs an old stone and earth dyke. The land has kept its characteristic division into *teigar,* long, narrow strips running parallel across the slope, following the contours of the landscape. This is how the land used to be worked all over Faroe, and only in Koltur is the *teigalendi* still intact. As there are now no longer any people living in Koltur, it may be preserved as a kind of agricultural museum of the old ways of cultivation.

Koltur used to be known as a good place for growing corn, and people would even come from other islands to get seed corn. To keep the land so

The beautiful and striking shape of Koltur

fertile took a lot of effort. As the western side of the island was so low, the sea would at times wash right over the land, necessitating the gathering of much seaweed for manure. The number of sheep allowed was only 166 so that, like their neighbours across Kolturssund, the Koltur people had to supplement their diet by fishing. Bird-catching was at one time important, but the guillemot, which used to be caught in large numbers, has for some time been scarce. Another drawback was the lack of fuel. Originally people would go to Syðradalur in Streymoy for peat, but then they had to start going to Skopun instead, and that meant a long and difficult voyage.

Still, in the 1950s there were twenty-one people living on four farms, and with seventeen cows the island was a net exporter of dairy produce. At that time people would come to Koltur from all over Faroe to have a boat built, as the king's farmer Niclas í Koltri was the most sought after and most highly respected boat-builder and craftsman in all the islands. With their neigh-bours in Hestur the islanders shared a teacher, who would spend six days out of every month with them. Sometimes he might be weatherbound for two or three weeks in the wintertime.

A fine knitting-wool produced on the island was known as *kolturstógv.* Koltur was also known for the clay that could be found in between the basalt layers in the hill. Mixed with the white of sea-birds' eggs to make it more workable, it was used for a kind of domestic pottery known as *koltursdøllir.* 'In the northern mountain there is a hard green clay, which the inhabitants mould with their hands and without a wheel into small chunky pots, without glazing, which they fire and then use for boiling milk' (Landt). At Heimi í Húsi lies a stone known as a *gandasteinur,* or troll stone, which it is not wise to move. Some young men once defied this warning, but they put it back soon enough after their boat overturned in the surf, and they only just made it ashore.

24

VÁGAR

This is the third largest of the Faroe Islands, but strangely it is not mentioned in *Færeyinga Saga,* and very little is known of its early history. It is named for the *vágar* or fjordlike bays that are characteristic of the island. The scenery contrasts strikingly between the idyllic and the awe-inspiring. This island has it all: lakes, streams, broad valleys with green patches of cultivated land, as well as black, volcanic areas with bird cliffs and wild crags. The archipelago of the south-western coast, with the island of Mykines as a dramatic backdrop, is unique.

Sørvágsvatn, or Leitisvatn, is about seven kilometres long and one kilometre wide and is the largest lake in Faroe. It pours into the sea through the magnificent Bøsdalafossur, 100 metres long with a sheer fall of 30 metres into the sea. The high, fierce seas of winter roll all the way into the end of the lake, bringing saltness into the water. The valley of Klovin, which is shut in on both sides by rather high rocks, connects Sørvágsvatn with Fjallavatn, the other large lake of Vágar. At 100 metres above sea level Fjallavatn is a mountain lake, and it empties into a stream which runs down the mountain side and falls into the Atlantic as Reipsáfossur.

As both lakes are rich in trout they have long been a favourite haunt of sports fishermen, especially the British. Vágar is not among the best bird islands, but for the experienced field walker the northern coastal area offers beauty and solitude. Two abandoned *bygdir* are found on the now empty north coast. At Víkar there was at one time a small settlement. The pasture there is very rich, and in the summertime it is perhaps the most beautiful place in Faroe. But this could not compensate for the isolation and bleakness of life there in the wintertime, and so it was left. In the north-east we can still see the *bygd* of Slættanes; from a distance it looks like a thriving village, until we realize that there are no people about. It was abandoned as late as 1964 because it was considered too difficult to connect it to the electric grid.

The southern part of Vágar has much in common with Sandoy, and it is here that we find the main settlements. In the old days most of the traffic with Streymoy would go between Kvívík and the small inlet of Fútaklettur, where an old Nissen hut remains as a memory of wartime. The entrance to the underwater tunnel planned across Vestmannasund will be in this area. But since the road in 1965 was extended north to Oyrargjógv, the almost continuous ferry traffic from Vestmanna has come ashore at the pier there. The east coast along Vestmannasund is empty and inhospitable, cut through by numerous clefts.

Guarding the twin bays of Sandavágur and Miðvágur is the slim, 313-metre-high needle of Trøllkonufingur – the Witch's Finger. It is possible to land at the foot of the Witch's Finger, but as it is exposed to every wind and current sweeping round this south-eastern part of Vágar, it is not often wise to do so. Attempts to climb it are even rarer, and reputedly there has been only one success: in 1844 a young Faroese climbed to the top during a royal visit. He got safely down again, only to discover that he had left his glove on the summit. Exuberant at his initial success, he climbed back up to get his glove, but this time he lost his footing and was killed. However, there is no written record of this accident, and the whole story may be another legend.

The *bygd* of Sandavágur is historically as important as Kirkjubøur and Gøta. From 1555 until 1816 the farm of Steig was the seat of the Løgmaður, the highest authority in the islands. The first Løgmaður to live at Steig was Guttormur Andrasson, and how this came about is one of those old stories which have been told so many times that they take on the characteristics of a fairy tale. Sent to the king in Copenhagen to plead the cause of his father, the Løgmaður, Guttormur elegantly solved a knotty legal problem for the king, and in return was allowed to choose any farm in Faroe as the Løgmaður's seat. He chose Steig, which has had the reputation of being one of the best farms for growing cereals in all the islands.

Subsequent Løgmenn were also colourful characters. Among them is Jón Heinason, the elder son of Heini Havreki. He is remembered for ruling that all women who had children before the proper time had elapsed since the wedding should 'bera rót', that is carry a wooden collar around their neck as though they were dangerous bulls. Ironically the first person this rule applied to was Heinason's own daughter, but he was consistent. She was in fact not only the first but also the last person subjected to such a treatment. Jón Heinason later lost his office as Løgmaður, probably because his half-brother Magnus Heinason fell out with the authorities in Copenhagen. But even without Steig he was the greatest landowner in Faroe at the time.

Another legendary Løgmaður is Sámal Petersen, known as 'Gamli Løgmaður' – the Old Lawman – as he was in office for almost fifty years, from 1706 to 1755. He was famous for his knowledge of sheep and for having six beautiful daughters. According to another old story a ship full of French pirates came into Sandavágur one Easter morning around 1715. The skipper became infatuated with Anna Margreta Sámalsdóttir, the youngest and fairest of them all, and refused to leave without her. He sent two boats ashore, one filled with liquor for a wedding-feast, the other with barrels of tar to set the village on fire, and Sámal could choose which to have. But Sámal outsmarted the skipper of the *fransaskip*– the French, or pirate ship – by hiding his daughter in a peat-stack and sending for Peder Arrheboe, the minister of Vágar, who was said to know the Black Art. He drove the pirates out to sea, and the people of Sandavágur were left with the liquor and the tar, and both were put to good use. The cause of it all, the fair Anna Margreta, later married Arrheboe's successor as minister of Vágar.

The farm of Steig was in 1822 divided into eight small farms and sold at auction. Jørgen Frants Hammershaimb, the last of the Løgmenn, was still at Steig when his son Venceslaus Ulricus Hammershaimb was born there in 1819. He worked for many years as a minister in Nes in Eysturoy, and is recognized as the father of Faroese letters. He collected and wrote down ballads and folklore, and after making a thorough study of the language spoken in the various islands he worked out a standard form for the Faroese literary language, which he was the first to use. In 1919, on the centenary of his birth, a large memorial stone was raised in Sandavágur, his home village.

Inside the tall wooden church of 1916 there is another interesting memorial stone. It is a rune stone with the inscription: *'þorkæl onondarsun austmadr af ruhalande bygde dena stad fyst'* – 'Torkjell Onundarson, an easterner from Rogaland, built first in this place'. The stone, which is believed to date from *c.* 1200, was found in 1917 at Eingjartoftum in Sandavágur, and later a small settlement was discovered close by. The farmer who found the stone meant to break it to pieces, but he was busy, and the stone just lay there and was washed clean by the rain. One day a young boy carrying a heavy load of manure was passing, and after sitting down on the large flat stone to rest his legs he noticed the inscription. He called in the local poet Mikkjal á Ryggi, who could read runes and knew at once that an important find had been made.

The bay of Miðvágur makes a good anchorage for ships, but is perhaps better known for all the *grind* (whales) that have been caught here. The *grind* are easily enticed into the bay, and when at ebb tide the sea recedes they are left stranded on the sand. Miðvágur is in fact considered the best place in Faroe for catching whales, and stories are still told of the great *grind* of 1899, when 1,500 whales were killed in the bay. In the old days the men would drop whatever they were doing and rush to the boats when whales were sighted in Vágafjørður, but the women knew from experience that they need not start baking the bread or putting the food on to cook for the men until the whales had been driven past the point known as Presttangi.

In the old days the island Ting would meet at Miðvágur, which has always been an important centre. Today it is the largest settlement in Vágar. The north side of the bay has taken the weight of housing development, but even so it is possible to see the division of the old *býlingar* of Hús, Ryggur, Kirkjar and Eirikstoftir. One of the sights of Miðvágur used to be the botanical garden laid out at Ryggi by the *kongsbóndi* Hans Kristoffer Joensen. It was the work of a lifetime, begun around the middle of the nineteenth century when he was a young boy. There were many rare plants, and their fate was uncertain, as they were completely at the mercy of the climate.

> The garden lies on a slope facing the sea, and when the great sou'easters rage, I wonder how any mortal plant can survive. But even when mourning some damage done, I remember what charm this sharp decline gives the garden, with the lovely tints of sea, sand and sky as a background for the blossoms – more than any garden I know, it is an epitome of the life of the people.
> *Elizabeth Taylor*

As William Heinesen's grandmother came from Ryggi, he spent many of his childhood summers there, playing in an enchanted garden. But later *kongs-bøndir* lacked interest in the garden, and today there is not much to show for the life work of Hans Kristoffer Joensen.

The childhood home of the writer Mikkjal á Ryggi (1879–1956) has been bought by the local community to serve as a museum for local writers. Mikkjal á Ryggi was inspired by the movement for self-government and wrote a number of songs about political freedom for the islands, but much of his poetry is about Faroese nature and life in general. He worked as a teacher in Bøur and Gásadalur.

High up above Miðvágur lies the small croft of Kálvalið, which is now another local museum. It is a very old house, which belonged to the parish church for 300 years. For much of this time it served as a dower farm for the widows of ministers. The best known of them is Beinta, who has become legendary, not just for her own exploits, but more so for being the model for Jørgen-Frantz Jacobsen's famous novel *Barbara*, which in 1939 was published posthumously in Copenhagen. In this novel eighteenth-century life as it was lived in Vágar and Tórshavn is colourfully described, and the people of that time come wonderfully alive.

The Barbara of fiction is an enchantress, who may be wilful but draws men to her irresistibly through her spontaneous joy in life. The Beinta of legend comes across as both a witch and a bitch; she is beautiful, but mean. Her real name was Bendte Christina Broberg (1668–1752), and she first married Jonas Jonassen, the minister of Viðareiði, and lived with him in the manse of Onagerði. He was much older than Beinta, and when she tired of him she made his first wife haunt him by putting earth from her grave under his pillow. After his death she became betrothed to the young minister at Nes in Eysturoy, but her meanness scared him off. Her second husband was Niels Aagard, the minister of Vágar, and at first he let her have her way in most things, as he was a peace-loving man, but that only seemed to make her worse. Once she tried to hit him with a heavy brass candlestick; she missed and hit a beam instead, and a large piece fell out of the foot of the candlestick.

Today this candlestick stands on the altar of Miðvágur church; it has been mended, but traces of the old damage can still be seen. At one time a male servant got so incensed with her behaviour to her husband that he ducked her in the urine tub – there used to be one at most farms, the urine being used for fulling the wool or for making soap. Till quite recently, many women swore by this soap as the best there was for washing their hair; such a tub can be seen by the door of the dower house at Kalvalið.

According to legend Beinta set her cap at the new minister of Vágar, Peder Arrheboe, from the moment he arrived. She tried to keep him away from the beauties in the Løgmaður's seat at Steig, but she could have saved herself the trouble, as he fell hopelessly in love with her at first sight. He married her in 1707, during his second winter in Vágar, and they had a long life together. He seems to have had bouts of madness, for which people blamed his wife. He fell out with one of the local farmers, and later at his funeral he made a travesty of the Lutheran burial ceremony when he threw earth on the grave and said, 'As a thief you lived, as a thief you died, and as a thief you will rise again.' Peder Arrheboe was defrocked for his behaviour towards this farmer, and strangely it was Beinta's erstwhile fiancé who presided at the ecclesiastical court that removed him from the living. Beinta and Peder Arrheboe spent the rest of their lives at a small croft in Sandavágur. The manse where Beinta lived with her minister husbands was called Jansagerði, and most of the land on the south side of the bay belonged to it. Today it is in ruins. A new and more centrally placed manse was built in 1921 on the other side of the bay.

The walk from Miðvágur across the hill to Vatnsoyrar is easy and gives a lovely view. Vatnsoyrar lies at the end of Sørvágsvatn in an area that used to be a marshy bog but has now been drained and reclaimed. The *bygd* was first built around 1920, and is the only settlement in Faroe without a view of the sea. The easiest route to the northern part of Vágar goes from Vatnsoyrar across a 113-metre-high watershed to Fjallavatn.

During the Second World War the British Royal Engineers carved a military airstrip out of the slope west of Vatnsoyrar. Vágar was the most strongly guarded military area in Faroe, with some 9,000 men stationed there at one time. Civilians had to carry identity cards, and visitors from other islands were not admitted without a permit from the security office of the military authorities. This embargo on Vágar lasted until 1944. This is the only part of Faroe where left-hand driving was ever permitted and practised because the roads in Vágar were completely dominated by British jeeps, but on missions to other islands the British had to keep to the right-hand side of the road.

Since the war the airstrip has been used for civil aviation. It has been modernized and extended, and a new terminal and a control tower have been built. Today not only do international companies have flights to Vágar, but the Faroese-owned Atlantic Airways have daily flights to and from

Copenhagen in modern British Aerospace-built jet aeroplanes. Annually some 100,000 passengers use the airport. The approach along Sørvágsfjørður is breathtaking, especially at night; on leaving the airport we get a no less spectacular view of Gásadalur and Mykines. However, in the summer the airport can sometimes be closed for days at a time because of fog.

Sørvágur lies at the end of a long and narrow fjordlike bay. This very picturesque *bygd* was until recently the largest settlement in Vágar, and is still an important trade and business centre. The quays are on the southern and more sheltered side of the bay, where once a whaling station used to be. The harbour is good but difficult to navigate. An irregular sea bottom scares off the whales, so that the beach is not suitable for *grindadráp*.

From Sørvágur the eastern part of Mykines is visible on clear days, and four times a week the *Súlan* brings the mail out to the island. But the Mykinesfjørður is notorious for its violent eddies and currents; in a storm the water will rise like a fountain five metres or more straight up in the air, and any small boat caught in such seas is doomed. Once the people of Mykines had to wait for their Christmas cards until around Easter time! The story goes that some years ago a convert to the Plymouth Brethren wanted to walk on the water from Sørvágur to Mykines, and if he was successful, to go on to Israel. The storm raged for days. A lot of people gathered on the beach at Sørvágur, some to pray and some to jeer. The local *sýslumaður* was frantic, but had no legal power to stop the attempt at a miracle. Instead he gravely asked the prophet whether he would be kind enough to take along the mail that had been accumulating in Sørvágur during the bad weather. The prophet did indeed drown, not in the sea but in laughter. He gave up the attempt.

At the entrance to the fjord lies Tindhólmur, with its characteristic profile of sharp peaks for which the island is named, *tindur* being the Faroese word for a peak. The southern side is a precipitous rock wall where the birds thrive; the northern side slopes steeply into the sea. According to tradition this island was once inhabited, but was left when parts of it were overwhelmed by the sea. Tindhólmur is separated from Vágar by a sound full of stacks known as Drangarnir. One of these has a hole in its base large enough for a boat to pass through in calm weather. Tindhólmur and the neighbouring island of Gáshólmur give very good pasture for the sheep which graze there.

Probably no other *bygd* in the islands has such an impressive view as Bøur. The archipelago off the western coast of Vágar looks like a playing-field for the giants of folklore; engrossed in their play they did not notice that the sun was rising, and so they turned into stone. Bøur is an idyllic cluster of old tarred and grass-roofed houses, and is protected by the high mountains behind it.

The road continues past Bøur to the site where a tunnel is planned to connect Gásadalur with the rest of Vágar. Gásadalur is for many reasons one of the most interesting places in the islands. It is the only village in Faroe

Drangarnir and Tindhólmur, Vágar

without a road, and thus exemplifies life as it used to be in most *bygdir* not so very long ago. The old mail route across the mountain from Bøur is still in use, and is the best approach for anyone seeing Gásadalur for the first time. Suddenly the mountain opens up, and 300 metres below, like a promised land, lies a colourful cluster of houses in an intensely green valley. The visual impact is stunning. The valley ends at a precipitous brink 100 metres above the sea; in crossing this brink the river Dalsá becomes a magnificent waterfall.

Landing is possible, but extremely difficult, at the small promontory known as Reyðastíggjatangi. Not only is the coast exposed to the Atlantic, but the waters there are full of reefs. To secure the boats it has been necessary to keep them out of the reach of the sea. They have therefore been winched up along a steep flight of 103 steps! But in spite of being a natural fortress Gásadalur has had its share of pirate attacks in the past. The pirates even tried to get the cattle up the track to Bøur, but had to give up. Most heavy goods are now transported by helicopter.

According to legend Gásadalur is named after a woman called Gæsa who around 1100 owned the large farm at Kirkjubøur. She had a richly decorated

stone church built there, said to have been dedicated to the Virgin Mary. Gæsa was hospitable to Gudmundur, who became the first bishop appointed to live and work in Faroe. He stayed with Gæsa at the farm and they got along well, but a young priest sent to assist him as he grew older thought it beneath the dignity of the Church to be beholden to a woman for its upkeep. On the pretext of her having eaten veal during Lent he had all of Gæsa's property expropriated by the Church. Gæsa had to go and stay with her nephew in Vágar. He gave her the *bygd* of Gásadalur, and the remains of the farm she built there can still be seen high up above the present *bygd*. Another less romantic explanation of the name is that it derives from *gás* for goose, as this part of Vágar used to be a great haunt of wild geese in the breeding season.

Gásadalur, the only bygd without a road. The postman on the mail route across the mountain to Bøur

Gásadalur is surrounded by the high mountains of western Vágar. For the intrepid a path goes north along the river and crosses the mountains in a pass between Árnafjall and Eysturtindur. There the path divides: one track goes down to Víkar, where the old fields are used as pasture for sheep by Gásadalur farmers, and the other goes east towards Fjallavatn. This area is a beautiful but lonely part of the island.

25

MYKINES

'And now you want to go out to Mykines! I can assure you that no minister has ever spent Christmas at Mykines. If you go there you'll risk the sea playing up and you won't get away from there for months! You must have taken leave of your senses!' But the minister of Vágar chooses to do what he considers his duty, and when the wind turns he becomes weatherbound on Mykines for eleven days. When he returns to the manse at Miðvágur, his wife has left him for another man. Thus the Faroese novelist Jørgen-Frantz Jacobsen works the weather and landing conditions on Mykines into the plot of his novel *Barbara*.

Despite modern transport, travelling to Mykines, the most westerly of the Faroe Islands, is still a matter of chance, as landing conditions for both boat and helicopter are extremely difficult. In a south-westerly wind as often as not the boat will not set off at all from Sørvágur in Vágar, but it can also happen that the boat has to turn back when it gets to Mykines because the surf is too strong or the wind is turning. Visitors who then decide to play safe by going to Mykines by helicopter the next day may find that in the meantime the fog has come down and it is impossible to land. In the old days the island might be cut off for weeks, even months, at a time, and it was not unusual for the Christmas mail to arrive sometime in March.

> One winter we were without connection with the outside world for seventy days. Food was getting very scarce by the time supplies finally reached us. There was also the Christmas mail, which was two months late. The relief was overwhelming. Mykines was swinging with joy and happiness.
>
> *Sámal Joensen-Mikines*

At one time a boat crew had to stay three and a half months in Sørvágur waiting for the right weather to return.

The coasts of Mykines are steep and inaccessible, with beautiful basalt formations. The island is surrounded by numerous holms and skerries, and underwater reefs make it difficult to approach it. The highest mountain is Knúkur (560 m), which on its west side slopes steadily through the valley of Djúpidalur down to Mykines *bygd*. On its north side, in the valley of

Korkadalur, are numerous caves said to compare in beauty with the caves of Staffa in the Hebrides. Like enormous organ pipes basalt columns rise here to some 60 metres. Because it looks rather like an ancient spruce forest it has been given the popular name of Steinskógir – the stone forest.

An old story explains how the forest became petrified. When men from the Faroe Islands were visiting King Olav Haraldsson the Saint, he asked them, after expressing concern that the amount coming in taxes from the Faroe Islands was so small, what grew there? The men told the King there was nothing but rock and stony ground. When King Olav heard this he said *'so verði, sum frá er sagt!'* – 'let it be as you have told me' – and it was at this moment, according to the story, that the forest in Mykines turned into stone.

Towards the east a narrow ridge called Oddarnir separates the two *botnar*, Kálvadalur and Borgardalur. Landings have sometimes been made at Álaberg in the north-eastern part of the island, but it is considered both difficult and dangerous to land there. The landing place at the extreme western end of the island is a cleft in the cliff, littered with jagged reefs. It is open to the Atlantic, so that even a moderate wind from the west or south makes landing impossible. There is almost always a surf, or *brim* as it is called, crashing against the cliffs, and it used to be said that the Mykines people talk so loudly, because they need to be heard above the sound of the sea.

From the landing place a steep staircase leads up past the old boat-houses

Mykines, the bygd

Mykines. The landing place at the extreme western end of the island is a cleft in the cliff, littered with jagged reefs

and green meadows to the *bygd* which lies snugly in a green hollow with a river running through it. According to tradition all the Mykines boats were lost on a stormy day in about 1690, leaving women and children only in the community. Men came from elsewhere, mostly Vágar, to join them. When the small white-painted church was built towards the end of the nineteenth century nearly 200 people lived in this *bygd*. In the 1960s the community was changing: there was as yet no electricity, but there was a school, a dance-hall, a swimming-pool, a hotel and three shops. Today the land is not farmed as it used to be, and the island is threatened by depopulation. People coming back for some weeks in summer keep up the houses, which have the spick and span impersonal look of second homes. But on the face of it the *bygd* has not changed much since 1932, when the famous picture known as 'Mykines Bygd' was painted by Sámal Joensen-Mikines.

It is perhaps not to be wondered at that the colours green and black, with touches of blood-red, dominate the paintings of Sámal Elias Joensen-Mikines, as to him they symbolized his native island of Mykines, to which he returned again and again. 'Without this sense of belonging and this world of images I would lose my identity both as an artist and as a human being'. When he was born in 1906 as one of the sons of an *óðalsbóndi* farmer, Mykines *bygd* was a closely-knit community where each season would bring its tasks, from lambing to puffin catching. Young Sámal had a pure singing voice and was only eight when he was first asked to sing at funerals.

Together with several grown-up men and women I went into the room of death, and with my hand on the chest of the corpse I said a prayer, and after that we sang. This was the only ceremony at a Mykines funeral. The deceased was never taken to church, but straight from home to the burial ground. On the way to the graveyard I walked in front of the coffin singing.

The genius of the young Sámal Elias, or Sámalias, Joensen was recognized, and in 1928 he began studying at the Academy of Art in Copenhagen. To the other students he was always known as Mikines, so that as time went by he began using the island name as part of his own. When he left the Academy he came back to the Faroe Islands, and spent much time at Mykines: 'My paradise, the island in the open sea, which is like a part of myself. The scenery and the colours here cannot be found anywhere else in the world'. At this time the island was a place of grief. In a shipping disaster off Iceland in 1933 some forty Faroese fishermen were lost, and of these nine came from Mykines. In such a small community the blow was crippling. Struck by this tragedy Joensen-Mikines painted his austere 'Sakn', a picture of three women who seem petrified with grief. It is not surprising that so many of his early pictures circle around the theme of death; among them 'Pieta' from 1937, which portrays a coffin with a dead man surrounded by dark, mourning figures.

On a high point known as Bønhúsberg, characteristically placed facing the sea just above the landing place in Mykines *bygd,* are the remains of a medieval chapel or *bønhús.* Excavations have shown that it was very well built as a 5 metre by 3.5 metre rectangle; the floor and the entrance area were paved with flat tiles. West of the *bøur,* by the path to the tiny island of Mykineshólmur, are traces of old cultivation in what is known as í Klingrugarði. Long narrow field strips are divided by low banks of earth, which on excavation have proved to be stone dykes made in a way that is reminiscent of the west coast of Ireland. There is no tradition or story connected with these fields, but it is possible that they were first cultivated by Irish monks as early as in the seventh century.

Today these fields are *lundaland* – land of the puffins. There are thirty species of birds nesting on Mykines, but no other bird is as numerous as the puffin. All along this western part of the island the ground is completely excavated by their burrows, and the smell of guano is overwhelming. The puffins sit in front of their holes, and do not seem to be worried by people walking quite close to them. Snoring sounds come from some burrows where the birds are comfortably asleep, but they are at risk of being rudely awakened and dragged out by the tool known as a *lundakrókur – a* puffin hook. Although it has been a set rule that no puffin carrying fish to its young should ever be taken, one rarely sees puffins returning from the sea with fish, and chicks lying dead outside the burrows are not an uncommon sight. Still, the number of puffins has always fluctuated, and there have been catches of as many as 60,000 puffins one year and only 10,000 the next.

At some point Mykineshólmur became separated from the island itself by the deep, narrow cleft of Hólmgjógv, and of course there is a story attached to it. A giant in Gásadalur wanted Mykines for himself and tried to kill Oli, who farmed there. He landed in Borgargjógv on the east side of Mykines, where his footmarks can still be seen in the rock. Oli saw the giant come down from the mountains and ran as fast as he could westwards, but the giant was catching up with him, so he cried out for a chasm to open – *'rivni gjógv!'* – and that is just what happened. Today a narrow cable bridge spans the *gjógv* some 40 metres above the sea, and in good weather the crossing is simple and safe. At one time there was only a rope, so that anyone wanting to go to the holm had to swing by the arms like a commando. During the bird-catching and sheep-gathering seasons the men would go out there and have food sent across to them.

From its highest point at 133 metres Mykineshólmur slopes southwards. The smooth surface is covered in lush grass, which is said to be the best in Faroe. Certainly the oxen that always used to graze here when the *bygd* was still being farmed were famous for producing the best beef there was. They would stay there all the year round until the time came to take them to market in Tórshavn to be sold. Now their place has been taken by sheep.

The lighthouse at the western end of the holm was first built in 1909 and was later extended. It is one of the most important lighthouses in the islands, with a radio compass station. Constructing a firm foundation for the light-house was quite an engineering feat as the violent onslaught of the surf is enough to wear away the strongest building materials. There used to be three lighthouse-keepers with their families living at Mykineshólmur, and a small school was kept there. Today the lighthouse is automatic and the families have departed.

The steep cliffs of Mykineshólmur and the western stacks of Gáadrangur, Píkarsdrangur and Flatidrangur are the home and breeding ground of the gannet – *Pelicanus Basanus* – or *súla,* as it is called by the Faroese. This gannetry is the only one in the islands. The currents here are violent and very dangerous, so that year by year the foundations of the stacks get more worn down. As the *súla* was important as food, it was the custom to go across in April to the breeding grounds to take the adult birds when they had made their nests but not yet laid their eggs. Then the birds were left alone until September, when the chicks are almost ready for flight, and are fatter and heavier than the parent birds. The gannet catching would always take place at night while the birds were asleep, and could be very dangerous. In calm weather the Flatidrangur would be accessible from the sea, but the Píkarsdrangur offered a real challenge to the hunters, as it was necessary to dangle at the end of a rope, then creep along slippery, guano-covered ledges

Mykines. A narrow cable bridge spans the gjógv *some 40 metres above the sea, to Mykineshólmur*

in order to go about the bloody business of killing birds. The first man up had the dangerous task of fastening a rope at the top. Attempts were made to fix iron chains to the top of the stack, but in vain – everything was always washed away. Lives were sometimes lost on this hunt, which was socially significant not only as a test of manhood but also as a big village event; the record catch was some 1,100 birds, weighing about 4,500 kilos! That was as large a booty as the Mykines people would allow themselves, as intelligent harvesting of these riches was essential.

With few people now spending the winter on Mykines the old way of life, with the many tasks shared communally, is no longer possible. Perhaps it is no longer necessary either, as electricity and modern appliances make living simpler. The storms and the isolation are still part of island life, and the environment is a challenge in itself, but people who enjoy being close to nature will find pleasure and adventure in this very special island.

26

SKÚVOY, STÓRA DÍMUN AND LÍTLA DÍMUN

These three islands are known for their bird life and are often grouped together. We are told in *Færeyinga Saga* that the three islands of Skúvoy, Stóra Dímun and Lítla Dímun belonged to the brothers Brestir and Beinir, who were chieftains of half of Faroe. Today Skúvoy and Stóra Dímun are part of the parish of Sandoy, whereas Lítla Dímun belongs to Suðuroy farmers.

Skúvoy

The island rises gradually from the east towards the west, to end abruptly in 400-metre-high vertical cliffs teeming with bird life. Here we find Knútur (392 m), the highest point. In the north the promontory of Høvdin seems almost like another island. The southern part of the island is rather marshy, and is known as Tjarnaheiðar – the heaths of the tarns. Numerous rivers flow towards the east. Three rivers meet in the hills and fall into the sea as Árdalsá. This is where the fertile land is, and where the only *bygd* can be found.

Skúvoyarbygd, or just Bygdin to those who live there, is a colourful cluster of houses on the north side of the river. The land ends abruptly in a bare rock wall, some twenty metres high. There are rock shelves below, but even so landing conditions have always been difficult. Boats usually have to be pulled up, it being necessary in the wintertime to winch them up to the top of the rock wall. Going to sea was therefore always a combined operation, requiring many men. A staircase of ninety-four steps cut out of the rock face was once the way up to the *bygd*, but now there is also a modern road from the pier.

There are just under a hundred people still living in Skúvoy. The number has declined somewhat, but it was never a large *bygd*. Thus when tragedy struck in 1900 and an *áttamannafar* on its way home from Sandur ran into bad weather and capsized, the accident was a crippling blow to such a small community, leaving thirty-seven children without a father.

Skúvoy is named after the *skúgvur* or skua, which were once found in great numbers on the island. The colonies of guillemots and razor-bills have also inexplicably declined in recent years, although there are still large bird colonies of numerous other species. Thousands of birds and eggs used to be taken here every year, mostly by climbing the cliffs from the sea. There is only one place where the cliff is lower and the climbing can be done from above. This is in Fagradalur in the north-west, close to Høvdin. The egg-taking in early June was, in nice weather, almost a picnic and everybody took part. Some 7,000 eggs could be taken in one day. They were shared according to strict rules: every man who climbed the cliff had sixteen eggs and 10 per cent of the rest. What then remained was divided into three equal shares. One-third went to whoever owned the land, the remaining two-thirds were shared equally among all who were taking part.

Fagradalur means the lovely valley and it is aptly named. It is often spoken of as '*norður á Dal*' – north in the valley. This is the scene of an old island story with a distinctly fairy-tale quality. Back in the fourteenth century the whole of Skúvoy was one big farm. The farmer lost his wife when his daughter Rannvá was born. He soon got married again, to a farmer's daughter from Leynar in Streymoy. She was an evil stepmother to the girl, as she wanted the farm for her own child, and her husband did not stand up to her. Rannvá was therefore packed off every spring and summer to a summer pasture in Fagradalur called Setrisgarður, to mind the bulls. One summer while she was there the Black Death came to Skúvoy and killed everyone in the *bygd,* and thus Rannvá came into her own again. Her son took over the farm after her, and according to tradition it was not split up until some time in the seventeenth century, but always inherited by one heir alone, as the *óðalsbóndi* felt constrained by some kind of unwritten bond. The remains of Rannvá's croft can still be seen in Fagridalur, and a spring close to it is known as Rannvákelda.

Although some of the events ascribed to Skúvoy in *Færeyinga Saga* must really have taken place in Stóra Dímun, there is no doubt that the island was important in Norse times. Here was the ancestral farm of Sigmundur Brestisson, and here he was set on by Tróndur í Gøtu and his men. The farm was set on fire, but Sigmundur swam to Sandvík in Suðuroy where he was killed by a farmer. It seems strange that Sigmundur would choose to swim to Sandvík when the Sandoy coast is so much nearer. Probably he meant to try for his fortress-like farm at Stóra Dímun, but was overtaken by the *vestfall* current, which took him straight to Sandvík.

It was here in Skúvoy that Sigmundur in the year 999 built the first church in the islands, and here he is buried: 'Later Sigmundur and Tórir were buried by the church in Skúvoy that Sigmundur had built.' The old churchyard, í Ólansgarði, is south of the present church, and this, according to tradition, is where Sigmundur's church stood alone. When it was decided to use this churchyard again some digging was done and a stone floor with steps leading up to a choir was found, but the stone was used to repair the wall. Sigmundur's grave, on the other hand, has always been known, as it is marked by the large cross-marked stone known as Sigmundarsteinur. An archaeo-

Gamul mynd av skúlabørnunum
í Skúvoy, umleið ár 1908:

aftasta rað: lærarindin Anna Sofia á Rýnuni,
úr Skúvoy
Poulina undir reynum, av Sandi.
Tina niðri stovu.
Sunniva niðri stovu
Jóhanna niðri í búð.
Katrina í gcilini.
Kristina í nýggjubúð.
Anna í garðinum.
Olivia í Skálagarði.
Inga í Stórastovu.
Frida niðri í stovu.
Olivia í Fógvanstovu.
Hansina í Dímun.
Aksel í Brekkunum.
Jóhan Hendrk niðri í stovu.
Sofus í garðinum.
Heinrikur niðri í búð.
Oli niðri í búð.
Jóhan í Brekkunum.
                    öll úr Skúvoy.

School photograph and list of pupils from Skúvoy, 1908. Photo: Føroya Fornminnissavn

logical investigation in Skúvoy might perhaps bring to light remains of the Viking Age farm complex as well. When the story of strife in the saga is finally over, we are told that Sigmundur's great grandson Steingrímur the Halt 'lived on Skúvoy and was considered a good farmer'.

Stóra Dímun

An aura of romance surrounds the island of Stóra Dímun, which has been called one of the strangest islands in Europe. Some English writers refer to it as the Great Diamond but, judging by the way they describe it, they might just as well have called it the Great Demon. It looks awesome when seen from the sea. The west side is one long vertical cliff with the highest point Høgoyggj (396 m) at the very cliff edge. The top of the island is a flat grass-covered plateau which slopes slightly towards the east. The only farm lies on the southern slope. This is lower than the rest; geologists think that it was at one time the bottom and north side of a *botnur,* but that much of the land was eroded by the sea long ago.

   The almost vertical cliffs that are nowhere lower than 100 metres make Stóra Dímun a natural fortress, and the bands of daredevil pirates who at one

Overleaf:
Tróndur Patursson –
The fight in Dímun: Gøtuskeggjar, Brestir and Beinir.

time harassed the islands never tried to scale them. There are two possible ways up the cliffs. One route not commonly used is at Breiðanes on the eastern side. The usual one, known as Kleivin, is on the southern side. A landing can be made quite close to this, but only in calm weather or when the wind comes from the north. There is another landing place in a cleft in the rock further north on the western side. During the winter the island boat used to be kept there, tied up 25 metres above the sea; even so the waves swept it away every time. This is the reason why fishing was never carried on from Stóra Dímun.

The climb to the top of the cliff is difficult, and to fall means certain death. It is not without reason they say that nobody has been injured climbing this path. 'But the difficulties have been exaggerated. Anyone of ordinary activity, who is able to keep a cool head, can make the ascent if he wears Faroe footgear, has a good helper behind, and takes thought for each footstep' (Elizabeth Taylor). The path is about a foot wide and zigzags up the ledges, in part artificially made with steps hewn in the cliffside and wire railings.

The farm on Stóra Dímun has been called both the loneliest and the oldest surviving farmstead in the world. Perhaps the sight of it calls for superlatives, as the contrast to the world below is enough to take one's breath away. A vivid green slope seems suspended between sea and sky. The farmhouse is surrounded by solid walls two metres high and more, but even though they are braced by cables the walls have sometimes been broken down by the wind. When the winter winds are at their strongest it is difficult to walk outside the walls, but this is not necessary as all the buildings open out to a narrow lane, which can be shut off by heavy wooden doors at each end.

The Dímun farm has been considered one of the four best farms in Faroe. The pastures are good and the cows were known for the richness of their milk. At the height of its prosperity the farm had 40 to 50 cattle and 650 sheep, and supported 36 people. The bird cliffs yielded large catches, with thousands of puffins and guillemots being caught every summer. In a good year some 15,000 birds and 5,000 eggs might be taken.

The farm has been continuously occupied since early Norse times. To the Norsemen both the fertile land on the island and its inaccessible position would have been seen as invaluable. Probably the land here was settled quite early. It was on the rocks below Kleivin that the boys Sigmundur and Tórir saw their fathers killed. Havgrímur of Hov fell at the same time, and his son Øssur was later given the islands in compensation for the loss of his father. Øssur made Stóra Dímun into a real fortress, but it did not help him against the military expertise of Sigmundur and his men. Øssur was killed and his thirty men surrendered. Later the tables were turned when Sigmundur was set on by Tróndur í Gøtu and his men.

Place-names still remind us of the saga. Close to Kleivin is a place known as Leivs Lop where Leivur Øssursson is supposed to have jumped down during the battle. In the north-western part of the island a stack is called Øssursdrangur. Again according to tradition this is where the chieftain Øssur Havgrímsson lies buried, but so far no grave has been identified with certainty.

Once a woman called Annika was put to death by drowning in Tórshavn harbour. They say that she floated by her hair, so her locks were cut off, and then she sank. For three years she had evaded capture by the authorities on Stóra Dímun. Records show that her name was probably Anna Isaksdóttir and she was the daughter of the *sýslumaður* of Sandoy and married to the Dímun *bóndi.* She fell in love with one of the men working for her husband, and together they killed him. She would not accept the death sentence imposed on her, and set men to guard the possible ways up to the farm, but they grew careless and in the end she was captured. The story has it that it was her own father who finally arrested her, and she asked him what dress should she wear for Tórshavn, the red, the blue or the green? 'Don't worry', said the father, 'it is not a wedding you'll be going to.'

According to legend Annika's father lost her at cards to the Dímun *bóndi* one night when he was extremely drunk, and that was how her marriage came about. Perhaps that explains the biting irony of her question.

The farm was a lonely place in the wintertime, when months could pass without any contact with the outside world. To all intents and purposes the people were imprisoned in their island world. For the rest of Faroe it has also served at times as a real prison, a place where undesirable elements could be got out of sight. 'You shall be put on Dímun,' was the threat used by parents to rebellious youngsters. The system was still used at the beginning of this century:

> … often paupers, people who drink or for some failing or infirmity are not fit to live with their family or in a village are sent here by the Judge. They cannot get away from Dímun, and they work for the peasant as they can. Fourteen people, four with whooping cough, one with consumption, one blind, several brennivín addicts, several with doubtful antecedents. And indeed there were storms inside as well as out.
>
> *Elizabeth Taylor*

In the wintertime when it is icy nobody in their right mind would try to climb the path to the farm. Yet the minister of Sandoy and the crew of his *áttamannafar* once did. It was January 1895; they were on their way from Suðuroy to Sandoy when they got caught in a snowstorm. Miraculously a large wave flung them on to the boulders below the cliffs of Stóra Dímun. The path was glazed in ice, but the choice lay between the risk of falling and the certainty of freezing to death. Two of the men managed to cut away the ice with an iron hook and slowly made their way to the top; in the end the most difficult part was getting across the top of the cliff in the wind. At the farmhouse the people were assembled in the *roykstova* listening to a dramatic story, so it is no wonder they thought it was a ghost hammering on the door! Nothing like it had ever happened at the Stóra Dímun farm before. The minister and the rest of his crew were saved; the next day he had recovered sufficiently to hold a thanksgiving service in the small church, which could just accommodate twenty people. The *kongsbóndi* was later awarded a medal for bravery.

The *kongsbóndi* ruled in this little world, where he was not only the employer but also the teacher, the doctor and the minister. Every Sunday he would gather his household for a service in the small church. The Sandoy minister was duty-bound to come twice a year, but after the Rev. Jensen fell to his death after conducting the service in 1874, not every minister felt he could carry out this duty. The tiny grass-roofed church was pulled down in 1923 to make room for a larger one, but the *kongsbóndi* was killed before the work could begin. And this has been the story of the Dímun *bóndi* and his family: an endless tale of fatal accidents on the cliffs and at sea. It is said that since the tenth century only one or two of them have died in their beds.

The family of the present *kongsbóndi* came to Stóra Dímun at the beginning of the nineteenth century. Until recently, a world war could break out and they would not know about it. A helicopter pad close to the farm now makes it possible to bring mail and visitors to the island in most weather. Today, for better and worse, Stóra Dímun is no longer an island, entire of itself.

Lítla Dímun

Like a rounded cone Lítla Dímun rises from the sea to 414 metres at its highest point. It is the home of many sea-birds and numerous sheep, but it has never been inhabited – even the hardy Faroese were not tempted to settle there. It was here that Sigmundur Brestisson came in the summer of 1004 with two other men to fetch some of the sheep for slaughtering. They were fallen on by Tróndur í Gøtu and his men, but saved themselves by running away and taking Tróndur's boats with them. Tróndur lit a fire and was rescued from the island before Sigmundur could return in force. The south-western point is still known as Sigmundarberg.

Stories abound of men who, like Sigmundur, have gone to Lítla Dímun to find sheep or to catch birds. Then for some reason they have been marooned there, but survive quite well by killing birds and sheep. Sometimes the *huldufólk* come to their aid, and bring them food. In one of the old stories a man left behind on Lítla Dímun knows that Christmas is near and is very

upset that he cannot find out exactly when to celebrate. Then a voice speaks *Lítla Dímun* and supposedly puts his mind at rest: '*náttin ein og dagarnir tveir til jóla*' – 'one night and two days till Christmas'. We are also told that one winter a whole ship's crew spent several days on the island after their ship was wrecked.

Lítla Dímun used to be the home of a peculiar breed of wild sheep, until they were all recklessly slaughtered in 1866 to make room for the more common variety of sheep, brought in from the North Isles. The original sheep were black and had short and rather coarse wool. They were small and slight of build and could make long leaps but still land on their feet with the agility of cats. Nobody knew where they came from or whether they were the original sheep of the Faroe Islands; perhaps they were related to the North Ronaldsay sheep in Orkney. They were completely wild and had to be shot because they could not be caught. A stuffed specimen of the sheep can be seen at the Føroya Náttúrugripasavn – the Museum of Natural Science – in Tórshavn.

The sheep were probably killed because the island changed hands. It used to be all king's land until some farmers from Hvalba and Sandvík in Suðuroy pooled their resources and bought it in 1851 for the sum of 4,820 *riksdaler* – an enormous sum in those days. Probably they needed to graze their sheep there to give some return on the investment, which has in fact proved a sound one over the years. As many as 300 sheep have been grazing there at times.

27

SANDOY

As you might expect there is sand in Sandoy. The wide beaches of Sandur and Húsavík are perhaps the most striking characteristic of this island, which is the most fertile of the Faroe Islands. Nevertheless, when seen from a distance, Sandoy looks steep and inhospitable. Impressive bird cliffs run almost the whole length of the western coast. The east coast is dominated by the looming Skálhøvdi promontory. The highest mountain is Tindur (479 m). This forms a part of the mountain ridge that is the backbone of Sandoy, but it is divided into three parts by two lovely valleys running in two directions from Sandur, northwards to Skopun and eastwards to Húsavík. These valleys are relatively flat and there are several small lakes, so that in the interior Sandoy gives a softer and more rounded impression than most of the other islands.

At the north end of Sandoy lies the small island of Trøllhøvdi, which belongs to the king's farm at Kirkjubøur. It is separated from Sandoy by the narrow sound of Høvdasund, which is believed to be where *Færeyinga Saga* tells us that Sigmundur Brestisson once to his cost spared the life of Tróndur í Gøtu. This is a world of birds, mostly puffin, fulmar, and guillemot, where every year a lot of eggs used to be taken without causing a decrease in the bird population. Away from the cliffs gentle slopes give good pasture to some forty sheep, but to get these away from the island in the autumn is a challenge, as the only way down from the island pasture is a steep ladder bolted to the rock wall. When rounding up the sheep the men have to bring food for several days in case the sea becomes too rough to get back.

Trøllhøvdi appeals to the imagination, and has always done so; according to tradition it was once the head of a giant who wanted to join Nólsoy and Sandoy together. He drew a rope though the holes under Nólsoy and the promontory of Skálhøvdi and put it around his neck, but he pulled so hard that his neck broke and his head rolled to where it now lies in the form of a wild and rocky island.

The old road between Skopun and Sandur was completed in 1917 as the first motor road in Faroe, and Sandoy for a long time had the best network of roads: by 1963 all the seven *bygdir* were connected with each other. Today some 1,800 people live in Sandoy. The main *bygdir* are Skopun and Sandur, with roughly equal numbers of inhabitants.

Although a site of medieval remains has been found at í Alvabø, Skopun is quite a new *bygd*, as it was first settled by two families in 1833. The young Mikkjal Jacobsen from Sandur and his wife were among the first settlers, but when he was killed in the mountains while out catching birds she moved back to Sandur with her three sons. The other family came from Hestur. The *bygd* grew quickly, and by the turn of the century it had more than 200 inhabitants. Its rapid growth probably explains why the houses are more scattered than in most *bygdir*.

The settlers did not find much of a natural harbour in Skopun, but several small skerries close to the shore made it quite easy to build piers for a protected harbour. These have been added to and improved until today the harbour in Skopun is large and modern. Right next to it lies the helicopter pad, as well as the modernized fillet factory Sólarris which is the main business. The harbour also makes Skopun the centre of communications in Sandoy, and there is a ferry connection with Tórshavn several times a day.

A memorial to those who were drowned at sea or were the victims of accidents in the mountains has been erected close to the new road to the harbour. It has a frieze by the well-known sculptor Janus Kamban of an *áttamannafar* – a boat with an eight-man-crew – getting the boat out.

The old road to Sandur goes higher up the slope than the new one, and makes a nice walk up to the lakes of Norðara Hálsavatn and Heimara Hálsavatn. There is also a spectacular walk towards Gleðin, past Lykkjuvøtn and idyllic scenery rather like that of Shetland or Orkney. All the time there is a dramatic view of the rocky slopes of Hestur and Koltur. A shorter walk goes north to Sorngjógv, where the onslaught of the sea, as in so many places on the Faroese coastline, has worn down the roof of a cave to make an abyss. For a while enough was left of the roof to form a natural bridge high above the chasm, but the pressure of wind and sea caused it to collapse.

Sandur was once undisputedly the largest *bygd* in Sandoy, and in the old days the Ting for Sandoy was held at the farm í Trøðum, where a stone known as Tingborðið with the date 1789 inscribed on it still marks the site. Even today Sandur is the administrative centre where the minister, the doctors and the *sýslumaður* live. Most of the houses are found on the small peninsula that forms the two bays of Grótvík and Sandsvágur. *Grót* means stone, and a high, pebbly beach here separates the sea from the small Gróthúsvatn, which lies four metres above sea level. Sandsvágur has a wide, sandy beach with a vegetation that is unusual for Faroe. This is the only place where marram grass – *Ammophila arenaria* – grows. Behind the beach is Sandsvatn, a long and shallow lake rich in trout, and every spring the last resting place for whooper swans on their way to Iceland. Both lakes were probably at one time the upper ends of the two bays, but were dammed by the strong waves.

Sandur is also believed to be the oldest settlement in Sandoy, and is probably the site of the Sandoy farm we are told of in *Færeyinga Saga,* in a strange Goldilocks sequence. When the chieftain Havgrímur of Hov in Suðuroy fell out with the brothers Brestir and Beinir, we are told that he went with his wife and some of his men to Sandoy to see his father-in-law Snæulf and ask his advice. 'As they approached the island they saw no one outside on the farm or indeed on the island. They then walked up to the farm and into the house but found nobody there either. They went into the *stova*, and there a table was set with both food and drink, but still no people. They found this strange, but they stayed there overnight.' Later they came across Snæulf, but he was a man who was not afraid to speak his mind, and he emphatically refused to fall in with his son-in-law's plans of intrigue.

The church at Sandur has a prominent position right in the middle of the *bygd* and close to the sea. Archaeological excavations have been going on for years both inside the church and in the area around it. The site gives us an insight into a thousand years of Faroese history. When in 1863 a new grave was being dug in the south-eastern corner of the cemetery a collection of coins was found. It was the local *sýslumaður* M. A. Winther who found the treasure: 'When a grave was being dug yesterday in the local churchyard, I happened to walk by, and found there, in the turned up earth … the coins, which were almost all stuck together because the metal had rusted.' There were ninety-eight coins in all; of these one was Irish-Norse from Dublin, one was Hungarian, eighteen were Norwegian, four Danish, twenty-four Anglo-Saxon, and fifty were German coins minted in sixteen different places. However, it does not necessarily follow from such varied origins that whoever buried the coins had travelled widely; there was a lively trade between the northern countries and continental Europe, using a variety of coins.

For more than a hundred years scholars have disagreed as to when the coins were buried. They were probably buried as treasure sometime just after 1095, as one of the coins was minted in that year, and then somehow forgotten. Close by the site of the coins have been found the remains of a very fine stone floor, tiled in a pattern. Probably this floor belonged to a Viking Age farm – perhaps even the farm described in the saga. But it may go back even further; the first Norse settlers, who came to Faroe around 800, would not have sailed by such a site, and excavations have shown that the first church in Sandoy was built on this farm. Recent excavations just outside the cemetery wall have revealed a pre-Christian burial site, so this central part of Sandur has probably been in continuous use since the arrival of the first settlers.

During repair work on the church remains of earlier structures were found underneath the floor. Excavation began in 1969, and traces of no less than five older churches were found, the oldest one a stave church. This may have been brought across the sea from Norway. It was quite small: the nave was 5 by 4 metres, and there was a choir that measured 2.5 by 2.5 metres. This church corresponds roughly in type to the small Haltdalen stave church which is now at Sverresborg Folk Museum in Trondheim, and may also have looked rather like it. The first Sandur church is at least as old as the oldest stave churches yet found in Norway, such as the Urnes church. But it was built differently; the wooden staves or corner posts were set into the ground without a stone foundation, and this is an older building method, known to have been used in Norway for the first Norse churches. The stave church is contemporary with the farmhouse and has been tentatively dated to *c.* 1000, the time when Christianity was first introduced into Faroe.

Sometime in the twelfth century a larger church replaced the old one. The corner posts were then placed on foundation stones, and a solid wall surrounded the church. It had a door added for the priest in the south wall, and remains of stained-glass and a leaden frame have been found belonging to the second church. The third church was built at the time of the Reformation in the sixteenth century. It was long and narrow, and had a ground-plan of three squares, of which the choir was the most easterly. This church was also made of wood, but had protective stone walls in the south and the north. Parts of its stone floor are still preserved. The discovery of a broken clay pipe provides further dating evidence, as the smoking of tobacco was unknown in Europe until Columbus brought the plants back from America.

The fourth church of around 1700 covered a still larger area, probably made necessary because the congregation wanted benches to sit on during the service. The fifth church is well documented; it was built in 1763 and stood until the present church was built in 1839. This, the sixth church on the site, is one of the most beautiful of the old Faroese wooden churches, both on account of its style and its setting. The church caught fire a few years ago, and the altar painting as well as the wooden interior were damaged, but the church was fully restored for the celebrations in 1989 when it was 150 years old. It is not a large church 'but of an incredible, simple beauty. All the candles are lit when the service begins; but the church sways, the wind whistles, and one by one the candles are put out by the draught' (Grete Gravesen).

In the choir of the later churches were found some male skeletons, probably of ministers who were interred there. Stories are still told of Sandoy ministers; the island seems to have had its fair share of both characters and capable men. Most legendary of them all is Clemen Laugesen Follerup, or harra Klæmint as he was known locally, who when he died in 1688 had been vicar of Sandoy for forty years. When he first came from Denmark he had nothing; when he died he was one of the richest men in the islands, owning forty-seven marks of the best farming land. He had achieved this by lending money to people who pledged their land, which he took over when they could not pay. He also ran a kind of old people's home at the Todnes manse – the old and disabled were looked after there if they left him their worldly goods.

For 250 years the Sandoy ministers observed the old Scandinavian clerical custom of marrying their predecessor's widow or daughter, thus effectively taking care of the pension problem. Harra Klæmint first married the older daughter of the former vicar, and when she died in childbirth he married the younger daughter, by whom he is known to have had fifteen children. Later another minister, Jørgen Falk Rønne, who worked in Sandoy in the 1890s, wrote a novel about harra Klæmint and his family. In this book he tries to understand the human being behind the evil name that harra Klæmint had acquired in Sandoy. In many stories Falk Rønne describes the island and its people, but people in Sandoy felt that he did not do justice to the models he used for his characters, and were not pleased.

A nice walk towards the west takes us past Gróthusvatn and quite gently rolling country towards the uninhabited bay of Søltuvík. It was just south of Søltuvík that the America-bound steamer *Principia* was dashed to pieces against the cliffs on a stormy November night in 1895. The ship was on fire and had drifted helplessly for three days. Of all the passengers and crew on board there was only one survivor, who came ashore at Kirkjubøur after holding on to a plank for thirteen hours. This plank was later made into a table that can still be seen in the old *roykstova* at Kirkjubøur.

Place-names like Scalloway in Shetland and Skálavík may derive from the Norse word *skáli*, which was mostly used of a farmhouse, or from *skál* for saucer, and it is possible that Skálavík got its name because of its saucer-shaped bay. This opens into a wide and fertile valley, where we find several *býlingar*, although not as many as in Sandur, which is the *bygd* in Faroe with the most. The farm of Dalsgarður is one of the largest in the islands, and in the old days the Dalsgarður farmers had the privilege of burial in the choir of the church. This used to be in the old cemetery á Mølini, but in 1891 the present church was built in a more central location. The altar painting was given to the old church by Jákup Joensen, who was *kongsbóndi* of Dalsgarður and Løgmaður of Faroe (1677–9), and his wife Kristin, the daughter of harra Klæmint.

The story of how this painting came to the church at Skálavík belongs to the traditional lore of Sandoy. Jákup fell in love with Kristin at first sight, but she did not want to marry him, perhaps because she knew it was what her father wanted. But before she knew what was happening her father had got her married to Jákup and living with him at Dalsgarður. There she locked herself in the attic. Jákup at first tried to break down her door, but he met with fierce resistance. Although he then changed tactics and tried to woo her by showing her how much he loved her, she remained cold towards him. Then one day all the Skálavík men rowed out to sea, the Dalsgarðsbóndi among them. The weather turned bad, and the women gathered by the shore to look for their men. Kristin Klæmintsdóttir was among them, thinly dressed and very frightened. One by one the boats came back, but there was no sign of the Dalsgarður boat. And all the time the weather was worsening.

Then somebody shouted: 'Now the Dalsgarður boat is drawing near to Skálhovdi!' Kristin stood there until the boat was in the bay, and then she went back to the house. Nine months later the first child of Jákup and Kristin was christened in the church at Sandur. After he had become Løgmaður Jákup went down, as the Faroese put it, to Copenhagen on official business. He never came back to Skálavík and nobody could discover what had happened to him. His chest came back to Faroe after some time, and inside it were a copy of the Norwegian lawbook and an altar painting with the inscription '*Jacob Jonsen og Kristen Klemments-Datter*'.

From Skálavík a nice walk takes us across Heiðafjall to the ancient village of Húsavík. Down on the beach several old *gróthus* – storage sheds for fish and meat – have been beautifully restored with even the old wooden locks in place. In the *bygd* itself the house of Jóannes á Breyt has been turned into a museum, which gives us an idea of what the house of a labourer and fisherman looked like from the Middle Ages till quite recently.

According to local tradition the *bygd* was in the old days at Kvíggjagil on the southern hillside. The remains of houses can still be seen quite plainly in the fields where the main road to Dalur crosses the river Kvíggjagilsá. It has been said that the population of the old *bygd* was wiped out during the Black Death in 1350, and that the *bygd* was then moved to the other side of the river Storá by the legendary Hústrúin í Húsavík – the Lady of Húsavík – and got its name because of the great house she built there. In late medieval times the term *hústrú* was used in Norway of the wife of an esquire or a man of the same noble rank. There has been much guesswork about who the Hústrúin could be, as the stories told about her differ, but the six documents in the Diplomatarium Færoense about the settlement of the estate in Húsavík of Guðrun Sjúrðardóttir, widow of Arnbjørn Gudleiksson, do not really leave much doubt as to her identity. The documents are written in the years 1403–5 and paint a fascinating picture of life as it was lived by an upper-class family who felt as much at home in Norway as they did in Faroe or Shetland.

One of the letters tells us that she was the daughter of Sjurður Hjalt of Bergen. Hjalt was the name given to Shetlanders who had settled in Bergen to carry on their trade or craft. Quite often these incomers were so successful that they proved serious competitors to the Hanseatic merchants. Guðrun Sjúrðardóttir inherited a large estate, owning many houses in Bergen itself, and receiving rent from some twenty farms scattered along the west coast of Norway. She also received rent from Shetland, and one of the letters shows us that she left some of her property to one Ragnhild Hávarðsdóttir of Vindás in Jala, or Windhouse in Yell, as it is written today. Lady Guðrun's son and daughter both died before her, so that much of the estate seems to have been broken up. And a valuable estate it must have been; the inventory of her belongings, from fine tapestries to silver rosaries, is long and impressive.

At first glance there is little left of her property today, but the present *bygd* is really built inside and around the ruins of Lady Guðrun's farm Heimi á Garði. As the ruins show, several houses were grouped around a paved yard. On the south side of the yard was the *stórastova,* or main house, where Lady Guðrun lived. It was a *stokkastova,* probably rather like the one at Kirkjubøur, and here again there is a story that it drifted over from Norway. The house still stood there in around 1700, but today only the ruined walls are left, 18 metres long, 6 metres wide and 1 metre thick. Towards the east were two large outhouses, probably joined in the upper storey, thus enclosing the passage known as Løðulið, which leads down to the church. The present church was built in 1863, but parts of the church dyke go back to the Middle Ages. Beside the ruined walls of the old house stands a house called Skumpitoft, which is in itself a monument to life in the islands in the nineteenth century, as it was built of timber from a ship that foundered at Viðareiði.

Probably the farm complex was still more or less unchanged when on a moonlit night in 1534 a boat with six exhausted young men drifted ashore in Húsavík bay. They were divinity students, who a week earlier had set out from Bergen to visit friends further north, planning to have a leisurely cruise among the fjords on the way. Instead they were surprised by a storm from the east so violent that they could use neither sail nor oars, but were carried helplessly before the wind. Among them Heini Jónsson was the only one who

Susanna of Skumpitoft, Sandoy. Her house is a monument to life in the islands in the nineteenth century

knew enough about seamanship to steer the boat through the wind and the waves. According to tradition they were found by the young girl Herborg Arnbjarnardóttir. One of the students died from exhaustion, four others went back home, but Heini stayed, and became known as Heini Havreki – 'he who has drifted in from the sea'. He was one of the most romantic figures in Faroese history.

Heini married Herborg, and their son Jón Heinason later became Løgmaður of Faroe. We are told that a rich *óðalsbóndi* owned the Húsavík farm at the time. He claimed to be a sixth generation descendant of Lady Guðrun. Herborg must have been related to him, as legal documents show that at the beginning of the seventeenth century the farm at Húsavík had passed to her grandson Mikkel Joensen.

For a young divinity student these were dramatic times. The Reformation came to Denmark-Norway in 1536, and in the following year the archbishop of Nidaros fled from office. Ámund Ólavsson, the last Catholic bishop of Faroe, was not respected and it was no great loss when he was dismissed. Heini Havreki stepped into the breach and became assistant to the new bishop, and by all accounts the one who ran the show. Later he was appointed minister of Nes in Eysturoy, and when the bishopric was abolished be became dean of all Faroe. After Herborg died in 1542, Heini went back for a visit to his native Bergen. There he met an old sweetheart of his student days, Gyrid Gran, whom he brought back as his second wife. In 1545 a son was born to them; he became famous as Magnus Heinason, the pirate, in many ways a chip off the old block.

The road to Dalur is a narrow shelf high up on the mountainside, where meeting a lorry can be a nerve-racking business. But the first view of Dalur more than makes up for this; low in a *botnur* lies a colourful cluster of houses, with the *bøur* or infields sharply distinguished from the *hagi* by stone dykes. This is the home of some ninety people; since the road came in 1963 the number of inhabitants has increased and new houses have been built. As landing conditions were difficult, farming was always the most important activity, and the *bygd* is known for its fine sheep. Some of the old houses in Dalur show Faroese building practice at its best and most harmonious: natural stone, tarred timber, small-paned windows painted white, and all of them with grass roofs, close to a small river and surrounded by a garden with stunted trees and hardy flowers. There is also a well-preserved old mill in an idyllic setting by the river.

On the other side of the mountain lies Skarvanes. The name may derive from *skarvur* for shag and thus mean the promontory of the shags, or from *skarv* which refers to bare, stony ground. At Skarvanes the landing-place is exposed, and it has always been difficult to make a living here. Now there are few people left; the locked and deserted schoolhouse survives as a monument to life as it was lived here not so long ago. But few other places have a view like this: Skúvoyarbygd, Stóra Dímun and Lítla Dímun, even Suðuroy in the far distance. This was the home of the Faroese bird painter, Diðrikur á Skarvanesi (1802–65). He is known to have made one trip to Copenhagen, but was probably self-taught. He was born on Stóra Dímun, but most of his life was spent working as a farmhand in Skarvanes and, whenever he had a free moment, painting birds. Only four of his pictures still exist. Probably some of his bird watching was done by the idyllic Stóravatn, which is rich in trout.

In *Færeyinga Saga* the Sandoy farmer Snæulf refuses to get involved in political intrigue. To this day Sandoy people are inclined to keep their own counsel and to go their own way. Politically it has been a nationalist stronghold where the unionists sometimes did not even bother to do any campaigning before elections.

The idyllic Stóravatn, Sandoy

28
SUÐUROY

In many ways Suðuroy is a world apart. It takes a good two hours to get to the island by boat from Tórshavn, in a spectacular run past Stóra Dímun and Lítla Dímun. Although the population has stopped growing, this fertile island is still rather densely populated. It seems to have a climate of its own. Even the language sounds softer.

Some think the people are distinctive too: 'The inhabitants of Suðuroy are on the whole different in character from the rest of the Faroe people. They are livelier and quicker, but also more given to legal quarrels and lawsuits. Also in looks they differ from the other Faroese; they are more stockily built and mostly darker' (Jakob Jakobsen). Many reasons, such as the frequent brutal attacks by North African pirates, have been put forward to explain this difference. Traditionally the political views held by the Suðuroy people have not been the same as those of their close neighbours in Sandoy. In Suðuroy the Javnaðarflokkur and the Unionists have had such a strong position that it was difficult for the Home Rule Party or the Tjóðveldisflokkur to gain a footing there, and for that reason the island was at one time nicknamed Little Denmark.

Suðuroy is some 30 kilometres long. In the old days the island was divided into two parts: north and south of Mannaskarð. Apart from the *bygdir* of Fámjin and Sumba most of the west coast consists of steep, inaccessible bird cliffs that form a high bulwark against the Atlantic. Towards the east rocky areas alternate with small valleys running from one side of the island to the other. In some places bays and inlets have left only a narrow isthmus. In the middle of the island, around the 574-metre-high Borgarknappur, there is an area of lakes and rivers formed by glaciers during the Ice Age. Thus the scenery changes rapidly between fjords, cliffs and fertile, cultivated land.

And yet for the last century and more fishing and trade have been more important to Suðuroy than farming. When the time of the Monopoly was over, Suðuroy forged ahead, to become the busiest and wealthiest of the islands. In the first decades of the twentieth century there was a bustle, an initiative and an air of modernity to the principal village of Tvøroyri, so that it for some time actually rivalled Tórshavn in importance. At that time the income in Suðuroy from fishing was larger than in all the other islands put together, probably on account of the excellent natural harbours at Tvøroyri and Vágur, which made Suðuroy the centre of the Faroe fishing industry.

It was at the northern end of Suðuroy that Sigmundur Brestisson swam ashore in the year 1005, to be killed by Torgrímur Illi – the evil one – and his two sons, for the sake of a gold armring. At an assembly meeting in Tórshavn some time later they confessed to the killing of Sigmundur, and they were sentenced to death and hanged then and there. Torgrímur and his sons came from the farm of Sandvík, which was named for the wide sandy bay south of the mountain of Borgin. It is said that the farm was banned, as for centuries afterwards the place was empty. It was then spoken of as Hvalvík, because the bay was often visited by whales.

According to an old Faroe description the place was still deserted in 1800, and the writer deplores this, as it 'is a lovely valley with excellent soil, so that it is most suitable for a bygd' (Landt). Others must have thought so too, as in 1810 the place was settled once again. The name was changed back to Sandvík when the postal service was established, as there is another Hvalvík in Streymoy. For a long time the settlement at Sandvík was quite isolated. The shortest route to Hvalba was across Skálafjall, but this was very steep and could not be used when they had to carry babies for christening. The easiest way from Sandvík to Hvalba goes along the eastern slope of Eggin; it is still clearly visible and gives a good idea of what even the easy roads were like. The road to the west gives a view of the 97-metre-high Ásmundarstakkur and a dramatic coast. This is *lundaland,* where the *lundi* is found in great numbers. The Ásmundarstakkur looks like a blank, inaccessible wall, and the story goes that when it was climbed for the first time by Hanus í Dímun the puffins were so tame and unsuspecting that he could take lots of them with his bare hands and throw them down to the waiting boat.

In 1908 Sandvík got its own church. It had originally stood on the old medieval site in Froðba and was moved to Sandvík by fishing boat. The writer Martin Joensen (1902–66) is buried in the churchyard. In his novels he writes about the life of the Faroe fishermen, who would work for months at a time off the Greenland coasts. It is a life Martin Joensen knew from his own first-hand experience; he wrote about it away from the somewhat rarefied atmosphere of literary circles in Tórshavn and is perhaps the most realistic of Faroese writers.

The wide, fertile *bygd* of Hvalba was at one time the main settlement of Suðuroy, and even today it has some 700 inhabitants. It seems to have been a sought-after site for a long time, as there are traces of old cultivation on the northern slopes, believed to be where 'westmen' or Irishmen lived before the Norsemen came. When later its isolated position made Suðuroy a target of frequent and brutal attacks by pirates, Hvalba seems to have been especially hard hit. Thus in the summer of 1629 two ships of privateers from the Barbary coast of North Africa attacked Hvalba. As the story goes, one of the ships foundered and some three hundred bodies drifted ashore from the wreck.

These were buried along the beach, and today some mounds are still known as Turkagravir, just as the granite rocks called Turkasteinar are believed to have been ballast used by the pirates.

The Hvalba people had no defence other than flight into the mountains. The young Danish minister Poul Rasmussen had been in Hvalba for only two years when the pirates came. He saw his young son tortured and killed, and the shock was so great that he went mad and used to laugh all the time. He had to be pensioned off from his living within a year. The pirates killed six people and carried off some thirty women and children, to be held for ransom. In a petition that is still extant, the Løgmaður Jógvan Justinussen and three other island officials beg King Christian IV of Denmark-Norway to pay the ransom, as there was no way the Faroese themselves could raise the money. But nothing was done, and the captives never came back.

The poignant story of Snæbjørn also takes place in Hvalba and gives us another glimpse of island history. It shows how the commercial monopoly imposed from outside could affect the average man and woman. Snæbjørn had bought four kerchiefs from a passing Dutch ship and given them to his sweetheart, but the officials learned about it, and Snæbjørn was sentenced to four years' hard labour. He thought the judge was biased and went for him with his staff, but by mistake he hit the bailiff, who fell against a stone and died. For some three years he lived the life of an outlaw in a cave in Vatnsdalur on the south side of Hvalbiarfjørður. He escaped again just before discovery and it is said that he later turned up in Shetland. In Hvalba his sweetheart and their son had to fend for themselves, but that is another story.

Hvalba has access to the sea on the west side as well, but the boats have to be winched ashore. The old mountain track south to Trongisvágur is very steep. It crosses Káragjógv where we find the Sigmundarsteinar that Sigmundur Brestisson and his men are said to have carried up there. Anyone who walks through the triangle formed by these stones will be dead before the end of the year. But few are exposed to this temptation these days, as a motor road was opened on this stretch in 1960. This road had the first tunnel in Faroe; today there are thirteen of them, and they have radically changed all communication and transport. In Suðuroy there are three tunnels; of these the tunnels between Sandvík and Hvalba, and between Hvalba and Trongisvágur are one-lane, whereas the 3.2-kilometre-long tunnel between Lopra and Sumba is two-lane, as well as being the longest one so far.

The area between Hvalba and Trongisvágur is known for the coal-mining that has been carried on there since 1780. In Prestfjall just above Hvalba it is possible to see the entrances to some of the oldest mines. At the north end of the tunnel a road branches off to the mines that are still in operation, and just by the south end of the tunnel another road leads to the old coal-mine 350 metres above sea level at Rangabotnur. Altogether the coal covers an area of some 23 square kilometres. The coal is not of very good quality but, as it does

not have to be transported far, it has always been cheaper than imported fuel. *Setting off from Nes,*
Production reached a peak during the Second World War, when the coal was *Hvalba, on the old*
essential for domestic use. *mountain track*
south, to
Today the three *bygdir* on the north-eastern side of Trongisvágsfjørður – *Trongisvágur,*
Trongisvágur, Tvøroyri and Froðba – make up one large populated area, and *Suðuroy*
for some reason the name of Tróngisvágur has often been used for them all
in foreign descriptions. When it became obvious to the administration of the
Trade Monopoly that it was no longer tenable to have just the one store in
Tórshavn for all the islands, branch stores were set up in Vestmanna, Klaksvík
and Tvøroyri. This happened in 1836, and as this area has perhaps the best
harbour and anchorage in Faroe, it soon became an important trade and
fishing centre as well as the base for most of the domestic steamship traffic.
It was a popular port of call for foreign fishermen and cruise ships full of

tourists who found it 'a picturesque little settlement of typical Faroese houses, half wood and half stone, with turf roofs, lying at the end of a level fjord about four miles long, which for wildness of scenery, challenges some of the showplaces of western Norway' (Joseph Jeaffreson).

By the turn of the century Tvøroyri therefore was the second largest community in the islands and an important centre. The local Mortensen merchant dynasty had a fishing fleet of thirty ships and ran shops in many *bygdir*. The large wooden church with room enough for a congregation up to 600 people was given by the Mortensen family in 1907. It was made entirely at a woodworking factory just outside Oslo and was then transported in pieces to Tvøroyri. Fine houses were built, there was a flourishing cultural life and a newspaper was also started in this period.

A nice approach to Froðba is to walk up a set of very steep steps, which give a wide view of the fjord. Another more roughly hewn set of steps are those by the beach at Skarvatangi. According to legend they were made to ease the landing of Froði and his cattle sometime back in the Viking Age. Froði was a Dane who was on his way to Ireland with all he needed to start a new life. He ran into fog and drifted helplessly till he landed at Froðba, where he occupied the land west of the beach, and the *bygd* became named after him as the *bø*, or cultivated land, of Froði. His own farm was called á Laði and exists still. He is also said to be buried somewhere at the headland of Froðbiarnípa. A steep road serpentines to the top of Nakkur, the hill northeast of Froðba. It was built by the British during the Second World War.

Just north of Skarvatangi are the famous basalt columns that are formed vertically in the rock wall and strangely resemble an inverted fan. Some time in the distant past outpourings of lava burst into hexagonal columns here. Close by there is an old walled cemetery. This is the medieval church site, where the old parish church of Froðba used to be before it was moved first to Tvøroyri and then on to Sandvík. Here was also the fine old king's farm Niðri á Bø which demonstrated so well the old way of life, but unfortunately it was torn down just a few years ago, in an unbelievable act of disregard for the island heritage.

The writer Poul F. Joensen (1898–1970) came from Sumba in 1919 to work as a teacher in Froðba. Only eight years later he had to resign because his writings were considered blasphemous, and he took up farming instead, as it was difficult to live from his writing alone. He became one of the most controversial poets the Faroe Islands have ever had. Known both as a *'danska-hatari'* and a *'prestahatari'* – for disliking both Danes and ministers – he wrote a lot of shocking but none the less very popular songs. These days they are usually part of the repertoire of the well-known and well-loved singer Hanus G. Johansen. Perhaps the best known of his poems is *Jarðarferðin,* an outrageous epic about friends and neighbours carrying a dead man in his coffin to his final resting place in the cemetery. When starting off they have

Basalt, Suðuroy

already had a few too many, but they begin singing decorously the right Danish hymns:

Yndisligt danskt er, og Harrin forbjóði	Danish is lovely, and the Lord forbid,
at føroyskt í Føroyum fær livilig kor!	that Faroese should be free on Faroese soil!
Mong er tann sál nú í Himmlinum er, vegvíst av danskari tungu og presti,	Many a dead one to Heaven came, the way was taught him in Danish by the minister
men fá vit føroyskt! Eg svørji tað her:	but if we get Faroese! I swear it here:
til Heljar so fara teir flestu!	then most of us will go to Hell!

By the time they reach the cemetery they are roaring drunk and singing the old Faroese songs. The minister takes fright and flees, but somehow the coffin is buried!

The pirates that attacked Hvalba in 1629 made an attempt on Øravík as well, but the story goes that a resourceful woman, Marjun Lavarsdóttir, managed to scare them away. On a mountain slope above the *bygd* the local Ting for Suðuroy used to assemble. The Tingstead was known as Uppi ímillum Stovur and the site was probably chosen because it formed a natural amphitheatre ideally suited to the purpose, and because it was centrally located. It was at this Ting that Snæbjørn was sentenced for buying four kerchiefs. This conviction was felt to be so patently unfair because it did not stem from any conception of crime relevant to the local community or even to Faroese society in general, but only to outside authorities. Crimes like sheep-stealing, on the other hand, affected a small community seriously, and thieves were severely punished. According to tradition a thief was sentenced to death at the Øravík Ting for sheep-stealing. But no honest Faroese would act as executioner, so the Tingmen made this deal with the thief: they would let him go if in the future he would undertake to do this unpleasant job for them!

Towards the west through Øraskarð we find Fámjin, one of the loveliest *bygdir* in Faroe and for a long time one of the most isolated places in Suðuroy. It was reputedly called Vesturvík in the old days, and of course there is a story of how it came to be called Fámjin. The *bygd* was settled relatively late by a man called Doffin and his son who came there from Hov. One day a French merchant ship anchored off the shore, and the two men rowed out to the ship to sell fish. Two women wanted to inspect the goods but no sooner were they in the boat than the two men rowed away from the ship as fast as they could go, while the Frenchmen cried 'femmes' after them. The ship sailed back and forth for a week, but as the surf was too strong for them to go ashore the Frenchmen finally had to leave the women to their fate. It is said that they cried and made a fuss when they realized that they were cut off forever from family, friends and country. Doffin and his son married the Frenchwomen. Among their descendants were the strong and courageous Albert and Gilbert, popularly known as the Jansa-boys. According to the old stories they joined forces with the Hørg boys of Sumba in protecting Suðuroy against pirate attacks. Ever since there have been boys in Fámjin with unusual, foreign-sounding names.

Whereas the popular explanation of the name Fámjin is thus a rather exotic one, the linguist Jakob Jakobsen points out that a similar name 'í Fámara' is found further south on the same coast, and that the 'fám' element may refer to the rounded, undulating character of the whole area. But the origin of the name is still a mystery.

Fámjin is one of the few *bygdir* where fishing locally from small boats is still a way of life. There is a fleet of some twenty boats in the harbour and a long row of *neyst* still in use. A natural, underwater reef that is visible at low tide protects the inner harbour. Still the surf sends sprays of water far inland when the Atlantic is at its liveliest. A passage has been made through the reef to enable boats to go in and out of the harbour. The old harbour, used for centuries, is at Prestgjógv, a natural cleft north of the beach. This small bay is protected by 'a rune from Arild's time' from ever filling up.

In a glass case in the church hangs the first Faroese flag – the Merkið. The story behind it is very poignant. It was designed in 1919 in Copenhagen by Jens Oliver Lisberg of Fámjin, a young Faroese law student, and two of his friends, Janus Øssursson of Tórshavn and Pauli Dahl of Vágur. They were all inspired by President Wilson's tenets on the rights of minorities. The flag was first hung from 'Regensen', the students' hostel where they all lived. Jens Oliver Lisberg brought the flag home with him, and the first time it was flown in Faroe was after the church service in Fámjin on Sunday 22 June 1919. The flag has remained in Fámjin ever since; the frame and the inscription on it were made by the well-known sculptor Janus Kamban. Jens Oliver Lisberg died of the virulent Spanish influenza in August 1920, as he was starting his final year. Just outside the church door is his grave with a stone raised by his fellow students, and there are usually fresh flowers on his grave.

The altar painting cost the large sum of 600 kroner when it was commissioned back in 1875, and to pay for it the local fishermen decided to give the largest fish each of them caught whenever they went to sea. The silverware on the altar is a gift from the British government to the people of Fámjin for finding and burying the crew of a trawler lost at sea. The rune stone in the church is perhaps unique, as the inscription was made in the second half of the sixteenth century, and thus shows that runes were sometimes in use even after the Reformation.

As the name shows the *bygd* of Hov is very old. The Norse *hof* was a heathen place of worship not very different from an ordinary longhouse on the outside. At one end there was a structure rather like a chancel. Here the wooden figures representing the gods stood around the high table where the bowl of *hlaut* – the blood of the sacrificial animal – would be ready. The ceremony known as *blót* could then begin: the blood would be sprinkled on the figures and the devotees themselves.

Hov is a fertile *bygd* and it is not surprising that it was settled early on. In *Færeyinga Saga* we hear about the rich and mighty Havgrímur who owned one half of Suðuroy outright and had the other half in feu from King Harald of Norway. He lived at the farm called Hov and *'hann var blótmaðr mikill'* – 'he was a good heathen'. Havgrímur comes across as a quarrelsome and rather stupid man, who starts the endless strife described in the saga, and is one of the first to fall victim to it. He is killed on the rocky beach of Stóra Dímun, along with the brothers Brestir and Beinir. He was 'taken to Suðuroy and buried there according to ancient custom'. People in Hov have always known that his grave was high up at the edge of the infields, and that nobody should touch it. Nevertheless it was excavated in the 1830s by a local farmer, who apart from bones found some pieces of iron and a small grindstone of Viking Age origin. Close by are traces of a farm.

West of Hov is a large, relatively flat area of lakes and rivers, formed by glaciers in the Ice Age. Close by the river running between the lakes of Bessavatn and Vatnsnes we find the open valley of Ergidalur. The name in itself is interesting, pointing as it does to its use as summer pastures, and it therefore comes as no real surprise that an old farm site has been found here. On one side of a brook are the remains of an enclosure for cattle, on the other the site of a house. The brook was crossed by a bridge. The house measures 5.15 by 3.5 metres inside. By the raised fireplace lies a large basalt column that must somehow have been brought there to serve as a seat. Clay bowls found in the house date back to the Viking Age. The old inland track between Øravík and Vágur was close to Ergidalur, and it is said that people were always in a hurry to pass this stretch as it was a home for the *huldufólk*. It was not unusual to associate an old derelict house site with 'the other people'.

Like Fámjin the *bygd* of Porkeri was settled from Hov. But there must have been some kind of ancient settlement because burnt, heat-cracked stones are sometimes found when a new grave is dug in the cemetery. The strange name is believed to derive from Purkugerði – an enclosure for pigs, used by the farmers of Hov. *Purka is* a Norse word for pig, probably originally borrowed from Latin and obviously related to the Norman-English word 'pork'. Today Porkeri is the larger of the two *bygdir*, a very prosperous village with well-kept gardens and streets. The church was built in 1847 and is one of the most famous of the old wooden churches. The Faroese archaeologist Símun Arge examined it some years ago and found remains of two old churches under the floor.

Vágur is named for the long, fjordlike bay that cuts almost right through the island. Most of the settlement is found on the north side of the bay. It was here at the farm of Toftir that the legendary Regin lived around 1400. At that time quarrels were still settled by *hólmgonga,* especially if they concerned land boundaries. Regin was so strong that nobody could defeat him in that kind of duel, and so he had become the most prosperous farmer in Vágur. When the *bygdir* of Vágur and Sumba both laid claim to Lopranshólmur, Regin of Hørg in Sumba was sent against Regin of Toftir, who won the island for Vágur. But another legendary character, Jenis Reginsson of Laðangarður, the son of Regin í Hørg, could not bear his father's defeat, and took a very subtle revenge on Regin of Toftir.

The church in Vágur is the only votive church in Faroe. According to tradition the first church in Vágur drifted over from Norway, the timber all cut and ready to be put together. A woman in Norway, whose husband had died at sea, had promised to build a church to his memory. To fulfil this vow she let the timber be thrown out to sea with the prayer that it must land where it was needed. There were gifts with it too: a crucifix still spoken of in 1710, and a *grøðisteinur* which could heal all illness. The latter was thrown to the bottom of the sea by a man who regarded the idea as witchcraft. The dramatic origin of the church and also the fact that it was the church where the teachings of Martin Luther were first preached, by the minister harra Andras, have given it a reputation as the most holy church in the islands, and it has therefore received many gifts as alms for illness, childbirth or danger at sea.

North-west of Vágur, at í Botni, we find the first hydro-electric power station built in Faroe. Another steep road winds its way to the old Loran station at Skúvanes, with its wide view of the western cliffs. The Loran station was built by the Allies during the Second World War, but was closed down in 1977. At Lopranseiði the island is only 800 metres across. In Lopra the houses cluster round the whaling station that used to be the core of the village. Small compact whaling boats used to bring in their catches of harpooned whales and, although they gave off a sickening smell, the whales also brought bustle and prosperity. The crash of the Sjóvinnubankin in 1951–2 brought about the bankruptcy of the whaling station as well, with the loss of many jobs in the *bygdir* of Lopra and Akrar. In 1983 drilling down to 2,200 metres in Lopra revealed deposits of gas, but so far nothing has been done about it.

The tunnel that connects Lopra with Sumba turned out to be extremely difficult to build because there are pockets of water in the rock, which is so soft and brittle that it breaks in your hand. From a construction point of view it is the poorest rock so far found in Faroe; that it is porous can be seen from the fact that water in this area does not fall in cascades down the mountainside, but is absorbed into the rock.

The road rises steeply from Lopra. A branch road leads eastwards to the two small *bygdir* of Víkarbyrgi and Hamrabyrgi, divided by an idyllic little river. The rock faces above Hamrabyrgi are of a strange bleak grey that is very striking. On the whole this is an unusually beautiful place, although a smolt

plant on the beach brings home to us the fact that today nobody can make a living from small marginal farms. It is said that in this area in the early Middle Ages there was an important village and that it had its own church, but the population was wiped out by the Black Death. Only one woman was left, but she had become so fearful and wild that she would never have anything to do with other people. Food used to be thrown down to her from a cliff so that she would not starve. The ruins of her house are still pointed out. The area was resettled around 1830, but then as two *bygdir*.

Until the road came in the 1960s the people of Lopra, Víkarbyrgi and Hamrabyrgi had to cross mountains to get to church in Sumba. And it was along this way that the coffin-bearers described in Poul F. Joensen's song had to go – his song was based on a scandalous event at the turn of the century, although it must be said that he added rather than detracted from it.

Today Sumba is the southernmost *bygd* in Faroe – indeed the name means the southern cultivated area. At Akraberg there are traces of old habitation, but its origin is uncertain. There are vague stories of Frisian pirates living there. Until the road came through, this part of Suðuroy was fairly isolated, as landing conditions are difficult, the waters being rather shallow. There used to be a reef going from the beach out to Sumbiarhólmur. This was torn up some 200 years ago, at the same time as Saksun in Streymoy filled up with sand. Probably this was caused by a volcanic eruption in Iceland.

Isolation has made the dialect spoken in Sumba quite different in many ways from that spoken in nearby Vágur; in some respects it is very close to western Norwegian. Faroese dancing has remained popular and innovative in Sumba, which is known for its internationally acclaimed folk-dancing group.

The old farm of Laðangarður, which plays such an important part in old Faroe lore, does not exist any more. But high up at the edge of the *bøur*, which in Sumba is very green, lies the old historic farm that was once the home of Regin of Hørg. The name of Hørg is fascinating, as it refers to a heathen place of worship in Norse times. Whereas Hov refers to a house, Hørg indicates outdoor practices. The sacrificial stone actually stood there until a few years ago, when somebody took umbrage and smashed it up for religious reasons. This was the childhood home of the controversial Poul F. Joensen, but it is also the home of William Joensen, his younger brother, who as a Catholic convert has been introduced to the Pope. Faroe is indeed a land of contrasts.

The southernmost point of Faroe is made up of a group of skerries known as Flesjarnar and the 12-metre-high Sumbiarsteinur. The latter was once much taller; it was described in 1539 as being 35 metres high. It has always been a popular landmark, as it warns passing ships away from the Sumbiar maelstrom. West of Sumba is the 469-metre-high Beinisvørð, a striking-looking mountain that has not only inspired poets as a symbol of independence, but has in the popular mind been seen as standing watch and ward over all of Faroe.

Suðuroy. The Lopra end of the tunnel that connects with the bygd of Sumba, under construction

29

A FINAL CHAPTER

The last decade of the twentieth century was a stormy period in the Faroe Islands, with political confrontations both at home and abroad. The islanders faced national and private bankruptcy, followed by economic improvement and hope for the future. It is a strange and striking story of the coming of age of a small nation. Yet freedom and the responsibilities accompanying it were important themes in the islands all through the last century, in fact ever since Jóannes Patursson and others challenged the Faroese people to look after their heritage.

During the Second World War the Faroese did in fact have self-government for five years. Negotiations with Denmark after the war led to the referendum that was held on 14 September 1946, and resulted in a small majority vote for independence. This was declared invalid by the Danish authorities. Instead came the Home Rule Act of 1948, in which the status of the islands changed from 'a county of Denmark' to 'a self-governed community within the Kingdom of Denmark'. This act is still in force, with no changes made. The Home Rule Act was a political compromise, and today it does appear that the division of responsibility between Faroese and Danish authorities was never clearly defined. This may have led to some confusion in connection with political decisions, as well as a lack of control over the economy.

As early as the 1970s the Faroese government – Føroya Landsstýri – started giving generous subsidies to the fishing industry in an attempt to reduce the fluctuations in prices and give the fishermen more stable incomes. More and more funds were transferred, until the government was spending some thirty per cent of its income in support of the fisheries alone. Generous loan arrangements also made it possible to invest in fishing boats with hardly any private capital; this was at times profitable for the individual, but was catastrophic for the islands' economy once things started to go wrong.

In the late 1980s the Faroese government also stepped up the building of high-quality roads and long tunnels in the islands, and people bought cars for commuting on them. Low taxes and generous credit made this possible, and the consumption rate grew till the Faroe Islands, it is said, enjoyed the world's highest standard of living.

But complications were coming. Although a number of fish farm enterprises were established all over the islands in the course of the 1980s, the income from fishing in general fell drastically. This was due to falling fish prices as well as to a decline in North Atlantic fish stocks, which in the period 1990 to '94 fell by almost one third. The large number of fishing boats with high-tech equipment probably led to serious overfishing in Faroese territorial waters. In this the Faroe Islands were not unique: parallel crises have occurred in Newfoundland, Finnmark in North Norway, and Iceland, as a result of somewhat similar public policies.

The crisis came to the Faroe Islands in October 1992 – since known as 'black October'. The Faroese-owned bank Sjóvinnubankin turned out to be burdened with defaulted loans and supporting a large national debt – it was in fact bankrupt. The other large bank in the islands was Føroya Banki, in which Den Danske Bank owned the majority of shares. In March 1993 the Faroese government was offered the opportunity to take over Føroya Banki on the clear understanding that it did not need fresh capital. Five days later, the Faroese authorities took over the bank, only to be told after 48 hours by Den Danske Bank that the offer had been based on a misunderstanding: Føroya Banki did need fresh capital.

The banks were in serious difficulties and to bail them out the Faroese government borrowed first DK 560 million from Denmark, then another 1.3 billion. The Danes insisted on austere measures being taken in return: government taxation was increased, tough budget cuts were made in public spending, and wages were reduced. Føroya Landsstýri was de facto if not formally placed under administration and the Home Rule Act virtually invalidated.

For Faroese society as a whole 1993 was an 'annus horribilis', with most of the fishing industry facing bankruptcy. The unemployment rate rose to 23 per cent, some 500 families lost their homes, and soon more than 5,000 people – about ten per cent of the population – left the islands for Denmark, Norway or Iceland. The national debt amounted to the equivalent of £17,000 per person.

The Faroese became the whipping boys of the Danish press, which described them as spoiled and irresponsible. The Danish minister of finance, Mogens Lykketoft, is quoted as saying: 'It has been a question of irresponsibility on all levels in the Faroese community – from politicians and business people all the way down to the individual family.' But the Faroese had by then started asking questions about the purchase of the bankrupt Føroya Banki, and a documentary programme on Faroese TV in the autumn of 1993 concluded that the government had bought nothing more than a painted corpse.

Relations between the Faroe Islands and Denmark deteriorated, but at the election for the Løgting in 1994 the clear winner was still the Sambandsflokkurin with their policy of looking to the Danish government for help.

The Løgting is one of the world's oldest parliaments

They formed a coalition government with the social democrats, the Javnaðarflokkurin. But their financial demands were turned down by the Danish government.

After the election the Faroese Løgting unanimously resolved to ask the Danish authorities for an official inquiry into the bank question. When this was refused, suspicion and distrust grew in the islands, but, as it turned out, the Danish media were also starting to ask questions. An expert commission was eventually appointed to look into the matter. A journalist from the Danish newspaper *Jyllands-Posten* revealed a conspiracy – the bank crisis had been engineered and staged at the highest political level in Denmark. The report of the expert commission seemed to confirm this when it was presented in January 1998. In consequence the Faroese government sued the Danish state and Den Danske Bank. The conflict was solved politically by a reduction of Faroese debts and the grant of a loan, free of interest, to the Faroese government.

Perhaps only time will give a balanced view of what happened during the bank crisis. According to the Faroese politician Høgni Hoydal it was all an attempt 'to carry through a controlled bankruptcy of the country with the Faroese politicians as bystanders' (*Myten om Rigsfællesskabet*, 2000). The former director of the Danish national bank, Richard Mikkelsen, who orchestrated the crisis, maintains on the other hand that the aim was 'to get the Faroe Islands economically on their feet again in a situation where Faroese politicians had neither the insight, the will, nor the ability to solve the problems.' (*Færøerne i bankkrisens tegn*, 2001). Today tempers seem to have cooled somewhat; perhaps the fact that 'the painted corpse', now the new Føroya Banki, in 2001 had assets of some DK 2.6 billion has something to do with this.

The Turn of the Tide

As early as 1995 the Faroese economy was showing clear signs of recovery. The stocks of cod and herring were rising, and that year the annual catch in Faroese waters was back to what it used to be before the crisis. Fish processing plants were reopened as fish catches soared, reaching an all-time high of 375,000 tonnes in 1998. The population increased too, as the people who had left started returning.

The scandal associated with the bank crisis placed a serious strain on Faroese-Danish relations, and at the time of the election for the Løgting in April 1998 support for independence from Denmark was strong. The independence movement in the Faroe Islands had by then been organised through political parties for close on a hundred years, but only once before had they been in the majority. In 1998 the three pro-independence parties – the republican Tjóðveldisflokkurin, the conservative Fólkaflokkurin and the middle of the road Sjálvstýrisflokkurin – formed a coalition that was also backed by the one member of the Miðflokkurin, so that together they represented a majority in the 32-member Løgting.

The major goal of the coalition program was to make the Faroe Islands into a sovereign state by the year 2000 at the latest. The Landsstýri prepared a plan for the process, which they described as 'a democratic and civilised way to independence'. Their pattern for this plan was the negotiations held between Iceland and Denmark in 1918, which led to complete independence for Iceland in 1944.

The new løgmaður – that is, the prime minister – was Anfinn Kallsberg of the Fólkaflokkurin, a seasoned and experienced politician. The young politician Høgni Hoydal from Tjóðveldisflokkurin was appointed a minister in the Faroese Landsstýri with special responsibility for the independence process. His book *Myten om Rigsfællesskabet – vejen til en selvstændig færøsk stat* (*The Myth of the Union – the way to an independent Faroese state*) gives a chronological survey of recent Faroese history. Hoydal describes how the Faroese consider themselves a separate people with their own culture, rights and potential. He maintains that the Faroese economy was healthy at times when it was run autonomously, as happened during the Second World War and after the recent bank crisis. In his opinion the Home Rule Act of 1948 was designed to protect Danish unity and actually prevents balanced development in the Faroe Islands.

On 10 June 1998 the Danish government entered into an agreement with the new Føroya Landsstýri to negotiate a treaty for a sovereign state in the Faroe Islands. In October of the same year three expert groups were appointed to consider what was required for the Faroe Islands to become a sovereign state – the Faroese word used is *fullveldi*. The chief aim was to give the people the necessary information about what such a process involves and to create a realistic basis for the forthcoming negotiations with the Danish government. A central issue was the future of the Faroese economy.

The results of the research done by the expert groups were handed over to the Landsstýri in September 1999 in the so-called *Hvítabók*, or Whitebook. More than sixty people had worked on the book and their conclusions were positive. The plan was for Denmark and the Faroe Islands to begin negotiations in the autumn of 1999 to draw up a treaty that would set the framework for all future co-operation between the two countries. Once this treaty had been accepted by the Danish Folketing and the Faroese Løgting, the Faroe Islanders would vote in a referendum in spring 2000 either to accept or reject it. The final stage of the process would be to devise a constitution, also to be voted on.

So what happened? In March 2000 the Landsstýri had its first meeting with the Danish government to discuss future relations between the two countries. The Faroese had their draft treaty ready; to secure their position they wanted the treaty to become legally binding through the UN. But there were no negotiations; the Faroese version is that the Danish prime minister started the meeting by taking up his pen and scoring out the Faroese proposals in order to show how hopeless he considered them to be. And the situation grew worse as time went by. The Faroese proposal to call in help from a third party – the UN or another Scandinavian state – was flatly rejected.

On 26 October 2000 Anfinn Kallsberg announced after another unsuccessful meeting in Copenhagen that the Danish authorities were not willing to meet the Faroese halfway in their efforts for independence; they were simply not willing to negotiate at all. However, the Landsstýri would not give up their plans for Faroese autonomy; the question was how long it would take without Danish co-operation.

It seems obvious that the Danish authorities simply had not at any stage wanted independence for the Faroe Islands. In the spring of 2001 the Danish prime minister finally came out and said so during a debate in the Folketing. The Faroese had hoped that after their obtaining sovereignty the Danish government would continue with financial support on a diminishing scale for a period of twelve years, but the Danes agreed to four years only. Probably this is the reason why the referendum planned for May 2001 did not after all take place. But the road towards economic self rule for the Faroe Islands goes on: in his Ólavsvøka speech Kallsberg announced that from 2002 support from Denmark would be reduced to DK 616 million a year, as the Landsstýri was taking over the running of schools and social care in the islands.

In May 2002 another Løgting election took place in the Faroe Islands, with a record turn-out of 91.1 per cent. The important issue was once again whether to sever links with Denmark or not. The result was a dead heat, with sixteen representatives for each faction. The three independence parties remained in power as they were once again supported by the one representative of the Miðflokkurin, thus ending up with a majority of seventeen members.

In retrospect it seems clear that the Faroese mandate for the independence negotiations was very narrow and that a larger majority for independence among the people would have made the situation simpler. The Danish authorities also have a vested interest in hanging on to the Faroe Islands. It seems obvious that a change in their status would have a knock-on effect on Danish relations with Greenland.

The recent taking over of the school system as well as social care by the Faroese themselves has led to an expansion of the Føroya Landsstýri – from seven to nine members. There are also negotiations about the taking over of the church.

Oil

For the last five years and more the economy of the Faroe Islands has been strong, mostly due to increasing fish landings and high and stable export prices. This has made it possible to reduce the large public debt, most of it owed to Denmark. The total dependence of the Faroese on fishing does, however, make their economy extremely vulnerable, as there is always a danger of overfishing in the long term. Diversifying the economy is therefore a goal in itself.

Oil has been found in the area, and the Faroe Islands have exclusive rights to any oil and mineral finds made in their territorial waters according to a treaty made with Denmark in 1992. As Jógvan Sundstein, who was Faroese minister of finance at the time, tells the story, the Faroese themselves were speechless when the Danish prime minister signed the rights over to the Faroe Islands without any conditions attached.

But progress in the search for oil has not been rapid. A basic problem in looking for oil and gas in the Faroese section of the continental shelf is the fact that it is covered by a thick layer of basalts, which are hard, volcanic rocks. This basalt layer makes it difficult to get a seismic picture of the shelf. In some places the basalt layer can be 3,000 metres thick, and it would be time-consuming, though not impossible, to drill through this layer.

In 1998 the Faroese passed both a new petroleum law and a new tax law, with a view to oil activities, but there is still some scepticim about the oil business. There is anxiety about the environmental effects of an oil spill, and the 1993 crisis and its consequences also make people cautious. However, there is not really much opposition to the oil drilling, even among the fishermen. Everybody acknowledges that the finding of oil would lead to changes – the Faroese community would become 'more like Norway'.

Companies are lining up, among them Atlantic Petroleum (1998), Føroya Kolvetni (1998), the Atlantic Margin Group (AMG), an alliance of twenty-three companies and the Norwegian Statoil. The first well was drilled in 2001, but no profitable find was made. Altogether eight wells will be drilled around the Faroe Islands by different oil companies over a six-year period from 2000, when the allocations were made.

Culture – Some Recent Developments

A milestone in the history of Faroese culture was reached in 1998 with the publication of the first Faroese dictionary – *Føroysk Orðabók* – with synonyms and explanations also in Faroese. It was launched at the Nordic House with 400 people present to welcome it. The man behind the dictionary is Jóhan Hendrik Winther Poulsen, a professor at Fróðskaparsetur Føroya and the 'grand old man' of Faroese linguistics. He has worked most of his life for the preservation and promotion of the language, and began work on the dictionary in earnest in 1990.

The new dictionary runs to nearly 1,500 pages, and defines some 65,600 words. It is interesting to see the words that have been added to the Faroese language in recent years. The computer age has generated, for example, *telda* (computer) and *fløga* (CD). The dictionary is also available on CD Rom and will be an indispensable guide to the Faroese language for a long time to come.

Another important development for Faroese culture was the signing of an agreement on 10 June 1999 by the Danish and Faroese governments. The agreement ensured the return to the Faroe Islands of some 400 Faroese antiquities and historical documents that had been preserved in Danish museums since the early nineteenth century. Among the most valuable objects to be returned were the so-called 'Kirkjubø-stólarnir'- carved bench ends believed to date from the fourteenth century – from the medieval church at Kirkjubøur. There are sixteen of them, and after 127 years of absence they were in the summer of 2002 given a warm welcome at the Fornminnissavn (Historical Museum) that was recently established in Hoyvík outside Tórshavn for the purpose.

After 127 years of absence, the 'Kirkjubø-stólarnir', the sixteen carved bench ends, have been returned from Denmark

Another important repository of Faroese culture that is soon to return to the islands is the account books of the Royal Danish Monopoly Trade, which had the sole right to all trade in the Faroe Islands until 1856. These books are an important source of information about the old ways of life in the islands, and will facilitate the study of Faroese history.

'We do not live in the Faroe Islands for practical reasons', said the writer Heðin Brú at one time. Perhaps he meant that at least part of the reason would be the cultural life, which is amazingly rich and intense. The political and financial crisis of the early 1990s seems only to have strengthened Faroese culture, as an unprecedented flourishing of cultural activities followed in its wake.

Gríma, the only professional theatre group in the islands, has under its director Eyðun Johannessen reached a high level of artistic achievement. In the course of 2003 the group will present Ibsen's *Peer Gynt*, translated into Faroese by Axel Tórgarð, who has already received an award for his translations of Shakespeare.

The Nordic House, a gift from the other Scandinavian nations, was opened in 1983 and has become an integral part of Faroese life. There is always something going on at the Nordic House – concerts, exhibitions, festivals. Many events have already become established fixtures – the summer exhibition of new Faroese fine art, the art festival in August, and the biannual rock event Prix Føroyar.

Literature

From a literary point of view the last decade has been rich in the Faroe Islands. The Faroese language is gaining ground; the many newspapers use only Faroese, and for several years literary magazines like *Brá*, *Varðin* and *Bragi* supported the numerous writers working in the islands. For some time a literary award, the M. A. Jacobsen prize, has been given each year.

And yet there are very few Faroese full-time writers; they are practically all professional people who write books in their spare time. The exception is Jens Pauli Heinesen, who has been a full-time author since the 1970s, and has produced a considerable number of novels and short stories. Heinesen is considered a master of satire, and has received a Faroese cultural award for his work. His novel *Nú ert tu mansbarn á foldum* was in 2002 published in Germany as *Ein Kind hier auf der Erde*. This is the first time that a novel has been translated directly from Faroese into German; usually translation into German or another major European language has gone via a Danish edition.

Annually some 100 to 150 books are published in Faroese. Of these about half are original works by Faroese writers, some 15 to 20 of which are fiction or poetry. Altogether an impressive 4,169 books have been published in the Faroese language since the first one appeared in 1822. Although the tradition is still so young, it is fair to say that the written language has come into its own.

Poetry has been a more popular way of expression than prose among the younger writers, and comparatively few novels and short stories are published. In an attempt to change this the Faroese Arts Festival – Listastevna Føroya – invites contributions to a novel competition, offering a prize of DK 150,000. Although the country is really too small to give room for various literary fashions or 'isms', it is still true to say that modern prose is mostly concerned with social themes.

Every year a Faroese writer is nominated for the Nordic Council award for literature, which in the Nordic countries is second only to the Nobel prize in prestige. The candidate for 2003 is Hanus Kamban for his collection of short stories called *Pilgrims*, which has been translated into Danish. The protagonists of these stories are spiritual travellers undertaking some kind of existential or aesthetic quest. Kamban has been praised for his mastery of style and language, and according to a Norwegian reviewer, *Pilgrims* is marked by 'a Poe-like, threatening, shadowy and Gothic mystique and a modern critique of capitalism, combined with a poetical use of images.'

Besides writing fiction Hanus Kamban, formerly Andreassen, has also published collections of essays and has translated stories by, among others, Poe, Joyce and J.G.Ballard. Some of his short stories have an international flavour to them; this is strengthened by the many direct and indirect references to French, German and English literature. Kamban's three-volume biography of Janus Djurhuus (1881-1948) was published in the years 1994–97, and in a Danish translation in 2001. It describes a poet who perhaps better than anyone else was able to use the Faroese language to express the feelings and thoughts of modern man. At the same time the biography presents a picture of the development of the Faroe Islands – linguistically, politically and culturally – until the passing of the Home Rule Act.

The only Faroese writer to win the Nordic Council award for literature so far is Rói Patursson in 1986, for the collection of poetry called *Líkasum*. The Tórshavn poet Jóanes Nielsen has since then been nominated three times for the same distinction, most recently in 1999 for the collection of poetry called *Pentur*, or *Sting*, but so far he has not won the award. It may be that his realistic and outspoken imagery is considered too provocative by many, but in the Faroe Islands he is popular and perhaps the most widely-read modern writer.

He started out as a socialist writer in the 1970s; his daredevil brand of socialism combined with a masterly use of language could always hit a nerve and get the complacent reader up from his armchair in a fury. He is a declared Marxist as well as a Faroese nationalist – 'Føroyar, I love you with my open hand, but also with my closed fist.' But there is also an abstract, spiritual dimension to his poetry: he asks 'the wind for advice' and speaks of 'the summer of the trees'. He thinks a poem 'is stronger than / the poet himself / a voice that breaks glass.'

At times Nielsen grapples with the meaning of life, and a sense of the divine. His concept of god is far from Christian, but still central in the mystery of life: 'He is a god without a throne. / He is my god.' In one of his poems he sums up the essence of his writing thus: 'Maybe they will say of me / that I was one of those poets / who coupled the hose / to life, / heard poetry throb in the ground, / fly under the sky / and drip like dew from green leaves.'

The poem 'What shall we do with William Heinesen?', written for the 85th birthday of the distinguished Faroese writer, is in many ways typical of his audacious style – a style that appealed to Heinesen himself. In fact Heinesen made the illustration for the cover of the 1985 volume that contained this poem.

If a clerical collar had suited him,
He would have been able to say
– The money will go to the mission
Or preach at the funeral of a Tórshavn man.
Unless on impulse a tiny smile
would smash the respectful silence into smithereens.

Or as head of telecommunications.

He could have had a call box put up on Sumbiarstein.
And ask daily, what in hollow hell the pope did in Rome.

Or become an agent for nylon stockings.
– Excuse me, madam, but your varicose veins are showing.

Maybe he could have taught bicycling at evening school.
For the way he handles his bicycle
with the right leg flung stylishly over the bar
makes the Plantasjan thrushes ecstatic with joy.

There would have been no use in sawing him into pieces,
putting them in plastic bags
and throwing him in the freezer.
For the fishballs would soon have protested
And a sheep's head would baa the Marseillaise
and on top of a pile of frozen leeks
the leg of mutton would dance a waltz.

No, he should do as he always has done.
Hand out tickets to the finest stars.
Expose the dark men who burn fiddles and girls' plaits.
Soften the sorrow that sobs in solitude.
Lay on sugar candy in the magical summer evenings.

William Heinesen, drawn by Zacharias Heinesen

Apart from his seven collections of poetry, Nielsen also published a novel in 1991, entitled *Rubber Boots are the Only Temple Columns we have in the Faroe Islands*. His second novel, *The Easter Storm*, was published in 1996. In 2002 he received the Nordic Dramatists Award for the play *Is any Land Called Weekend?* This was staged with great success by the theatre group Gríma.

The contemporary writer Gunnar Hoydal is an architect by profession, as well as one of the finest essayists writing in Faroese. His work is varied, and includes poetry, short stories and articles, as well as two novels. In 1982 he published his first book, a collection of short stories, for which he was awarded the M. A. Jacobsen prize.

His book of poetry *Hús ur ljóði* (*House of Sound*) was nominated for the Nordic Council literary award of 1989. He is a sensitive and lyrical poet as well as a strict stylist. He had already published some of his poetry in a rather unusual way, making three records on which his sister Annika Hoydal sings his lyrics. *My Own Country* came out in 1981; it is partly a declaration of love for his native land and partly a personal journey backwards in time. *Dulcinea* (1991) is all about the here and now, although the title alludes to Don Quixote's Dulcinea – the woman of his dreams and the one he is fighting windmills for. *Dulcinea* is about the courage to dare and venture in an adult world, perhaps also about the moral duty to stand up for the weak. These two works together form a poetic cycle and belong together. A more recent work is *The Ocean*.

The novel *Undir Suðurstjørnum* (*Under Southern Stars*) is perhaps Hoydal's most ambitious book, as well as one of the major works of the new Faroese literature. It was published in 1991 and was nominated for the Nordic Council award in the following year. It is a mixture of memoir, fact and fiction. As a young boy Gunnar Hoydal moved with his family to Ecuador, where his father worked for some years for FAO as a fisheries adviser on the Pacific coast. Many years later he went back there with his sister and brothers, and this journey into the past and the present inspired him to write the novel. It takes the reader into both South American and Faroese culture, through poverty and riches, history and dream, and evokes strong emotions such as infatuation and jealousy.

Although by no means the first female Faroese writer, Guðrið Helmsdal set two records when she published her first book of poetry, *Mild Wind*, in 1963: it was the first book of Faroese poetry to be published by a woman, and it was also the first collection of modernist poetry in Faroese. The period before the turn of the millennium saw the coming of several women writers. Some of them write children's books, but most are concerned with the role of women in Faroese society.

Oddvør Johansen's novel *Lívsins Summar* (*The Summer of a Lifetime*) has been translated into both Danish and Swedish. It is the story of a year in the life of a young, not so ordinary family: Poulina and Ólivant and their family of three children. The story focuses on their ten-year-old daughter Nora, and is told from her point of view as she experiences life in the Tórshavn of the 1950s, a very difficult period in the islands. The family lives in rather straitened circumstances, but they are close-knit and dream of a house of their own and a workshop for Ólivant. At the end their dreams come true, when the bank gives them a loan to build a house of their own.

The book tells the story of people who enthusiastically take on tasks they do not know they can master. They are all fond of music, but cannot afford a piano, so why should not Ólivant learn to build one? And when the orchestra where he is so active needs somebody to play the trombone, he at once volunteers to learn. The female characters face more constraints; their role in life is to look after home, children and husband. But when Poulina is asked whether she has ever regretted that she gave up an artistic career for husband and children, she answers: 'No, never.' Poulina has made her choice voluntarily; another female character, Alvilda, chooses to break away and follow her talents.

Johansen writes in a restrained manner which is very effective; she does not preach or criticise, merely describes. In her later books she deals with the same theme of women's lives, as seen from different angles. Her 1996 children's book *Kongsdóttirin í Nólsoy* (*The King's Daughter in Nólsoy*) recounts the old tale of the Scottish princess, the daughter of James II, who in the fifteenth century settled with her lover in the Faroe Islands and left many descendants there. The novel *Tomorrow is Another Day* was nominated for the Nordic Council award of 1998.

In the successful novel *When I Have Painted the Summerhouse* (2001) Johansen describes how the crisis of the 1990s and the public bankruptcy that follows it affect her main character both socially and economically. For this harsh and intense novel she received the literary award of the city of Tórshavn. The story was also made into a popular series on Faroese radio.

Tóroddur Poulsen hails from Tórshavn, but lives in Copenhagen. He has been one of the most active Faroese writers in the last decade, and is an exciting poet, although difficult to categorize. Poulsen published his first book of poetry in 1984: *Botnfall* (*Dregs*). Society is viewed from beneath; this was to become a characteristic of his poetry. Two years later came *Drunken Angels* – the title alone was considered a provocation in his native Tórshavn. In his third collection of poetry, *Holy War*, his social criticism is, surprisingly perhaps, less harsh. His next three books of poetry are concerned with existential questions, and, in the process of reaching for the ultimate truth, many everyday inherited values are trampled on, without anything much taking their place, unless one is able to see a beauty in decay. On the whole his playing with words and with the Faroese language makes his work an ever-changing puzzle.

When he switched to fiction in 1994 with the novel *Reglur* (*Rules*), he had to some extent prepared the way for it in his two previous collections of poetry. The novel is as difficult to characterise by genre as the rest of his work, being a mixture of poetry, fiction and essay. It was nominated for the Nordic Council award in 1996. Since then he has published seven books, of which all but one were poetry.

'I cannot write / as a Føroyingur should / I got the sea in my mouth / and forgot to sink,' writes Poulsen in his latest collection of poetry, *Bloodsamples*, which was the 2002 nominee for the Nordic Council award. By this he perhaps wants to say that he must run with the current, and give words for blood. 'Of course Tóroddur Poulsen is a Føroyingur,' says a Danish literary critic, 'there is nothing else he could be – he has the wind in his mind and the salt in his eyes.'

Carl Jóhan Jensen is one of the most interesting writers working today, as well as one of the most complex. He is a modernist who not only adopts words from the old Norse language but also makes up his own as he goes along. His poetry is rich in allusions to Norse literature and Faroese tradition as well as to classical texts. Consequently, what he means to say is not always immediately clear. When he received the M.A. Jacobsen prize for his poetry, he actually had to defend his style on Faroese television.

Jensen holds a degree in Nordic languages, and his interest in the use of language is apparent in his writing. He considers it necessary to add new words, as there is a considerable difference between the spoken and the written language of today. The written language was created while most people still lived in the compact communities of the bygdir, but this has changed, and these days Tórshavn is definitely the intellectual centre of the islands. He states that the idea behind his writing is existential: 'The world is what the ego thinks, and language is the factor that brings structure to chaos. The world is shattered; the poet puts it together again by creating new meanings.' Ambiguity characterises all his writing; making it fascinating and challenging, but requiring close reading.

In 1991 Jensen was nominated for the Nordic Council award for his fifth collection of poetry, *Hvørkiskyn*. The title is again ambiguous, but can perhaps be interpreted as 'not understanding anything'. This uncertainty is repeated in the biblical quotation from St Mark (Authorised Version, Chapter VIII, verse 12), which is given a page of its own at the beginning of the book:

> Why doth this generation seek after a sign?
> verily I say unto you, There shall no sign
> be given unto this generation.

In other words, people crave a certainty they cannot have. The title poem expresses sorrow at the idea that the images a language can create do not exist in the world of reality; there are simply not phenomena in the world to fill the words. The writer then opens doors to the reader, who hopefully will appreciate what he finds.

Jensen was only 22 years old when he published his first prose story, *Afternoon*, in a 'stream-of-consciousness' style. In 1995 came the novel *Rúm* (*Room*), which was very well received. It has many points of similarity with classical literature. The story takes place at the beginning of the twentieth century, and is told from the point of view of a stranger who arrives in the islands.

Perhaps it is fair to point out that Faroese literature also has its lighter moments, and that even crime stories are produced there these days. The first one of the kind was written by Jógvan Isaksen, who lectures on Faroese literature at the University of Copenhagen. It is called rather romantically *Blíð er Summarnátt á Føroya Landi* (*Tender is the Faroese Summer Night*). It was published in 1990, and makes very good reading.

Barbara

In the late 1990s came the long-awaited new film version of *Barbara*. It is based on the only novel of the Faroese writer Jørgen-Frantz Jacobsen, which first appeared posthumously in 1939, but has since been published again and again in many different languages. The novel was first filmed in 1961, with the Swedish actress Harriet Andersson in the title role. In the new version the Norwegian Anneke von der Lippe plays Barbara, a woman who is always true to her feelings, wherever they take her. It is a difficult part to play as Barbara is perhaps one of the most complex female characters in Nordic literature.

Barbara is the eighth film directed by Nils Malmros, who is a Dane. He

Director Nils Malmros working with local extras on the film Barbara. *Photo: Torben Stroyer*

practises as a doctor in between making his award-winning films, and through working in the islands he has come to see the fascination of the Faroese landscape. As he considers the novel to be deeply melancholy, rain and fog (not unheard of in the islands) are used to create atmosphere. All the outdoor scenes were filmed on location in the Faroe Islands, most of them in Saksun in Streymoy and Húsavík in Sandoy. The rhythm of the old Faroese ballads of 'Karlamagnus' (Charlemagne) is used throughout the film.

Nils Malmros had always promised himself that he would never film a novel, but as he himself says, *Barbara* represents 'my intellectual awakening to literature. The theme of *Barbara* is close to my earlier films.' And the theme of all his films is the pain which is so closely linked to love, whether the story is acted out in the world of today or in the Tórshavn of the 1760s.

Music

Musical life is flourishing in the islands as hardly ever before, and its scope is impressive. In the third week of June every year the Faroe Islands Festival of Classical and Contemporary Music known as 'Summartónar' takes place at the Nordic House and all over the islands, in interesting places such as Gjógv. It lasts for about a week, and is a much visited event, with musicians coming from all over the Nordic world. The well-known composer and musician Kristian Blak is the artistic director of this summer festival. Another popular musical event is the annual Jazz, Folk & Blues Festival, which is held in Tórshavn during the first weekend in July.

Composer and musician, Kristian Blak. Photo: Rolf Ohlson

The leading musician and composer in the islands today is Sunleif Rasmussen. His work has become highly appreciated outside the islands too, so much so that he was given a three-year working scholarship, to give him peace and a chance to work his Nordic soul into his compositions. Perhaps that is what he succeeded in doing, for in 2002 he received the very prestigious Nordic Council music award for his 'Symphony No. 1', known as 'Oceanic Days'. It was first performed in the Nordic House, and was then played by the Icelandic Symphony Orchestra.

Another major work by Rasmussen came the year after: 'Ferðin' ('The Journey'), a composition for symphony orchestra and choir. It was based on the text *Ferðin* by Jørgen-Frantz Jacobsen. The composition 'Trauer and Freude' is closely related to a classical Kingo-hymn, and is one of the works performed by the Faroese music ensemble Aldubáran. The ensemble consists of ten young professional musicians who work in close co-operation with modern composers. Rasmussen is now working on a new Faroese opera, to be produced at the Faroese Arts Festival – Listastevna Føroya – in 2005.

One of the most productive poets and composers in the islands is Regin Dahl, who has composed some 450 melodies, among them many of the best known songs. His music is lyrical and at times reminiscent of Faroese dance-song melodies. Dahl is also outstanding among twentieth-century poets, and there are those who consider him the greatest Faroese poet of the last hundred years. His latest collection of poetry, *Trifles,* was published in the summer of 2000.

Another well-established musician is Jørgin Dahl; this grand old man of Faroese rock has been active since the 1970s in such well-known groups as Straight Ahead and Hjarnar, both from Klaksvík.

Pauli í Sandagerði who achieved popularity for setting some of Heinesen's poems to music, has since been active within the cultural community as a composer, conductor and organiser. Among his work the rock and classical musical 'Jesus og Makedonarin' should be mentioned; he has also composed cantatas, besides conducting choirs for nearly thirty years. Another promising composer is Tróndur Bogason, who won a contest for a cantata for the Ólavsvøka celebration.

A popular singer is Kári Petersen, who writes and composes his own songs. He publishes them under his artist's name of kári p. He was awarded the M.A. Jacobsen prize in 1995 – the first time it had been given to a song-writer. His work is of course mostly recorded, an exception being the large Faroese songbook of 1993, which contains many of his song texts. His songs are alive and hard-hitting, expressing sympathy with the disadvantaged in a rare blend of music and poetry. He is one of the most popular troubadours the islands have ever had; his LP 'Vælferðarvísur' is now considered the greatest Faroese musical release ever to have been made. Nowadays he seems to have put his guitar on the shelf, and is working as a psychologist in the Tórshavn hospital.

There is a large production of recorded modern music in the Faroe Islands today. The record company Tutl, which is run by Kristian Blak, can boast of some two hundred releases, and the output of CDs reaches about forty a year. Some of the old groups have remained at the top for a long time; Frændur, a tremendously popular band, is still going strong as a song and folk rock group. So is the group known as the Spælimenninir, without doubt the Faroese group that has travelled the furthest, with five tours of the American midwest. And Faroe Boys, the pioneers within Faroese pop-rock music, have recently re-released recordings from 1967.

Quite recently, a new trend has appeared – the use of traditional music in a new form and rhythm. The rock band Týr has received a lot of attention and praise for its new CD, 'How Far To Asgard', which in part has old Faroese dance-songs as its theme – using heavy rock rhythms. It is a demanding but melodious rock music with texts based on the old songs, Nordic mythology and history. The band went straight to the top of the hit list in Iceland, and they say that just about everybody there was humming Týr's rock edition of the old dance-song 'Ormurin Langi'.

A young newcomer to the musical life of the islands is Eivør Pálsdóttir from Gøta. She has a career as a singer as well as a song-writer, and works with her own band in Iceland as well as with the Nordic jazz group Yggdrasil, where Kristian Blak is the composer and the band leader. Her beautiful voice can be heard on their latest CD.

Eivør Pálsdóttir also participates as a soloist and as a lead singer with another popular band, Clickhaze. This band has been at the top of the Faroese charts recently, with strikingly original music that has obvious roots in old local tradition, but is played on modern musical instruments. They are inspired not only by the old dance-songs but also by the baroque hymns of Thomas Kingo which, with their powerful language and visionary religious rapture, have been so much loved and so often sung in the islands. In fact, they are still sung in the Faroe Islands three centuries after Kingo's death. The local church singers from the village of Tjørnuvík in Streymoy have been invited by the bishop of Copenhagen to sing Kingo psalms in the place where he lived and died in 1703.

Visual Art

In 1993 the Faroe Islands' original art gallery, known as Listaskálin, was re-opened in a new and extended form in a picturesque location close to the Plantasjan. The work was planned and carried out by the Listasavn Føroya – the Faroese Museum of Art – which had taken over the old art collection. Much of this will now be on view, giving an insight into Faroese history – the development of Faroese visual art from the works of Sámal Joensen-Mikines

and the bird painter Díðrikur á Skarvanesi to those of present-day artists. In *Etching of the* addition to the permanent collection there is room for exhibitions and *church in Nolsoy,* concerts, as well as studios where visiting artists can work. *by Marius Olsen*

The Nestor of Faroese sculpture is still Janus Kamban, whose portrait in bronze of the linguist V.U. Hammershaimb is on view at the art museum. It has the serenity characteristic of his sculptures, which can be seen in so many places all over the islands. Sadly, Kamban has not been able to work since he hurt his hand some years ago.

Like Kamban, the modern sculptor Hans Pauli Olsen shows people in his work. One of his most striking sculptures is that of the enchanting Tarira – the elf girl – dancing in an exuberant joy of life, of freedom on a stone in Plantasjan. Tarira is the creation of William Heinesen, and appears in his writing as well as in his paper collages, where she also dances to the music of a young man playing the violin at her feet. The sculpture of Tarira was unveiled on 15 January 2000, the centenary of Heinesen's birth, and the site was well chosen, as the park is close to the house where he spent most of his life; in his latter days he would often sit there, on his favourite bench.

Hans Pauli Olsen's two brothers are also well-known artists. Torbjørn Olsen has a special interest in portrait painting, but is also known for his townscapes, where the colour is warm and rich. The same is true of his monumental altar painting in the church of Miðvágur, where the crucified Christ is shown against a shimmering red background, which somehow seems to symbolise blood and suffering as well as love and comfort. Marius

Olsen, the youngest of the brothers, works exclusively with graphical techniques. Man is important in his work, and many of his pictures are self portraits.

Through most of the twentieth century Faroese nature was a central theme for painters, and a panorama of 'the bygd by the sea' was a must for any home. In the 1990s there was, however, a general flight away from the recognizable bygd to a more abstract theme, as well as to a reinterpretation of the motif. This shift towards the abstract can be observed at a rather early stage in the pictures of Ingálvur av Reyni. Everything superfluous is left out of his pictures, and he no longer paints a particular landscape. Neither does his son, Eyðun av Reyni. Their motifs can therefore be described as imagined landscapes.

Zacharias Heinesen, on the other hand, does not take his abstract style quite so far. Although he experiments as an artist, both stylistically and technically, his work remains representational. While his favourite theme used to be nature, and maybe to some extent still is, he also experiments in a new style altogether, in paintings like 'Paraphrase of Leonardo da Vinci's The Last Supper' and 'The Artist's Mother'.

Perhaps the most exciting artist in the Faroe Islands today is Tróndur Patursson, notable for his spontaneity both in form and content. For some time now he has worked much with glass, and finds it exciting because of its 'third dimension', the light that shines through it, but also because he considers glass a special material to work in, as it is never possible to predict what the final result will be. His first big commission working with glass was the staircase in the shopping centre SMS in Tórshavn, and later the glass paintings for the new church at Gøta. Architecture and art here work together, the church being sited with the choir and the altar facing towards the sea; this is where we find Patursson's large painting of Christ with fishermen – the Crucifixion merged with the Miraculous Draught of Fishes.

The interest on the part of the Faroese people today in buying paintings and sculptures has made it possible for a dozen or more artists to make a living from their art.

The Future

There were celebrations when the Vágar tunnel under Vestmanna Sound opened in December of 2002 – the first tunnel under the sea in the Faroe Islands. The next undersea tunnel will connect the Northern Isles with Eysturoy. Work on the tunnel to Gásadalur, the last inhabited bygd to be without a direct connection, has been resumed, and the project is due to be completed in the course of 2003. As with the Vágar tunnel, work had already started when the financial crisis came in 1993. To the people of Gásadalur the tunnel will mean a complete change of lifestyle, as the bygd will no longer be a world apart.

The Vágar tunnel has made the airport more accessible, so that traffic will increase. This has been foreseen by the Danish state, which owns and operates the airport, and modernisation has been going on for some time. The Faroese authorities would like to take over the running of the airport when it is finished. Of course, if oil is found, it might be necessary to build another airport, closer to Tórshavn. The new *Norrøna* ferry will, as before, run the North Sea circuit from Tórshavn, but as a year-round connection.

Through an improved communication network the islands will in many ways become a more integrated community, and the depopulation of the more remote bygdir will hopefully be avoided. Prosperity came suddenly to the Faroe Islanders, and in a generation they changed from being a community of fishermen in close contact with the sea to being a modern western state. The sea road may therefore in the not so distant future become replaced by a tunnel below it. To accept this is to face up to a change that has been coming for some time: the small fishing boat that at one time was the sole means of inter-island communication has been put in the shed for good. Today the fishing boat is brought out only on special occasions, and in the end maybe a tunnel is easier and safer to use than a car ferry.

In the old days the many words for wind and rain and waves would make it possible to relay exact weather information. Even so, changeable weather would make it difficult for people to make definite plans; it was often better to say 'maybe'. There may be no need in the future to know so many words for weather and waves, but if so, it is a comfort to know that they are preserved in the new Faroese dictionary!

GLOSSARY

amtmaður governor of a county

áttamannafar boat with an eight-man crew

botnur/pl. *botnar* cirque, a deep round hollow or natural amphitheatre

brekka/pl. *brekkur* large, steep hill, slope between two outcrops of rock

bygd/pl. *bygdir* settlement, village

býlingur/pl. *býlingar* a cluster of farms

bøur/pl. *bøir* infield, cultivated land

drangur/pl. *drangar* needle, in Faroe in the sea, in Iceland in the mountains

eystfall current going in an easterly direction

fossur/pl. *fossar* waterfall

føroying/pl. *føroyingar* a person from Føroyar, the Faroe Islands

gandur magic or witchcraft

gjógv/pl. *gjáir* gorge, deep cleft in the rock

glasstova the room with a glass window, the best room

grind whales and the hunt for whales

grindadráp the slaughter of the grind

grindaknívur knife used for the grind

grindarakstur the hunt for whales

gróthús a shed with outer stone walls

grøðisteinur a stone, especially soapstone, believed to have a healing power

hagi outfield, pasture

hamar/pl. *hamrar* crag, buttress

handil a (grocery) shop

heyggjur/pl. *heyggjar* hill

hjallur/pl. *hjallar* a shed with trellised walls for the drying of meat or fish

hólmgonga a fight to the death on a small island

hoyggjhús a shed for the hay

huldufólk the other people

hvast sharp

knettir large fish-balls

kongsbóndi/pl. —*bøndur* king's farmer, a tenant on Crown land

kongsjørð Crown land

kvøldseta/pl. -*setur* evening gathering

ljóari roof opening in the roykstova

lundi puffin

neyst/pl.(-) boat shed

niðagrísur a supernatural creature with a large head and small body which would roll around between people's feet, believed to be the ghost of a murdered child

óðalsjørð privately owned (inherited) land

próstur dean or provost, for long the highest church official in the islands

roykstova/pl. *roykstovur* a room with a fireplace for cooking, used as a family room

seksmannafar boat with a six-man crew

søgn/pl. *sagnir* a popular story, passed off as truth

skarð/pl.(-) gap, pass in the mountain

skerpikjøt dried, hung, unsalted mutton

skipari lead singer

skysskaffer (Danish) a person responsible for obtaining transport for travellers

stakkur women's national dress, for festive occasions

táttur/pl. *tœttir* satirical verse

teigur/pl. *teigar* field/*teigalendi* an area under cultivation

tíggjumannafar boat with a ten-man crew

trøð/pl. *traðir* a fenced-in plot in the outfields, used for cultivation

vestfall current going in a westerly direction

BIBLIOGRAPHY

Andersen, *N., Færøerne* 1600–1709, Tórshavn, 1964.

Annandale, Nelson, *The Faroes and Iceland,* Oxford, 1905.

Barthel, Sven, *Atlant med en återkomst,* Stockholm, 1963.

Bronner, Storm, 'Banebryteren i færøysk litteratur'. Interview with Heðin Brú, *Aftenposten, Oslo,* 15 August 1981.

Bruun, Daniel, *Fra de færøske Bygder,* Copenhagen, 1929.

— *Turistruter paa Færøerne* I–II, Copenhagen, 1915–19.

Brøgger, A. *W., Ancient Emigrants,* Oxford, 1929.

Brønner, Hedin, *Three Faroese Novelists,* New York, 1973.

Burton, Richard F., *Ultima Thule,* London, 1875.

Debes, Lucas, *Færoæ et Færoæ Reserata,* Copenhagen, 1673.

Degn, Anton, *Færøske Kongsbønder* 1584–1884.

Furseth, Astor, *Færøyene, Oslo,* 1975.

Færøerne. Publ. by the Danish-Faroese Society. Ed. N. Djurhuus. Odense, 1958.

Garborg, Hulda, *Songdansen i Nord-landi,* Kristiania, 1903.

Gravesen, Grete, *Lægekone paa Færøerne i 5 aar,* Copenhagen, 1941.

Gulbranson, C., *Paa hesteryggen gjennem Island, Oslo,* 1926.

Hammershaimb, V. *U., Færøsk Anthologi,* Copenhagen, 1891.

Harris, G. H., *The Faroe Islands,* 1927.

Hátun, Ølavur, 'The Faroese dance – the ballad', *Faroe Isles Review,* No. 2, 1977.

Haugen, Einar, Foreword to *The Ring of Dancers,* by Wylie/Margolin, Philadelphia, 1981.

Heinesen, Jens Pauli, *Færøerne í dag,* Tórshavn, 1966.

Heinesen, William, *Blæsende Gry* (Stormy Dawn), Copenhagen, 1934.

— *Færøsk Kunst,* Tórshavn, 1959.

— *The Lost Musicians,* New York, 1971.

— *The Kingdom of the Earth,* New York, 1974.

Hildremyr, Asbjørn, *Landet mellom hav og himmel, Oslo,* 1976.

Hoydal, Høgni, *Myten om rigsfællesskabet,* Copenhagen, 2000.

Jacobsen, Jørgen-Frantz, *Barbara,* Copenhagen, 1939, London, 1948.

— *Færøerne. Natur og folk,* 3rd ed., Tórshavn, 1970.

Jakobsen, Dr Jakob, *Diplomatarium Færoense,* Tórshavn and Copenhagen, 1907.

— *Færøske folkesagn og æventyr* (Faroese Legends and Folk-Tales), Copenhagen, 1898–1901.

— *Færøsk sagnhistorie,* Tórshavn and Copenhagen, 1904.

— *Greinir og ritgerðir,* Tórshavn, 1957.

Jeaffreson, Joseph, *The Faroe Isles,* London, 1898.

Joensen, Jóan Pauli, *Färöisk folkkultur,* Lund, 1980.

— *Fra bonde til fisker,* Tórshavn, 1987.

Jóhansen, Jóhan, 'A paleobotanical study indicating a pre-Viking settlement in Tjørnuvík, Faroe Islands', *Froðskaparrit* 19: 147–57.

John, Brian, *Scandinavia. A new geography,* 1984.

Johnston, George, *The Faroe Islanders' Saga,* trans. from Icelandic, Oberon Press, 1975.

Kielberg, Børge, *Færøfolk,* Copenhagen, 1946.

Kinck, Hans E., *Storhetstid, Oslo,* 1922.

Landt, Jørgen, *A Description of the Feroe Islands,* London, 1810; original edn. Copenhagen, 1800.

Low, George, *A Tour through the Islands of Orkney and Schetland* (1774), Kirkwall, 1879.

Mentze, Ernst, *Sámal Joensen-Mikines,* Copenhagen, 1973.

Mikkelsen, Richard, *Færørne i bankkrisens tegn,* Copenhagen, 2001.

Muir, Christine, *Orkney Days,* Edinburgh, 1986.

Nansen, Fridtjof, *Nord i Taakeheimen,* Kristiania, 1910.

Niclasen, Sanna Dahl, 'Søgan um nátasjukuna í Føroyum', *Fróðskaparrit,* 34–5.

Pløyen, Christian, *Reminiscences of a voyage to Shetland, Orkney and Scotland in the summer of* 1839, Lerwick, 1896.

Ryggi, Mikkjal á, *Miðvinga søga,* Tórshavn, 1940.

Rønne, Jørgen Falk, I *Sol og Blæst,* Copenhagen, 1936.

Skaare, Kolbjørn, 'To myntfunn fra Sandoy, på Færøyene', *Nordisk Tidsskrift,* 1986.

Stove, Sverre and Jacobsen, Jacob, *Færøyane,* Oslo, 1944.

Svabo, Jens Christian, *Records of a Journey in Faroe,* 1781–82.

Sørensen, Th., 'Færøerne' in *Danmark i Skildringer og Billeder,* Copenhagen, 1883.

Tarnovius, *Færoensia Textus & Investigationes,* 1669.

Taylor, Elizabeth, *Elizabeth in the Far Islands,* unpublished manuscript, Tórshavn Library, 1979.

Thomsen, Dr Severin, *En Vinter paa Færøerne,* Copenhagen, 1895.

Torfason, Hógni, 'Sámal Joensen-Mikines', Morgunblaðið, Reykjavík, 6 October 1961.

Trap, J. P., *Færøerne,* Copenhagen, 1968.

Weir, Tom, 'Bird Island of the Faeroes', *Country Life,* 28 September 1961.

West, John F., *Faroese Folk-Tales and Legends,* Lerwick, 1980.

Williamson, Kenneth, *The Atlantic Islands,* London, 1970.

Young, G. V. C. and Clewer, Cynthia R. *The Faroese Saga,* trans. from Icelandic, Belfast, 1973.

INDEX

261